1

The Father Factor

A spiritual <u>triage</u> for husbands, wives, fathers, fractured families,
and those considering entering God's marriage covenant*

Jim and Merry Corbett

"And he who overcomes (is victorious) and who obeys My
commands to the [very] end [doing the works that please Me],
I will give him authority *and* power over the nations..."

Rev. 2: 26

ISBN-13: 978-0-9817033-8-1

Original printing 2007
Second printing with revisions 2011
Third printing with revisions 2014
Fourth printing with revisions 2017

Contents

Intensive Care Unit I

Anointed Invitation – Page 21

Open My Eyes to See as You See, Lord

Intensive Care Unit II

ABBA Initiated Intimacy – Page 95

The Oneness of a Loving Father God with His Adoring Child

Chapter

Intensive Care Unit III

Advocate Action – Page 193

Living Significant, Overcoming, Christ-centered Lives

Chapter

For the Sincere Believer Only

The following pages are designed for deeply committed believers who choose to become all they are intended to be in Christ. They are not designed to come against a belief system on which anyone may have chosen to stake his eternal well-being, or for that matter, his non-eternal well-being if he so chooses to believe. If you do not believe in the Bible as the Word of God and do not claim to follow Jesus, this book is not for you. Whatever you choose to believe and whatever you choose to worship as your god is your right. You are living in a world that, until it turns completely dark as prophesied in the Bible, allows you the freedom to do so. However, if you are looking for answers to your life and you find yourself thinking they may be found in Jesus, then we urge you to read these pages with an open heart. The Lord may be calling you to Himself as an answer to your prayers.

This book is intended primarily for men who have given their lives to Jesus Christ and have a desire to more fully understand, according to God's Word, their place in His plan and His desire to make their lives significant. As you read, you will find four Intensive Care Units or sections pertaining to specific areas that need attention in the lives of most men. All units of this book are intended to provide answers for the Christian man who is searching for direction for his spiritual walk, his marriage or future marriage, his family, his immediate circle of influence; and ultimately for how to please God with his life and leave behind an honorable legacy that glorifies the work of the cross. Also included in this book are insights for the woman who is in need of godly perspectives regarding her role in marriage, whether she is married, divorced, or planning to be married.

A.W.Tozer

Adapted from <u>This World: Playground Or Battleground?</u>

The most critical need of the church at this moment is men – the right kind of men, bold men. We languish for men who feel themselves expendable in the warfare of the soul because they have already died to the allurements of this world. Such men will be free from the compulsions that control weaker men. They will not be forced to do things by the squeeze of circumstances. Their only compulsion will come from within, or from above.

This kind of freedom is necessary if we are to have prophets again in our pulpits instead of mascots. These kind of men will serve God and mankind from motives too high to be understood by the rank and file of religious retainers who shuttle in and out of the sanctuary. They will make no decisions out of fear, take no course out of desire to please, accept no service for financial considerations, perform no religious acts out of mere custom, nor allow themselves to be influenced by the love of publicity or the desire for reputation.

The true church has never sounded out public expectations before launching its crusades. Its leaders heard from God and went ahead wholly independent of popular support or lack of it. They knew their Lords will and did it, and their people followed them - sometimes to triumph, but more often to insults and public persecution – and their sufficient reward was satisfaction of being right in a wrong world.

Another characteristic of a true prophet is love. The free man who has learned to hear God's voice and dared to obey it has felt the moral burden that broke the hearts of the Old Testament prophets, crushed the soul of our Lord Jesus Christ, and wrung streams of tears from the eyes of the apostles.

The free man has nothing to protect, no ambition to pursue, and no enemy to fear. For that reason he is completely careless of his standing among men. If they follow him - well and good. If not he loses nothing that he holds dear. But whether he is accepted or rejected, he will go on loving his people with sincere devotion, and only death can silence his tender intercession for them.

Yes, if evangelical Christianity is to stay alive, it must have men again - the right kind of men. It must repudiate the weaklings who will not speak out, and it must seek in prayer and much humility the coming again of men of the stuff of which prophets and martyrs are made. God will hear the cries of

His people as He heard the cries of Israel in Egypt, and He will send deliverance by sending deliverers. It is His way.

And when the deliverers come – reformers, revivalists, prophets – they will be men of God and men of courage. Such men will be baptized with the Spirit indeed and through their labors He will baptize others and send the long delayed revival.

An Astounding Adventure – A Wondrous Privilege

In the Garden of Eden, when God commanded His new creation to go forth and multiply, He initiated the institution that to this day remains closest to His heart - the nuclear family. That command pertained to not only that generation but every one that was to follow. In God's eyes, the family is an incredibly important institution. The family that's in line with God's Word is an impenetrable fortress against all of the world's challenges, a safe place for wives to thrive and children to prosper; and a place for His Word to gestate and then be distributed throughout the nations.

God placed man in the most important position He has ever created—head of the nuclear family. He also created the second most important office of a helpmate, his wife. His design for their partnership is to develop offspring who learn His ways through parents who are spiritually in order and learning from God through an intimate relationship with each other and with Him. Their lives mirror the life of Christ, thereby creating significant legacies and overcoming lives that honor Him.

From the beginning, in an attempt to thwart God's plan, the enemy of everything God desires has masterfully deceived men to the point where they desire almost anything over the intimacy won for them through Jesus. The Father Factor is a positive and refreshingly candid look at the peril in which the body of Christ finds itself because of the spiritual impotence of its men, which has come about mainly through the lies and deception of the enemy. It is a step-by-step guide for men to use in reclaiming their offices of husband and father, restoring their spiritual significance before God, and rebuilding their family fortress or picking up the pieces of a broken marriage. It is the call of God for the true heart revival and valiant leadership that is needed in overcoming all the challenges of life and the perilous times in which we live. It is an incredible outreach tool to help men who are in need of answers for their lives and families, and for those men considering marriage in their future.

When men get in line with God's Word, and dedicate themselves to once again be in awe of God, their wives become free, their children are shown direction for their lives, families are protected and prosperous and walk in Christ-like power, churches become bastions of God's magnetic love and biblical power in a dying world, society is revived, and God's Word goes forth.

Children Learn Who God is by the Actions of Their Fathers

The Father Factor is far more than an exposé of the spiritual impotence of the men who call themselves followers of Jesus. It is a step by step blueprint for men to become valiant leaders, who live fearless lives that truly testify of the power of the cross and represent the character of Jesus in their circles of influence, no matter what peril they may face.

As said before, you will find this book to be a spiritual triage* in your Christian walk. It will take you on a journey in assessing your spiritual needs as a Christian man from God's perspective and lead you to definitive answers for your life in Christ. If you call yourself a follower of the ways of Jesus, if you desire to present a significant, world overcoming, life to the Lord on the day you stand before Him, if you need to understand what following Jesus really means to God, your marriage, your family, and your circle of influence, this may be the most challenging and important modern day book you will ever read!

Personal Significance to God vs. Judgment of Our Lives

[Personal significance was won for you at the cross. A significant life is won through continued submission and obedience to the ways of Jesus.]

Throughout these pages, you will become familiar with the concept of God judging the effect of our lives in Christ on the day we stand before Him. It is of the utmost importance to know the difference between our personal significance to God and the fact that He will judge how we lived while in Jesus.

The Word says that we are personally pleasing to God once we surrender to the Lordship of Jesus Christ. Our righteousness in Christ and all that has been accomplished through the life, death, and resurrection of Jesus is complete and ours because of Him.

On the day we personally stand before God, we will be totally accepted solely because of the blood of Jesus and our acceptance of what He accomplished on our behalf - not because of our works, not because of

13

our importance or standing in the world, and certainly not because of our religious activities. We have an eternal relationship with God through Jesus and Jesus alone. As His fully accepted and greatly loved children, we will spend all of the remaining eternities with Him. However, our lives and what we did in the Lord will be judged.

II Cor. 5:9-10 NIV So we make it our goal to please him, whether we are at home in the body or away from it.

10) For we must all appear before the judgment seat of Christ, that each one may receive what is due him for the things done while in the body, whether good or bad.

The truth that you are fully and completely loved by God must be held fast in your heart to weather the storms of conviction that will come through the Holy Spirit as you read the following pages, where your flesh, negative thinking, possibly your doctrines, and the self-worth crutches that sustain you are offended. Even though your heart will be broken as the Holy Spirit makes you aware of how far you may have fallen from God's perspective of a significant life in Christ and exposes the wood, hay, and stubble, the understanding that God loves you completely will sustain you as you press on step by step to the life to which Jesus has called you to live if you say you follow Him. Awareness, conviction, and repentance are good things! They lead to spiritual healing.

*Triage: the assessment of a patient's needs and the prioritizing of treatment, which is designed to maximize the number of survivors through an impending peril or a present time of disaster.

MASH icu
(Men After the Savior's Heart intensive care units)

"Living for Others with Brothers We Trust"

It is our belief that the only way to overcome any season of difficulty or peril - concerning you, your family fortress, and your circle of influence - is to own the wealth of the bridal heart of Jesus. Valiant, positive, Christ-trusting men, who are completely sold out to the ways of their Lord, are the unstoppable, overcoming servant leaders He can use to guide and direct those He loves to the only true safety found in God alone.

Our experience is that most books, retreats, weekly men's meetings, and prayer breakfasts soon become history once they are completed, which leaves many weeks of little support for the individual wanting to go deeper with Christ. We have, therefore, developed this book with its study questions and a daily support program of interactive resources as companions to what is written. We call the support system for this book MASH icu.

What is MASH icu?

MASH icu is a Companion Support Protocol
for Building Biblically Sound Husbands and Fathers

The church of Jesus Christ is a series of interconnected field hospitals (fellowships in whatever form they take) in the middle of a war zone (the world). Each group is supposed to function as a MASH (Mobile Army Surgical Hospital) unit on the front lines of a battlefield, available to those wounded and broken by the warring world, receiving them, restoring them to wholeness, and preparing them to reach out with bridal heart power to others who are in need of Jesus.

Focused, Sold-Out, Spiritually Healthy Men, Who Oversee
Healthy Families, Will Build Strong Fellowships

At present most fellowships are ill-prepared to handle the much-needed heart revival and subsequent harvest that we're convinced will accompany the astounding difficulties that loom on the horizon. Strong, spiritually sold-out men and women, healed families, and vibrant youth are being prepared to function as Christ did to address this timeframe and help lead the church body back to wholeness. Thriving fellowships begin with strong, focused men who have reestablished their offices of husband and

15

father, and taken servant leadership roles within a formal church setting or parachurch group.

MASH icu (Men After the Savior's Heart intensive care units) is an international organization of independent, committed men or men's groups, that are established within churches, fellowships, or home groups. These men have chosen to become all they can be in Christ Jesus. Having made a commitment to do whatever it takes to allow the Holy Spirit to empower their marriages, families, or those in their circle of influence, they have chosen to overcome the world and its ways by reclaiming their God-given offices of husband, father, and servant leader.

Like David's mighty men, they are ready for any battle sent their way because God's Holy Spirit power is alive and well within them. They see every challenge that comes their way not as some worrisome potential for defeat, but as an opportunity for the Lord to reveal Himself strong on their behalf. Like David's mighty men, they know that only when peril is faced head on will they see God's glory, so they have chosen to submit to the refiner's fires He allows in order to prepare them to live a fearless and devoted life.

Using the metaphor of the church as a field hospital, this vigorous training can be clarified in medical terms. One must undergo many "operations" while in training.

First of all, there must be a heart transplant to replace a self-serving, fearful heart that can't be trusted in dangerous situations or moved with the compassions of Jesus. That comes from the full and complete surrender to the Lordship of Jesus Christ. There may be a need for some radical amputations, a severing of associations and ways that hinder you from walking as Christ walked in this world. Cancerous habits and infected tissue caused by wounds from your past must be placed on the operating table in God's throne room for complete removal.

In addition, physical therapy, reconstructive surgery, and crisis intervention may be necessary to walk in the fullness of God as His mighty spiritual warriors, trustworthy to stand side-by-side with Jesus to affect a dying world as He did. There is need for the three R's—a Representation of Christ, a Restoration of marriages and the family unit where possible, and a corresponding Rescue of children from the world and its ways to bring them into the protective covering of a family that represents and honors God.

You will find MASH icu questions at the end of each chapter and a more complete description of other support systems at the end of this book. Make sure that you sign up for our blog and the accompanying library of MASH icu teachings on our website www.the101group.com.

A Woman's Perspective with Merry Corbett

You may already be asking "Why is a woman writing the introduction to a book written for men?" For both my husband Jim and me, the most important reason is that we were impressed in our hearts it was the Lord's idea, not ours. Beyond that, I would like to share that we have been in the process of living out the contents of this book by the mercy and grace of God over the years, and have continually experienced the biblical reality of what is presented here. Not only can these pages help to point you toward a significant, overcoming life in Christ but your entire family as well.

Do we claim to have all the answers? Absolutely not! We're in process just like everyone else and there are always new things to learn and additional changes to be made as the Lord continues to work in our lives for His glory. We pray the contents herein will be one of the ways in which the Lord will exhort, encourage, and equip you to become all He intends as a husband and father. May you have joy in the journey! May the changes be eternal and fruitful!

(Wives, if you are led to read this book, may you develop the compassion and mercy of Christ toward your husband and pray for him with new vigor for his sake, so he might honor God as he functions in the offices of husband and father. He needs to know you are for him, not against him. As the Lord continually works in his heart and makes changes, the entire family will benefit.)

Are we presenting a quick fix? Sorry. The heart of God is that you experience lasting changes. Those rarely come the easy way. (So, yes, it will involve more than a bouquet of roses, a night out at a fancy restaurant, and taking the family to the amusement park.) It seems that so many approaches available today that aim at making you a better person and improving your relationships only apply a bandage rather than really get to the root of our problems. It's usually a case of trying to complete in the flesh what God has begun in the Spirit, which the apostle Paul warns us is a foolish thing to do. God wants so much more for all of us and it's a shame we will settle for so little. What's really sad is that I believe we settle in great part because we just don't want to do what it will take to experience significant, lasting change. God is certainly willing to work needed changes in us, but are we willing to have Him do so?

You may look at the contents of this book and come to the conclusion it's a sheer impossibility to truly become the husband and father God desires. I'm sure Jim would tell you he's had that thought on more than one occasion. I can tell you I've had the same thought concerning becoming a godly wife and mother; and if we try to accomplish change in our own strength, it is impossible. However, with God, all things are possible!

We have learned two things over the years that have helped tremendously on the road to developing a significant life in Christ. The first is best explained by this question and answer illustration. Q: How do you eat an elephant? A: One bite at a time. It's important to keep that in mind, especially on the days when you may feel overwhelmed by life. (We may take a vacation from time to time, but life never does.)

The second thing will help you to remember that the Lord will be faithful to bring about the changes that need to happen in you and your family. He showed us that our lives are a series of "yeses" to Him. As we say "yes" in agreement with what He shows us, He is faithful to change us and we can honor Him through our obedience. Only God can make changes that last both now and for eternity.

From our family to yours, we highly recommend the adventure with God we have outlined in the following pages. We are firmly convinced it's important to Him that you embark on this journey even though the road will more than likely not be an easy one to travel. You can trust Him to work not only for His best interests, but also on behalf of you and your family. That is the ultimate win-win situation as you take these very important steps toward a life that's significant to God!

Merry Corbett

A Young Woman's Perspective with Jubilee Corbett

As a young adult, I look back in such thankfulness for the kind of home environment my parents have provided over the years. I can't remember a time when my parents weren't leading me toward Jesus. They made it clear that anything we become or do must have Him as the foundation. The best example of that in my life is their choosing to live out what that looks like. At times, it's been pretty challenging for all of us in the process of walking through life together before the Lord; but it's because of those challenges that I've known such joy in having the opportunity to live a fruitful life that depends on God in all things. Because of my parents' dedication, humility, and love, I've been able to witness and learn what it means to be a follower of Jesus, a godly woman, wife, and mother, and to know what a godly man, husband, and father looks like. Though no one in our family is perfect, we've all chosen to follow Jesus full sway as best we can. That's the heart of this book. My testimony and encouragement to you is: Giving all to Jesus is completely worth it.

18

Although this book is intended to help men return to their first love for Jesus so they can address the very critical needs within the body of Christ, I feel it's very important that we initially discuss the role God has intended for women to dismiss some of the misconceptions so prevalent within the church and their impact on marriage and family in the eyes of God.

So, How Prepared Are You?

How prepared are you as a husband and father to love your wife and lead your family through the coming perilous times? What is life really all about? What is your place in your marriage, your family, your workplace, and your immediate circle of influence?

Let's start over and rephrase the same questions from God's point of view. How prepared are you to lead your family with spiritual wholeness, powerfully glorifying God through the coming times and love your wife as Christ loves His church? What is your life really all about in the eyes of the Lord? Why has He placed you in your marriage, your family, your place of business, and your circle of influence for this generation? Have you fulfilled His plans in those areas? When you stand before your Father in heaven, these are some of the questions you really should be prepared to answer without stammering.

God is raising up His special forces out of the ashes of refiner's fires to restore the powerful family unit. He is giving those men, who choose to hear His voice, certain footing in a very uncertain world. He is giving them the spiritual power to overcome a dead and dying world.

What Is Important to God's Heart?

I believe the spiritual impotence of a man along with its impact on his marriage, his family, the work of God, and the restoration of that man is of paramount importance in the heart of God. I'm also convinced most Christian men sincerely believe they're living significant lives in God's eyes, while He actually sees them wasting their days in living a life that does not mirror the life Jesus exhibited to the world. Many of us say we follow Him and His ways, but look and act almost nothing like Him.

However, God will always have a people. Throughout the Word, God is shown in a relentless pursuit of men who will set aside their ways and choose His ways, men through whom He can show Himself strong. In every generation since the cross and in every spiritual season, He searches out those who will exhibit a powerful presentation of His Word and a proper representation of Jesus to a world that's dying and out of answers. He asks them to live in His kingdom with Him while they breathe the air of this earth, just like Jesus did.

In this day, out of the ashes of this season's refiner's fires, I am convinced God is calling His men to address their lives from an eternal perspective, being sensitive to His desires in creating them. He is calling men to realistically face their spiritual impotence and inability to even desire to live as Jesus did in front of those who need Him.

In His mercy, God is asking men, who can hear His heralding, to reclaim their offices of husband, father, and community leader. He is calling those with shattered marriages and disrupted families to find a way to repent of whatever happened in the past and begin to function in truth from this day forward. He is asking for the one contemplating marriage to truly investigate it from His perspective and determine to enter it with His heart for the best interests of his future mate, and chart a course so that each spouse can wholeheartedly undergird one another for God's best interests.

If they respond, He is removing the spiritual impotence that has held His men captive. He is in the process of restoring an eternal significance to the lives of those who choose to shake off their spiritual bondage. In truth, God is rebuilding His men to make their lives significant in His eyes, one day presenting a proper heritage to Him.

Final thought: Remember and own this fact. If you are in Christ, your old, unworthy, impotent nature is dead. It has been crucified with Christ. It no longer lives, unless you choose to give it life by continuing to remain in the stupor of old thinking and your old way of living. Submit to the power of the Holy Spirit to change the way you think and act. Begin to determine to walk in covenant partnership with your Father God, as He destroys all that's in the way of you fulfilling your offices of husband and father, and being a representative of the life, death, and resurrection of His Son.

Enjoy the ride!

Jim Corbett

*Find the very center of the will of God
and flow in it with all of His available power.*

Intensive Care Unit I

An Anointed Invitation

Open My Eyes to See as You See, Lord

God is in the process of calling His men to an intimate relationship with Himself. This invitation is from the Holy Spirit directly to the hearts of those He desires to restore and use in implementing the plan He has for these end days of His calendar. If your life has become dull, full of questions and very few answers, and you are beginning to desire a vibrant, first love kind of relationship with Jesus once again, you may very well be one of those who are being called. Do not push aside this invitation. With that call comes an anointing to accomplish all that needs to be done in you, your marriage, and your family. You are being taken to a deeper level of life in Christ as you learn His ways and submit to His power that's alive in you.

Gal.2:20 I have been crucified with Christ [in Him I have shared His crucifixion]; it is now no longer I who live, but Christ (the Messiah) lives in me; and the life I now live in the body I live by faith in (by adherence to and reliance on and complete trust in) the Son of God, Who loved me and gave Himself up for me.

From Our Father's Heart

Unfolding your life for you is a joy every heavenly moment.
I relish the idea that you will eventually be the person
that I have planned for you to be.
I see how you stumble and wander and wonder.
I love how you are seeking for truth.
It pleases Me that you are coming to Me more often
for that truth.
You need to know that I am pleased with you.
I understand how far you have to go.
I appreciate the struggles that you are going through.
I knew how many times you would fail
long before you were born,
and still I gladly invited you to be with Me for eternity.
If you have any doubt that I would ever leave you or forsake you,
eliminate that doubt forever in your mind.
It is all a lie of the enemy.
I have created you.
I have called you.
Now I am forming you.
I will invest My time in you because I believe in who you are.
You are valuable to Me.
It delights Me to know that I am becoming more valuable to you
each and every day.
This is only the beginning.
You should see what I have in store for you.
Run your race hard.
Focus on your calling.
Prepare as a bride in waiting with every fiber of your being.
It will all be worth it.

Chapter 1

The Litmus Test

Finding the wisdom and courage to follow hard after God

Nick closed his cell phone with disgust, placing it back in his carryall. "I'm gonna kill that kid," he spat angrily.

"What's wrong?" Barry queried as they walked toward the racquetball court.

"It's my boy," Nick began. "He's in trouble again."

Dropping his head and slowing his pace a bit, Nick began thinking about what he could do to discipline Tony this time. Nothing seemed to work. No matter what Nick did, his son continually got into trouble. This time it was pretty serious.

"I don't think I want to play today," he began, looking at his co-worker. "That was Judy. She said Tony and some of his friends were picked up by the police in a stolen car. They were drunk and had some minor girls with them."

Nick stopped and looked at Barry, tears welling up in his eyes. The two moved to some bleachers in the gym near the courts. Barry climbed about four rows up and sat down. Nick followed, but sat on the third row.

"Maybe it's time we talked." Barry looked intently into the face of the distraught man in front of him and continued. "Maybe it's time I told you about my daughter and our family."

Nick really didn't want to hear about someone else's troubles and started to protest with his eyes. Before he could say anything, Barry proceeded past his expression. "You knew that my family and I moved into this area about two years ago, didn't you?"

"I guess so," Nick responded. "I heard you had some kind of trouble with your daughter and decided to pack up and move here. I guess I never asked what happened and you never volunteered any information, so I just left well enough alone."

"Sarah, that's my daughter," Barry responded. "Well, Sarah was on a road to some pretty dark places. Somehow she had changed. When she was young, she was an incredibly bright, beautiful girl, full of smiles, love, laughter, just a good kid."

Barry shifted his position and leaned back on the bleacher above the one on which he was sitting.

"But then things went bad. When she started seventh grade, she went behind some kind of cloud. She isolated herself, kept secrets from us, and hung around with some unsavory friends. They weren't real bottom dwellers, but they just had a bad influence on her. We even found small items missing from our house after they came over and money began to disappear from Connie's purse." Barry sat up, tracing his index finger over his racket strings as he chose his next words.

"Over a period of time, things kept getting worse. I'll spare you the details, but she started lying to us about everything and would get angry whenever we asked any kind of question regarding her life. Connie and I knew we were losing her. There was no talking to her about her friends. She wouldn't hear it. All she wanted to do was listen to her music - man, I hated those ear-buds, and be on the phone with her friends. There was so much more. Making a long story short, she was in deep trouble and something had to be done."

"What did you do?" Nick asked, sitting up straight as he looked piercingly at Barry.

"Well, we prayed long and hard, asking the Lord how we could get Sarah to change." A small chuckle escaped his lips. "We were pretty surprised at the answer He gave us."

Nick couldn't wait for the next words to come out of Barry's mouth.

"The Lord showed me that one day I would answer to Him for her life, because He placed Sarah under my care. I would be asked if I had done all I could to provide a fertile place for Sarah to grow in Him." Barry looked down and twirled his racket a few times.

"That shook me up pretty good," he recalled. "I mean, I knew God had given Sarah to Connie and me, but I guess I never thought God was actually holding me accountable for her." Barry looked purposefully into Nick's eyes. The two men briefly stared at each other before Barry continued.

"I thought my job was to provide a good home, keep food on the table, and give my kids what they needed to stay on top of everything. I thought by having a big house in a great neighborhood I was doing my job. Connie was working. I had a thriving business. We had everything we needed. I thought we had made it, ya know? The Lord showed me that while I was busy working and playing so hard, I lost my daughter in the process."

Nick waited for a few seconds before he asked the question that burned in his heart.

"What did you do?"

"Well, that's why we're here," Barry answered. "God showed me Connie and I were the ones who needed to make some changes so we could rescue Sarah. He showed me she wasn't capable of making proper decisions at that time, and that we needed to help by creating a place of safety for her. She needed a protected place where she could rest from the things that were harming her while she was being healed. It was really important to God that

24

we did what was necessary to bring her around, so she could grow up strong and straight, spiritually sound in Him."

Nick became really interested now, and moved onto the bench, seating himself next to Barry.

Barry continued. "Connie and I prayed together quite a bit, but I knew that because I functioned in the offices of husband and father – something very important God gives to men - I was responsible to Him. I would answer to Him for Sarah's life. He showed me I was incapable of helping Him to reproduce the life of Jesus in Sarah, because I had been distracted by my own needs and wants. I wanted the successful business. I wanted the big house, the new car, money. I never even gave much thought to the fact that Sarah was on her way to throwing her life away and then burning in hell for eternity because I was too busy with my own life to stop her. That really scared me. It scared Connie, too, when I told her."

"So, what did God tell you to do?" Nick asked with great anticipation.

"Well, things became pretty clear after awhile. The stuff we treasured for so long became pretty useless to us once we surrendered everything to Him, especially in light of Sarah's need. We looked around, and then looked at Sarah and her pain, and the path was pretty well laid out for us since we were going to answer to God for her life."

Barry got up to stretch, then sat down again. Nick didn't move. He couldn't wait to hear what steps Barry and Connie took.

"Within a matter of a few months, I sold my business, Connie quit her job, we sold our house, and moved here. I took a job which allowed me to spend time with my family. We bought a much smaller house, traded in our cars for really good used ones; and now Connie home schools Sarah."

Nick was dumbfounded. His mouth dropped open and he just stared at Barry. "You must be kidding," was all he could muster as his mind reeled.

"No, we got Sarah back," Barry said with a smile. "She hated us for a little while. We had to build some pretty strong "love fences" around her in the beginning —move her away from bad influences, take away her headset so she'd start to communicate, monitor her computer and phone time, you know, stuff like that, all the time praying real hard for her. It was pretty much touch and go at first, but we got her back. Now we live in a family fortress of love and compassion designed by God—one the world can't touch. We laugh, love, communicate, and have a great relationship. She's in tune with the Lord and wants to reach out to kids her own age. She's really happy again and our times together as a family are special no matter what we do. " Barry stopped for a brief moment to reflect on some of the wonderful things God had done. It brought a big grin to his face and gave Nick a little time to think.

"The changes we had to make cost us in many ways. What's so amazing, Nick, is even though we had to make some very difficult decisions that often times seemed wrong, and now have far less of the things we used to feel were so important, Connie and I have never been happier. *Our* relationship has changed. Our relationship with God has changed. Something happened inside of us in knowing we've done what's right in His eyes. We wouldn't trade our lives for anything."

Slowing his next words almost as if commenting to himself, he looked at Nick with a brightness Nick had never seen in any of his other friends. "It's almost like the Lord threw that in as a bonus for us just because He could."

Barry quietly got up from the bleachers and started to walk back to the locker room. Nick sat on the bench a little longer, pretty much absorbed in what Barry had shared. Catching Barry about midway to the lockers, he asked one final question.

"What if it hadn't worked? What if she hadn't come around even after all you did?"

Barry looked at the floor for a moment and then up at Nick.

"God showed me it was my job as a father to do whatever it took to save Sarah. She was more important to Him than anything else I would do. No matter what I might do to try to please Him after that, it would be second best if I stopped short. He showed me that Jesus never got off that cross until the work was done. I promised Him I would do the same for Sarah, no matter what price I had to pay. He liked that."

Barry reassuringly laid his hand on Nick's shoulder and then resumed his walk toward the locker room. Nick made his way back to the bleachers and sat there until the sun went down.

[Children understand who God is by the example of their fathers.]

Before Barry detailed the way in which he'd won his daughter back, Nick didn't have any idea how to rescue his son Tony from the grip of the enemy. He was absolutely impotent to solve the challenge before him because he had no idea that God's place of safety for wives and children is the family whose head is serving God. All he could do was react, get angry, and build some kind of temporary fence around Tony to somehow contain him, one that would be tall enough to hold him - at least until Tony became stronger than that fence or learned how to climb over it. Then, another fence would have to be built, followed by others, until Tony was old enough to bear the consequences of his actions and be on his own, eventually reproducing offspring who would only know how to build fences of their own around their children rather than nurturing and guiding them to wholeness.

And so the Christian community goes. Men, (who are leading spiritually insignificant lives and attempting to fill their offices of husband and father while absolutely impotent in reproducing spiritual offspring who attain significant lives in the eyes of the Lord,) reproduce themselves in their children, who are then as impotent as their fathers, and reproduce more of the same.

Nick had no ability to understand, nor could he even care about, the eternal impact of Tony's actions. They were not in the realm of his thinking. He also had no idea how to rescue Tony from himself, nor was he capable of deciding to pay whatever price it would take to do so.

All Nick could see, up until this very moment, was the social impact his son's actions had on society and on his success as a father. The idea that Tony's actions were indicative of his son's horrible spiritual condition never crossed his mind. The idea that Tony was in grave eternal danger, should anything catastrophic happen to him, was impossible for Nick to comprehend because he was blind himself to his own impotence and incapable of thinking beyond the immediate need for some kind of solution - a temporary solution at best and at the very worst, a solution useless to God and his plan for Tony's life.

Nick was blind to the fact that he was unable to love Tony, or anyone for that matter, the way Jesus loved, although Nick considered himself His follower. He called himself a Christian, but actually living the life Jesus lived - obedient to His Father's will, passionately and compassionately relating to His Father and those around him - was a nebulous concept to him. It had never occurred to Nick that as a steward of his son, God expected him to see Tony with spiritual eyes and act toward him with the heart of Jesus.

Even though Nick somewhat understood that Tony was given to him by God, he just didn't spend time with the idea that God had a very specific plan and purpose for Tony's life and that it was his job to help Tony find that plan and purpose. The accountability of stewardship, the fact he would answer to God for the way he either did or didn't nurture and guide his family, loomed large in his mind for the first time.

Up to that moment, he had been a blind guide, incapable of playing his part in the reproduction of the character of Christ in Tony because that character had eluded him also. He was a spiritually impotent man, unable to understand the plans and desires God had for his son (in fact, for any member of his family including himself) and too overburdened with his own life - the things he owned and that owned him - to even be concerned with what God had for Tony.

[The road to everything is intimacy with your Father God.]

One of the most overlooked events in the life, death, and resurrection of Jesus is the tearing of the veil in the temple. It was rent from top to bottom, a task impossible by anyone but God. That single act rings with the mercy and love of God. It was symbolic of our invitation into the unthinkable – access into the very presence of God. Even more amazing, we, as believers, not only have access to God; but we are now accepted by our Father in heaven with the same love, intimacy, and acceptance that Jesus has with Him!

In today's Christian society, it seems as if we've somehow managed to sew the veil back together in our minds. We reject the thought that God has offered us entrance into a warm Father-son (daughter) relationship with Him. For some reason, many of us - especially men - fail to grasp the concept that even though He is a sovereign, almighty, glorious God, we are welcomed to enter into His presence, sit on His lap, so to speak, and suck our thumb. Few of us feel free to enter His presence as needy, broken failures who, at times, have no answers. Few of us have the joy of understanding that our bankruptcy opens the compassionate heart of our loving Father, Who is waiting to embrace us with loving acceptance and turn us into powerful godly representatives for our family and those around us.

When God tore the veil, He gave you and me permission to feel so small in our own eyes, that we'd be able to really need Him for everything in our lives. He gave us permission to fail Him over and over again, and still be accepted. He told us He would never condemn us or remove us from His heart. He invited us into an incredibly close relationship, one that permits us to walk together in the spiritual kingdom of heaven on this earth as companions with Him throughout our lives, and then throughout all eternity. As you go about the business of reclaiming your offices, you need to settle it in your heart once and for all that you are cherished. You have permission to love Him unashamedly and He promises to love you back - forever.

As you read the following pages, men, I challenge you to put aside all your wounds, and the misrepresentations and misunderstanding of Who our Father God is, and embrace the truth that He loves, cherishes, and accepts you at all times. I challenge you to believe in your heart that He gives you permission to fail and have no answers. I challenge you to trust Him to love you just as you are, while walking with you so you can become who He intends you to be - a mighty warrior with the honor of glorifying Him with your life, marriage, and family.

After reading, hearing, and gaining understanding from Him as I wait in prayer, I'm convinced Father God is raising up a very special league of men who are reclaiming their positions as husbands and fathers. He is raising up leaders who will show others the love of their Father, and they, too, will reclaim their offices. If you choose to reopen the veil and enter into God's kindness, as a child would go to a truly loving father, you can become one of those valiant leaders who can show others His love.

Getting Started

The spiritually impotent man has little knowledge of his offenses against God and therefore, probably has not spent any time trying to discern what they are. Thinking he's a good Christian, he spends time in the Word, goes to church; and prays daily for assistance in his challenges and tasks. There have been few times in his spiritually impotent life, however, that he's spent enough time in fellowship with the Lord and in the Word, to be sufficiently convicted to even want to change the life pattern he has determined for himself, much less exchange it for a life pattern that mirrors Jesus.

In the life of a spiritually impotent man, there may have been times of crisis or seasons of need when this man sought God diligently to fix a problem or give him a solution to his dilemma. Because Father God in His great mercy answered the prayer, this man now moves on thinking things are OK, basing his peace on his physical life being temporarily restored. If told to go deeper with God inwardly, however, to do whatever it takes to actually function in his world as Jesus would function, he would find the request an unnecessary distraction to the needs and demands of his daily life. In fact, he has shaken that kind of conviction off enough times that it no longer bothers him. He is spiritually immovable, even by God, if he considers the price too high to pay for anything he is called to do.

[The spiritually impotent man actually harms the work of God.]

Men, if you are typical of the Christian man of today, you function as if you are unable to recognize your spiritual impotence to the point you do not desire to see the character of Christ reproduced completely in you or in those around you as your priority in life. As a typical Christian man, you have chosen to set aside God's desire for your life in order to fulfill your own concept of what your life should be, or maybe just survive in an incredibly difficult world. You feel you're spiritually comfortable and adequate, and see no need to consistently act as Jesus would act and love as He would love in your family.

Like a gelded horse that no longer has an interest in mares, most of you have little Christ-like spiritual enthusiasm toward the people within

29

your circle of influence or for your part in God's plan for mankind. *Remember, we are talking priorities.* If you would really get honest with yourself, your thoughts are not continually on where others will spend eternity or on who they could become in this lifetime through your influence on them by the way you represent Jesus. Even the spiritual well-being of your family, those God has entrusted to you as His steward, falls somewhere behind economic challenges, your job demands, the home and yard work, the toys you want to acquire, and the sports teams you idolize. If this is you, you are impotent in discerning the things that are important to God.

As an example of your impotency, if you sports fans would also get honest with yourself, you'd admit you focus more on whatever teams you follow than on the spiritual condition of your wife and children. Even if you do care about their spirituality, you probably have little ability, little desire, and few tools to foster their spiritual growth, to do whatever it takes to have them able to present a significant life to God. If you are not that heavy into sports, you can substitute the word "sports" with any other personal god, such as "worry," "fear," "work," "success," money," or "worldly power," etc., to which you've pledged your allegiance.

[Even attempting to gain a significant life for your own good shows your spiritual impotence.]

If you take that same "getting honest with yourself" and carry it further to the point of "getting honest with God," you will have to admit that the things that are important to God have been placed somewhere behind the things that give you some semblance of purpose for your life here, not eternally. Focusing on your personal fulfillment for so long, you may have actually become impotent in even discerning the things that are important to God.

Think of the eternal impact of those last statements if they are true for your life. Ask the Lord to reveal how accurate they might be for you. They may not be exactly where you stand with God; but more than likely, they're quite close to the spiritual impotence you experience every day, if you are like Christian men in general. To whatever degree you are dealing with spiritual impotence in your life, the sooner you realize and admit it, the sooner you will be on your way to a significant, world-overcoming life in God's eyes.

The typical Christian man of today is more focused on the physical appearance of blessings than on the actual development of Christ-like character within himself and his family. Having children who haven't killed anybody, having a stable but mediocre marriage, giving your ten percent and living on the ninety percent to satisfy your own personal wants is simply not the way God would have you function as ordained

30

representatives of Jesus, either within your family or in society. Whether you know it or not, whether you like it or not, God has called you to be like Jesus within your circle of influence if you say you're a follower of His ways.

[The life of Jesus is the plumb line, the only example after which you and I are to pattern our lives if we want to fulfill God's plan and present our lives as significant in His sight when we stand face to face with Him.]

I John 2:5b-6 AMP By this we may perceive (know, recognize, and be sure) that we are in Him:

6) Whoever says he abides in Him ought [as a personal debt] to walk and conduct himself in the same way in which He walked and conducted Himself.

How far is your everyday life from the exemplary life Jesus lived? How often have you dismissed this Bible verse as one of those unattainable, nebulous verses that applies to someone else? How often have you pushed this verse aside and tucked it in the back of your mind so you could deal with it some other day?

Well, today could be the beginning of that "other day" if you choose to heed the clarion call the Holy Spirit is presenting to the men who claim to be living their lives as followers of Jesus, but have had no desire to go any deeper with Him or are light years from mirroring His life to their family and the world around them. This present day could be either the very first day of a life that will be considered significant to God on the day you stand before Him and He weighs all that you have done in the name of Jesus, or it might be just another day which produces insignificant works accomplished in your flesh – important to you, perhaps, but quite possibly meaningless to Him.

If some of the above statements are true for you, do you want to continue to offend God by your impotent life, (especially when He is calling for valiant, world overcoming leaders, leaders who will do whatever it takes to be in line with His Word,) or do you want to have Him classify your life as significant in His eyes on that final day? Only how you have actually lived out your life will count, not how good your intentions may have been or how ignorant you were concerning His plans for you. I pray you'll make the right decision to acknowledge your impotence and then read on with great hope and expectation.

I Am in Process Myself!

Before we go any further, I believe I need to make some things quite clear. It's been over thirty years since I gave my life to Jesus. In those years, I have probably offended God as much or even more than you. It's only by His great mercy and grace that I'm not screaming in hell for eternity. I know what it is to be overcome with sin personally living in deep spiritual impotence, incapable of overcoming the incredible amount of sin in my life. I lied to God for many years, telling Him I loved Him and wanted only to serve Him, and then discovered my only real goal many times was to serve my own lusts, ambitions, and desires after I had called Him Lord.

I have been the hypocrite of hypocrites, the liar of liars, and the fool of fools, wasting many years of God's time while He, in His mercy, nurtured me to health in Him step by step, mercy by mercy. I know what it's like to fail God over and over, but be so cold of heart and impotent of spirit I couldn't understand my desperate situation and consequently care enough to do what was necessary to honor Him with a life He considered significant. I was in the league of the still born of God, claiming to know Him, yet light years from surrendering to Him completely. All of the time, my loving Father God was intervening in my life to make me more and more like He wanted me to be!

Philippians 3:10-16 NIV I want to know Christ and the power of his resurrection and the fellowship of sharing in his sufferings, becoming like him in his death,

11) and so, somehow, to attain to the resurrection from the dead.

12) Not that I have already obtained all this, or have already been made perfect, but I press on to take hold of that for which Christ Jesus took hold of me.

13) Brothers, I do not consider myself yet to have taken hold of it. But one thing I do: Forgetting what is behind and straining toward what is ahead,

14) I press on toward the goal to win the prize for which God has called me heavenward in Christ Jesus.

15) All of us who are mature should take such a view of things. And if on some point you think differently, that too God will make clear to you.

16) Only let us live up to what we have already attained.

Through God's miraculous healing power and living mercy, He broke my heart and allowed me to see His broken heart over the state of my life and eventually the state of His church, especially his men, over and over until I could grasp what He was attempting to get through to me. He allowed me to understand how much the words "that none should perish" really mean to Him. He also showed me the "poor, blind, and naked" condition of my life, even though I felt I was spiritually in need of nothing

32

from Him. As a man who claims to follow the ways of Jesus, He asked me to buy gold from Him, refined in the fire of adversity to my flesh.

Over the years of God dealing with my heart, He has allowed me the privilege of becoming a student of His heart and a blood bought son who gained the knowledge and assurance that He greatly loves me. The more time I spent in becoming aware of how often I had broken His heart and then repented of my actions, the healthier I became and the more I began to desire to know what pleases Him and what causes Him pain. The process of awareness, repentance, and healing continues to this day as I respond to Him. I have by no means arrived, but I am learning to submit all of my failures to Him and place them under the Lordship of Jesus Christ.

Even as I write these pages, He is cleaning the dust from the corners of my life and directing my life along the path to significance. As Paul said, *"Not that I have already obtained all this, or have already been made perfect, but I press on to take hold of that for which Christ Jesus took old of me. Brothers, I do not consider myself yet to have taken hold of it. But one thing I do: Forgetting what is behind and straining toward what is ahead, I press on toward the goal to win the prize for which God has called me heavenward in Christ Jesus."* *(Phil. 3:12-14 NIV)* We are all in this together.

[Not one of us has attained perfection. God, however, is using every one of us to help the other while we are submitting to His healing.]

Some Observations Attained Over the Years

The Impotent Perspective of Success

According to the standards of most Christians today, the accumulation of personal success in its many forms is often the litmus test for spirituality. To most, personal security or the appearance of having need of nothing means that things are going well in their relationship with the Lord. In contrast, if someone has great personal need, continues to have trials, or has little of the world's goods, it's generally determined that somewhere in his or her life, God is not pleased and some sin has to be dealt with before He can prosper that person - a foul lie from the pit of hell that permeates the church body of today and a distortion of what true prosperity really is.

In times of petitioning prayer for men to become more involved in the things that are important to God, He revealed to me that some of those who were most proud of their achievements in life or for the Lord were the ones farthest from His heart. What they had accomplished had been done with their own abilities and skills, which led to personal ownership of their achievements, rather than the full submission of those successes to the Lordship and subsequent ownership of Jesus Christ.

In my prayers, I believe the Lord indicated He was grieving over their spiritual state. He showed me they either did not spend enough time with Him to know His will, or were too dim because of the spiritual and carnal clutter in their lives to notice the need for any kind of change in their hearts. Often, He would lead me to places and have me interact with the different men in His church, those who please Him and those who are oblivious as to how far they are from His perfect will for their lives - even though they think they are in the center of His will.

Over time, He also showed me that so many of His pastors and teachers were imparting the lies of the enemy regarding true wealth, our covenant partnership power, true significance, and true stewardship. Some compromised what they taught, so that men would remain with them to help them build their own visions; rather than speak the truth, potentially offend their flesh, and watch them leave. Some had become so spiritually impotent themselves that they had nothing to impart to anyone who craved the deeper things of God. The idea of the powerful crucified life had become a thing of the past in their lives and, therefore, something for another generation, another time.

We Little Resemble the First Church

Today, the church in general, once motivated by the early morning discovery of the open grave and empowered by the blood that was shed on the cross, is a mere shadow of what it once was. In most cases, the church of Jesus Christ is ineffective against the sin in their midst. Christians - those who say they are followers of the Lord of all that ever existed, those endowed with the same power Jesus had when He walked on the earth, those who can call upon the Almighty, Supreme, Everlasting, One True, Living God any time they want - are placed on the same level in the eyes of the world as those who believe in the gods men make with the imaginations of their hardened hearts and minds.

The very sad fact is we deserve to be there. By our weak, selfish lives, we exhibit to the world a powerless, ineffective, religious Jesus who is incapable of delivering us from the challenges, lusts, and bondages of the world in which we live. There is no visible distinction between most of us and those who follow their man-made gods.

Today, the character and integrity of the first followers of Jesus the Christ, those who may even have witnessed the cross, are nowhere to be found in most fellowships, most families, and most marriages. Remnant believers, those who do want to live only as Jesus lived, have a difficult time finding places to feed their starving spirits. Programs to entertain and occupy have replaced the pursuit of having face-to-face contact with Jesus.

34

School systems have become our children's life teachers rather than their parent's exhibition of the life of Christ Himself. Selfishness has replaced service and fleshly gods have our allegiance rather than the God of the heavens. Families reel under the lifeless direction of spiritually impotent husbands and fathers, which causes societies to be little impacted by those called of God to teach them His ways.

It seems the war against those of us who say we follow Jesus is well on the way to being won by the enemy, making us oblivious to our own peril and the peril of our families and sphere of influence. We have relinquished our godly offices of husband, father, and leader to the ways of the world and the lusts of the flesh that consume us. Jesus deserves more!

It's time to reclaim the high ground of a life that exhibits the wonder and character of Jesus Christ, if we call ourselves His followers. It's time to love without limitations. It's time to determine to build a legacy that's honorable and important to God.

[You need to remember that you are loved, as you are challenged to make changes! You are going through the temporary discomfort of change simply because it is your time to become truly prosperous as God sees prosperity. It is your time to reclaim the offices of husband and father through the power of the Holy Spirit. It is your time to truly affect your circle of influence and your generation with the love of Jesus. It is your time to prepare to present a significant life to God on the day you stand before Him. You can be confident your Father in heaven will guide you through this and any other difficult work by the power of His Holy Spirit. That is a very good thing! It pleases the heart of your Father God.]

Chapter 1
MASH icu Study Questions

Answer the following questions honestly, realizing the Lord already knows the truth of your answers.

1) Are you ready and willing to hear the real truth about your relationship with the Lord from the Holy Spirit, as He convicts your heart of needed changes? Y/N

2) Would you be willing to do whatever it takes to become the man God has designed you to be, no matter what the cost? Y/N

3) Are you willing to surrender everything you have, everything you need or want, everything you are, and everything you are not to the Lord to do with as He pleases? Y/N

4) Are you willing to be exposed for who you really are in the light of God's truth through the power of the Holy Spirit? Y/N

Father,

I have no idea how far I really am from Your perfect will for my life, but I am willing to find out if it pleases You. Help me to walk through this time of exposure as You mercifully show me who I really am. I choose to trust You will guide me into truth, show me what is needed to make my life significant in Your eyes; and then accomplish it in me through the power of Your Holy Spirit.   Thank You, Lord!

Signed _____

Chapter 2

The Grand Design

What is God's intent for your life? What is yours?

Genesis 1:27-28a AMP So God created man in His own image, in the image and likeness of God He created him; male and female He created them.

28a) And God blessed them and said to them, Be fruitful, multiply, and fill the earth, and subdue it [using all its vast resources in the service of God and man]...

God began with man in the Garden of Eden. God gave him a companion - woman. The cross of Jesus made them equally acceptable in His eyes and gave them the same opportunity to serve Him. In the spiritual realm, all hearts are treated in the same manner with no respect for gender.

As with all of His other creation, however, there is an order. The planets follow the order He has established. The angels follow the order He has determined for them. Mankind must also follow the order He has marked out to truly live a significant life.

Every group must have ranking and organization in order to function properly. The Word exhibits various types of angels. In the heavenly realm, angels come in different sizes, ranking, and power. There are archangels, ministering angels, and others. Each type of angelic being is designed to function a certain way under a specific authority, all of them under the supreme authority of God and the Lordship of Jesus Christ.

In the same way, governments and laws of operation have been established by God for mankind. Just as in other arenas, leaders are put in place and a chain of command ensues so society as a whole can function properly. No matter which office a person holds, both men and women are, first of all, answerable to God. They are accountable to God for the way in which they function in their given offices. If God's human creations function properly in their God-ordained offices, His order is maintained.

His spiritual government, with its unique standards and laws, must preside over all physical governments. Surprising to most people is the fact that the family unit also takes precedence over all other physical governments in God's eyes, because kings, presidents, governors, leaders of any kind all have their start in the family unit. As the men and women in any given family unit embrace or reject the plan of God, so goes their society, their government, and whether or not their society will accept or reject the plan of God for their lives.

The man, in the office of husband and father, presides over the family unit for its protection and safety. This office is ordained by God to be one of complete obedience to the plan of God and one of whole-hearted service to the wife and children - the same heart of service that Jesus has and one that lives in the man who has accepted Christ's Lordship. This office is never to be one of dominance, but one that exists to foster the best interests of those close to him, and to further the plan of God.

The family unit that functions as God intended is the springboard for all governments necessary to maintain order in a society and it is the unit that God desires to use to display the life and nature of Jesus so that anyone with an open heart might see and embrace Him. In doing so, that individual comes into the perfect plan of God in his/her heart and becomes the next vessel so others can see Jesus and embrace Him, whether within or outside of his or her family. Thus the plan of God continues!

It's no wonder that Satan has targeted the family to either destroy it or redefine it so that it's unrecognizable when compared to what God originally created it to be. It's no wonder that he's targeted the offices of husband and father to minimize their effectiveness and reduce their power to govern within and through the nature and character of Jesus.

From Our Father's Heart

*Don't you think that I would love to give you
everything that you would like from Me?
Do you for one moment believe
that I do not see your need
and desire to meet those needs with all of My heart?
I would!
You see, however, we have an agreement.
You have agreed to allow Jesus to be Lord over
everything that you are,
all that you own, and every situation in your life.
I have agreed to conform you into the image of Jesus.
Those two commitments
are working together to accomplish truth for your life.
You have no ability to become anything
other than what you have always been.
You need Me to change you,
so I place you in situations, bring people into your life,
and allow hardship to come your way
to carve away at the person you used to be
in order to allow room for your new inner being
to come to the forefront.
I am never far from fulfilling all of your desires.*

However, your desires need to be conformed to those of Jesus.
When that is accomplished,
it allows you to fulfill your commitment to Me
and My promise to you.
It is allowing everything to work together for good.
Is it not time for you to stop asking Me for things?
Those will all come as you grow up
and I am able to send them your way.
Begin to work with Me
and allow My promise to come to pass in you.
You will be amazed at how delightful your life will be.
Be assured that I will keep My promise to you.
While I am doing that,
I am helping you to keep yours to Me.

The Deceptive Road to Spiritual Impotence

If the plan of God is for man to savor only the things of God and desire only to fulfill God's plan for his life while he presides over the family unit under the complete Lordship of Jesus Christ, then any distortion or compromise of that perfect plan minimizes its effectiveness. If men can be fooled into desiring taste buds for anything other than God and His desires, the enemy is well on his way to minimizing man's effectiveness and rendering the offices he holds powerless.

In nature, when a male of any species undergoes emasculation, he no longer seeks to fulfill the natural, God-given desires inherent in his makeup. In the same way, when a man becomes spiritually impotent, he no longer has a desire to fulfill his God-given offices of husband and/or father in the manner God intended, nor does he take on the longing or compassions Jesus has for souls in the way God intended his new nature to function.

The things that stirred the heart of Jesus - absolute obedience, the desire to fulfill the will of His Father, the desire that none should perish - no longer move the spiritually impotent man. He is not stimulated to pursue the heart of God, the life of Jesus that had no compromise, the passions that drove Jesus to the cross on behalf of others, or the joy of pleasing his Father in heaven with exuberance. He is spiritually impotent as God sees it. Because he is blinded spiritually, he goes about the "business" of being a Christian, oblivious to how far he is from what God intended for his life.

Ezekiel 13:7-8 AMP Have you not seen a false vision and have you not spoken a lying divination when you say, The Lord says, although I have not spoken?

8) Therefore thus says the Lord God: Because you have spoken empty, false, and delusive words and have seen lies, therefore behold, I am against you, says the Lord God.

Spiritual impotence begins when you accept and embrace anything that is not completely acceptable to God. In both the individual and in society as a whole, this acceptance happens a little at a time, choice by choice, rebellion by rebellion. From the moment Jesus accomplished His Father's will and made a way for man to again be in right relationship with God through His death on the cross and His resurrection, Satan has been about the business of attempting to spiritually emasculate society, trying to make us dull to the desire for all of God and turn our hearts away from the fullness of Jesus' life. Society in general - still under the dominance and the delusion brought on by the initial rebellion and transference of allegiance in the Garden of Eden - is hopelessly heading in the direction of eternal separation from God.

Although people in society believe they're making illuminated choices, they're completely deceived and totally impotent to fulfill the plan of God. Thinking they're free to successfully determine their own destinies, they are pawns in Satan's game of deception. This book will not address them, nor attempt to change their hearts or sway their thought process in any way. That is up to God and the power of the Holy Spirit. With that in mind, let's focus on men who believe they are serving God through Jesus Christ.

The moment after a man accepts Jesus as Savior and Lord, Satan attempts to reinstate taste buds that are natural to the old man and unnatural to the spiritual nature that now resides in the man, knowing he must divert the man toward impotence. He attempts to modify a man's spiritual desires so that his thoughts are not God's thoughts, his plans are not God's plans, and his longings are not the desires of God's heart; namely, that none should perish.

[If this really is a spiritual deception, it is impossible to overcome it with conventional wisdom. It must be spiritually overcome.]

As stated before, the plan of God is for mankind to follow Jesus throughout life into eternity. If Satan can get mankind as a whole - especially as he picks each man off one by one – to crave anything other than what motivated Jesus, he can minimize the effectiveness of not only each man and his circle of influence but society itself.

Once these fleshly cravings establish a foothold, they will eventually begin to override the spiritual life God establishes when someone truly commits his life to Jesus Christ as time is spent in their pursuit. This is very logical because every one of us is shaped very much by where and on what we spend our time.

Even the church is not immune to this eroding process. Once Satan has established his tactics in the lives of individuals, they bring them through the church doors and try to incorporate them into God's plan. It's like trying to mix oil and water, spiritual with fleshly. It never really works. At best, this counterfeit to God's real plan consigns people to doing good things but not necessarily God-ordained things. There is a form of religion exhibited but no real power, obligation but no real commitment, following the rules but not truly living the life of Christ, compliance but no true obedience, a certain amount of caring and concern but no unbridled compassion and love toward those very dear to God's heart. Is it any wonder the world cannot see Jesus in those who claim to follow Him?

If the body of Christ does not function distinctly different than the world – and we don't when we continually try to use its methods in the spiritual arena – then what could possibly motivate someone to cross over the line into a true commitment to Jesus Christ except the Holy Spirit Himself? And then, where can God send that person to be nurtured in the things that are important and significant to Him? To the body of Christ, you say. Yes, but do we in the body of Christ actually know what God's plan is or have we been duped by Satan as he methodically uses God's own to introduce the world's methods into the body of believers?

Where Do You Stand?

A spiritually impotent man gives no thought as to how much he's offending the heart of God, little thought to the fact that he will answer to a holy God on the day his life is judged; and much less thought to the lie he is living, while calling it Christianity. In fact, when confronted directly about his life, he is offended. When asked if he's a follower of Christ, he's assured that he is in league with those who are called the children of God and relatively confident he's pleasing God with his actions and lifestyle.

If the Holy Spirit does have an opportunity to break into the thinking of the spiritually impotent man and convict him of every area that offends God, he may initiate a concentrated effort to change and walk in it for awhile; but the price he'll be asked to pay to become a truly holy man of God is eventually seen as much more radical than necessary. Shortly thereafter, he ceases his efforts, labeling them spiritually zealous and unnecessary; and trades them in for the comforts afforded him in his "business as usual" atmosphere, without considering or caring how inadequate his life is in furthering the true plan of God and fulfilling his role in it.

The spiritually impotent man is the epitome of a blind guide, who leads others into the destructive nature of his own self-manufactured beliefs,

43

unaware that he's offending God by his religious activities and ignorance. Not only that, he unwittingly offends others by his spiritual immaturity, because he can give them little hope for their eternal well-being since he is so impotent in knowing and walking in the plan of God himself, something others should be able to learn by his example.

It's Time to Begin to Find the Heart of God for Your Life

Answer the following questions as best you can. As you progress through this study, a godly pattern will emerge that can be applied to every area of your life. Only after you have submitted all areas to Him as you become aware of them will your complete pattern for change be revealed. Be patient with yourself. God will be patient with you as He brings you to repentance for who you are not and for the things you are doing that He wants to remove. Remember that you have been given the mind of Christ, and an inner being that only responds to the resurrection power of the cross. All the resurrection power of heaven is poised to explode against the enemy on your behalf if you determine to walk in the life God has given you. Choose today to be immersed in the Lord's mighty work that's being done in you, as you align your life with His plans.

It might be wise to begin a journal for this study, someplace where you can refer back to insights the Lord gives you as you progress through different sections of this book and prayerfully use them in dealing with specific people and situations in your life. You may want to add your own questions, statements, or notes in addition to the questions below. Remember, you are a work in progress, a delight to the Lord as you shake off your impotence and set your course to know and serve Him.

Chapter 2
MASH icu Study Questions

1) Do you fully understand that the works in your life are going to be judged by God?   Y/N

2) Do you fully understand the difference in these three things: the value that God places on you vs. the value He places on the work you have done in the flesh vs. the works you have done under full submission to Him? Take the time to express this concept in your own words.   Y/N

3) List the priorities of your life in order of importance to you. Include the areas of your relationship with Jesus, your work, your marriage, your children, your fellowship, your community activities, recreational activities and anything else that is part of your life.

Start with #1 as being your most important priority. The easiest way to do this is to use the last six months as your guideline. What your priorities have been in the recent past will generally be a great indication of your priorities at present. This is not a test, but a starting point. Be truthful. God knows your heart. He just wants you to understand where you are at this juncture in your relationship with Him and say it out loud.

4) Find a Bible verse or verses that clarify what the Lord desires to do in you. Find those that encourage you. Find those that confirm what He determines as significant and clarify the direction He has for you.

5) What have you claimed as your own that is really owned by God?

Make a list of what you are willing and/or unwilling to acknowledge as completely His. You might ask yourself questions which include the portion of your income that you believe is yours to do with as you please, the amount of time in your day or night that need not be directed by Him, the areas of your business or job and the ethics you employ that are not under His jurisdiction, etc.

6) Do you fully understand all of heaven is for you as you shake off your old way of living, because you are a blood-bought child of God? You are entering into the life that delights His heart as you choose to live as the new creation He has made you. Determine to walk with Him as He teaches you to think His kind of thoughts and walk His kind of walk.

Father,

Please help me to fully understand how significant my life is to You. Remind me often how important it is to You that I make significant decisions throughout my days. Give me the wisdom and power to live significantly in Your eyes. Thank You, Lord.

Chapter 3

And the Bean Is Under Shell #1?   #2!!   #3??

It is vitally important to pursue truth at any cost.

Acts 17: 29-31 NIV "Therefore since we are God's offspring, we should not think that the divine being is like gold or silver or stone—an image made by human design and skill. [30] In the past God overlooked such ignorance, but now he commands all people everywhere to repent. [31] For he has set a day when he will judge the world with justice by the man he has appointed. He has given proof of this to everyone by raising him from the dead."

I don't know for certain if this story happened in my home town or not. I heard it from someone locally that I trust. The information in the story I'm about to unfold may have changed a bit even to the point of some inaccuracies, but the concept is such a marvel of deception that it bears repeating, discrepancies and all, in introducing this chapter.

A man purchased a new barbeque grill. It was beautiful, one of those monuments of grilling machinery that makes most of us men water at the mouth just thinking about the culinary masterpieces we could conjure up to impress our neighbors. Bringing it home in all its immensity, it evoked awe in the guy next door and sent terror into the hearts of the neighborhood children who feared it would somehow devour them before they had a chance to grow up.

He set the grill in his backyard in a prominent place, where he could look at it periodically and dream of winning first place ribbons in the minds of all those who were fortunate enough to experience his expertise, nay, his art form of providing unforgettable, succulent treasures for the discriminating palate. Tomorrow, he was going to fire that baby up and let the whole neighborhood salivate as the smell of his edible creations wafted across physical lot lines and into the nostrils of envious observers of his newly purchased tower of one-upmanship. (OK. So, I got a little descriptive; but, hey, I'm a story teller!)

Anyway, the guy bought a grill, set it in his back yard and went to bed, possibly dreaming of the ultimate barbeque experience. The next morning, lo and behold, there was an empty spot where the grill had been situated. The man's potatoes were burned. He kicked something, threw something else; and stood in the corner of his garage with his thumb in his mouth, plotting revenge for the time when the police caught the person who would dare do such a thing. (Well, maybe not!)

About two days after it was stolen, the grill miraculously reappeared in the place from which it had been taken. The man was thrilled. Opening the cover, the owner saw that although the grill had been used, it was cleaned up very nicely and looked almost as good as new. On the grill rack was an envelope with a note in it that read something like this:

"Hi, I'm sorry I took your grill. We had some surprise guests from out of town and I discovered my grill wasn't working. I borrowed yours and I hope you don't mind. Please forgive me and accept this token of my gratitude."

The letter was signed, "An Embarrassed but Grateful Neighbor in Need."

Inside the envelope along with the note were four front row tickets for the local professional basketball game the following night - one for him, his wife, and their two teenage boys, who loved the team and the game. All of a sudden, the missing grill was no longer a problem.

The following night the whole family went to the game and enjoyed it immensely. After laughing and cheering and having a whole lot of fun throughout the evening, they returned home to find their house almost completely empty. Oops!

It seems the "embarrassed neighbor" had set them up quite nicely. Knowing that the entire family was gone and approximately when they would return because they listened to the game while emptying the house, the very cunning thieves took the liberty of helping themselves to much of what the family owned. Pretty slick deception, huh! Surely the thieves enjoyed a few good laughs at the expense of the owner of the grill.

Awareness

Satan is the master of deception and delights in the ease with which we fall for his plans and schemes. If the deception above surprised or startled you to some degree, even though you were tipped off it was coming, you more than likely function in some areas of deception as far as your life is concerned. I believe we all do. We are no match for the enemy's wiles. In fact, most of us have bought his cunning at one time or another, hook, line, and sinker. Personal experience tells me the Lord spends a lot of time in getting the light bulb to go on over our heads.

Just as the family was gleefully unaware of the deception in which they were involved as they enjoyed their good fortune, we as men have bought the lies of the enemy as to what it is to be a man and how we are to act, especially if we are blessed by the successes of the world. We blindly go about our days building this, deciding that, buying whatever, worrying about another impending disaster, planning for stuff in the future - all the

48

time oblivious to how spiritually bankrupt we are as far as God is concerned.

[If it really is important to have a significant life in God's eyes, we first of all need to know what that life is and what changes we need to make so we can flow in it.]

Most men - those who don't have the peace that comes from knowing Jesus - spend their days attempting to find purpose and/or importance in their lives. Each of us, as men, wants to be significant. We all want to believe our lives have made a difference to someone, that there's purpose for being alive. Someone once said that most people marry so they have a witness to their lives.

In Christ, the Bible tells us that each of us has incredible significance with God and is fully accepted by Him. Somehow though, that does not seem to be enough. Even when we are with Him, we strive to find acceptance with others and have a need to own things with our hearts. In most cases, we need to be the fastest or the best. We are on a mission to be successful by the world's standards. More often than not, we are delighted to be accepted for what we have accomplished and how many toys we have, rather than for who we have become in Christ. Gaining His attributes seems to be far less important than what we own and much further down the line behind our own achievements.

Although each of us is very important to God because of the blood of Jesus, most of us don't have a clue as to what He considers a significant, world-overcoming life. Most of us haven't even thought about it. That's how creative and masterful the enemy's deception is. We live in spiritual impotence and complete blindness every day, never knowing that our spiritual home is being methodically ransacked.

God has given us our breath to use on His behalf. Shouldn't something as important as the fact that God considers our actions of great significance and will eventually judge them compel us to make it our priority to find His will and function in it? Instead, we play in the dirt of personal selfishness, while He mourns the loss of those we are intended to touch for Him.

From Our Father's Heart

Many in My church have been lulled into a complacency
that is certain death to the kind of deep spiritual life
that I desire for them.
They observe that their "big" sins are gone,
so they think that everything is in order.
They do not know how far they are from the truth.
They don't know how much of a hindrance

their complacency is to My work,
because they have not sold out enough
to hear My voice above their works-oriented religion.
They can only see through eyes that are carnal,
so they understand little about what I call "big" sins.
Big sins to Me have little to do with the visible sins of the world.
Removal of initial sins is part of My covenant promise
because of the cross.
The undiscerning see themselves being healed of obvious sins,
layer after layer, and stop pressing in deep enough
to allow Me to show them a mightier walk,
a walk that I wish all of My children could experience.
A big sin to Me is compromise,
which is caused by rebellion to My ways.
Another is keeping what is Mine
so that they can pad their comfort areas.
One that is prevalent now is a complacency
toward the seasons in which they live.
I grieve over a prayer-less life.
You who do see, you who have sold out,
you who are surrendering fully
must understand that only radical intrusions
on the comfort areas of those in rebellion
will shake them loose from their sin.
Do not spend your time attempting to teach
those who choose not to be taught the crucified life.
It will only cause you frustration and hardship.
They do not understand your devoted life,
so they must judge you by their standards.
Concern yourselves with souls,
those who need to hear and be saved.
Cultivate young hearts to fully submit to Me
before they are swayed by the cold church.
Save them from complacency
by exhibiting the life of My Son before them.
Serve the teachable.
Set aside those who choose not to see the times and seasons.
They are not willing to do what it takes to be ready
when I need them.
You find those who will hear and see.
I will soon deal with those
who have chosen to go the way of complacency.

The following Bible verses from Revelation might as well have our names at the front of them. Go ahead, put your name there. If you don't believe the verse pertains to you, you soon will if you allow the Holy Spirit to really deal with your heart as you complete the different sections of this book.

"(Your Name,) *I know your deeds, that you are neither cold nor hot. I wish you were either one or the other!*

16) So, because you are lukewarm - neither hot nor cold - I am about to spit you out of my mouth.

17) You say, 'I am rich; I have acquired wealth and do not need a thing.' But you do not realize that you are wretched, pitiful, poor, blind and naked.

18) I counsel you to buy from me gold refined in the fire, so you can become rich; and white clothes to wear, so you can cover your shameful nakedness; and salve to put on your eyes, so you can see." (Rev. 3:15-18 NIV)

I always thought those verses were for someone else, some reprehensible Neanderthal, until one early morning the Lord convicted me of my own blindness. The prospect of being lukewarm was not a very pretty picture. Poor, blind, and naked started to scare me. Being spit out of the mouth of Jesus brought me to my face for quite some time.

"Wait a minute!" I thought after praying for a while. "I'm saved. I gave my life to Jesus. What's this 'spit you out of my mouth' thing?" Then I said it out loud and hoped I wouldn't hear a thunderstorm manifest itself in my area. After much prayer, the words "about to" struck my eye. "About to" meant there was still hope for me. It meant I still had time to change so I wouldn't become a projectile from the mouth of God.

That morning, I started on a quest that took some twenty years so that I could arrive at a reasonable conclusion. I wanted to know the heart of God for men like me who have difficulty grasping things like intimacy, love, commitment; and, yes, feeling distasteful to my Lord Whom I want to serve with whatever capabilities He has given me.

I began to see the mercy of God in verse 16. Although God has many purposes for His Word, for this study He was warning those to whom He was speaking and He was warning me there was more He desired from me. But how much more and how would I get there?

Over the years, the Lord has guided me through a lot of both spiritual and religious stuff, the same as He has done in your life if you are seeking any truth at all. He has allowed His Word to divide what was real and beautiful in His eyes from those religious activities I did to impress Him and my friends, those things that took on a spiritual aroma that did not please Him.

Those days and years held some pretty interesting - and sometimes quite surprising - revelations as to what pleases Him and what doesn't. In my own life, I found that a lot of the things spoken by those who are heralded as people we need to follow are pretty much designed to have us help them build their large churches. Their words also provided a kind of gospel that told me what I wanted to hear, so it was only natural that I would support their ministries, causing them to appear successful. As the Lord continued to reveal things and I was able to start understanding His heart, I chose to look a little closer in His Word to see what God considers important.

I began to realize that if God is real, the epitome of truth, and has all the answers, it would behoove me to see how much I lined up with the truth. I was challenged to ask Him to reveal areas in which I walked in deception by following the teaching of those who had less than my best interests - and God's - at heart. Pretty sharp, huh! Talk about brain surgery!

Deception is a funny thing. Not funny ha ha, but funny in the fact that it does its job so well that you don't see it's happening until the Lord starts working on His end. I finally realized that most of the time, we - especially as men - are deceived, we just don't see deception weaving its web around us. I remember times when I'd find myself defending something in which I truly believed, only to have to later undo the damage that had been done while I was confused in my thinking, flowing in the spirit of foolishness.

That kind of deception is bad enough, especially if you are someone who proclaims his deception loud and clear for everyone to hear while under the influence of stupidity. The deception that's really quite frightening, however, is the kind that causes the dulling of one's senses, rendering one blissfully ignorant of the surrounding danger. It's the kind that causes a young child to want to walk across a busy highway to pet the cute doggy on the other side, having no inkling as to the imminent danger of speeding cars; or the kind that would prompt that same child, in his immature thinking, to grab the shiny handle that peeks at him from on top of the stove - something very wondrous from his perspective, but not in any way linked in his thinking to the very hot liquid in the pan to which the shiny handle is attached. That kind of deception is not only dangerous in general life situations; it is extremely hazardous when applied to spiritual situations that have eternal consequences.

For many years, I was so dull in my thinking I gave little consideration to what really pleases God. What did He consider a significant life? Would He consider my life significant when I stood before Him to give an account? These were questions I never thought to ask myself and no one else asked me, as best I can remember.

Sure, there were teachings about Jesus and His desires to only please the Father. I heard many stories about people who lived their lives in complete obedience and stories of the great saints of the past who lived exemplary lives; but the thought that my Father in heaven considered my life and the things I did while living it of great significance and would judge them never crossed my mind. I was saved, I dealt with the sin the Holy Spirit showed me, I desired to please Jesus most of the time; but generally, that's as far as it went.

I eventually discovered that somehow, sometime, someplace in the past, I was rendered incapable of having – or even desiring to have - taste buds for only those things Jesus embraced. I was spiritually walking across the busy highway to pet the cute little doggy, unaware of the impact of the spiritual traffic that had been hidden from me. I was deceived and the "beauty" of my deception, as with any masterfully contrived lie, was the fact that I truly believed I was walking in truth. That's what makes it so insidious (having a gradual and cumulative effect.)

<u>Chapter 3</u>
MASH icu Study Questions

1) Is it possible you might be deceived as to what it means to please God in regard to your life, your marriage, your career, your circle of influence? Y/N

2) Are you tired of attempting to be better or more spiritual? Y/N

3) Are you a little perturbed that it has taken you this long to comprehend your deception and you'd like to see some changes take place in you that would allow you to glorify God with the rest of your life? Y/N

4) Do you understand that it's not in your power to initiate and complete these changes? Y/N

Father,

I realize I don't even know what You want me to desire as a priority in my life. Please make me aware of what I need to know. Please heal me of my spiritual impotence. Give me a desire to want what You see as significant. Give me the heart of Jesus. Thank You, Lord. Amen.

Chapter 4

The Vital Importance of Understanding the Plan of God

You are important and greatly loved by God.
Even so, your actions and motives will be judged.

II Cor. 5:9-10 NIV So we make it our goal to please him, whether
we are at home in the body or away from it.
10) For we must all appear before the judgment seat of Christ, that
each one may receive what is due him for the things done while in the body,
whether good or bad.

According to the Bible, somewhere in the timeless eternity past, sovereign Father God spoke the universe into existence, simply because He desired it to be done. Galaxy upon limitless galaxies were formed by His Word undeniably going forth. Each was positioned as He commanded.

In one of these vast galaxies, God selected a small planet called Earth, (a place where a portion of the fallen, rebellious angels are free to roam,) to play out the drama of His next creation- mankind. The stage set, the players in place, He was ready to develop a creation that was to wholeheartedly serve Him out of love for all eternity. The drama of free will, free choice, rebellion, and a subsequent salvation opportunity for this fledgling creation was an integral part of the plan of God to establish willing, loving servants, who would be available to Him and any future creations. Willing obedience – whether past, present, or future – is the key in God's relationship with man and is very dear to His heart.

From Our Father's Heart

I wish that none should perish.
That is the priority of My heart for your creation.
It is the reason that I have set everything in motion
since the fall of Adam and Eve.
Their fall was no surprise.
The need for redemption was no surprise.
Every action by every individual born of woman was no surprise.
All that has happened,
is happening, and will happen is right on My timetable.
There are no surprises
when it comes to those who are to spend eternity with Me.
Where each of you spends that eternity

is My heart behind My Word.
It is the central focus of all that I have created thus far.
Consider this.
Pause quietly and think on what I am about to say.
Before any of My other creation processes will unfold,
the redemption of your generation must be completed.
That is how important each and every day of your existence is.
With that in mind,
I would have you consider your reasons
for everything that you do
compared to My reasons for your life.
What is the purpose for your every action?
I have a specific plan for your birth.
Have you taken the time to really find out what it is
and function in it with the same importance
that I place on your days?
Look at the life of Jesus.
He is your example.
For everything that He was,
for all that has been said about Him,
most people have not applied His zeal
for the fulfillment of My plan to their lives.
His every breath was dedicated to My desire
that none should perish.
That is the way I want you to live.
Your specific task is part of the overall fulfillment of My plan.
If you get in line with My heart from now on,
everywhere you go and whatever you do
will have that purpose in mind.
Turn now from every other distraction.
I need you.
So does everyone around you.

The Fall

In God's plan, rebellion (or sin) had to be established and then exposed. Once the same choice that the previous angelic creation had made came into play - for the tempter was the same tempter that challenged the angels who fell - the stage was set for God to continually prove that mankind could not be faithful without God Himself intervening. It also provided the formula for mankind to make a choice to serve God as intended or to continue to serve his new master because of the allegiance established at the fall.

Four thousand years of failure to serve God, repentance, failure, separation, failure, mercy, failure, exposure, failure, hopelessness, etc., positioned the rebellious heart of mankind to become aware of its inability to understand God's ways. The continual personal failures softened the collective heart of mankind enough to accept the fact that it was impossible to serve Father God faithfully without supernatural intervention. These many years of God coming to the rescue of helpless man proved to mankind that he had no capability of being a trustworthy servant of God, fit for either earthly or eternal service, in his own strength.

II Samuel 14:14b NIV "But God does not take away life; instead, he devises ways so that a banished person may not remain estranged from him."

The Merciful Intervention

By initiating a plan whereby mankind could freely choose whether or not to serve Him and then infusing anyone who made the choice to serve Him with His very own reliable nature, God reestablished the originally intended, reliable form of creation. God, in the form of the man named Jesus, made Himself visible to anyone who chose to see Him. From the smallest child to the most prominent of men, everyone had the opportunity to see in Jesus how God intended life to be lived. All of mankind could, for the first time since Eden, observe the benchmark of what God considered a significant life, a life with which He wanted to spend eternity. They could observe firsthand true obedience (even unto death,) unbridled passion for doing the will of Father God, purposeful love for everyone (even the lowest ranking of fellow human being); and limitless energy to fulfill the plan of God by living the kind of life He intended for everyone from the very beginning.

With the visible presence of God came a promise. For anyone who would embrace the life God made available through Jesus, God Himself promised to dwell in that person with the same presence that dwelt in Jesus.

Person after person, generation after generation now had the same opportunity to see what God considered a significant life – just like those in Jesus' generation - because He was now supernaturally present in anyone who made the choice to embrace His life.

With the acceptance of His life came another promise from God. All who fully embraced the life He offered - with its new obedient nature, its heart for also fulfilling the plan of God; and its desire that none should perish but also make the same life-giving choice offered by God - would be given a place in future eternities with the God they chose and embraced, all after an incredibly fulfilling life of service on earth.

John 4:34 NIV "My food," said Jesus, "is to do the will of him who sent me and to finish his work."

As you are hopefully beginning to see at this point, most of us rarely regard this life as a rehearsal, so to speak, for what is to come once we finish our lives on earth. This world is a place of preparation where we learn how to rule and reign with the Lord for eternity. We usually look at this life as a means to an end; that somehow if we just hang on long enough, we will receive our reward, stroll on streets paved with gold, and live in our mansions while plucking our harp strings. What are we thinking? There is so much more!

God has placed us on this earth to prepare all who will respond for what is to come, not have us flounder around for a lifetime and then be rudely surprised when we stand before Him because of our fruitless lives! He is looking to develop priests and kings who will rule and reign for His best interests, not court jesters on the world's stage who amuse and placate the crowds. We are to be the anointed, powerful representatives of His plan for all of mankind, proclaiming to everyone what truly matters – the importance of a life devoted to Jesus being prepared for eternity.

Second Best

Because all of mankind, through generational ties, was included in the choice to serve self when the very first of mankind sinned, they were all now under the fatherhood and authority of the ultimate self-server, the father of lies, Satan. Angry, jealous, and vicious, with a continual vendetta to minimize the number who will serve God, he lies in wait to stop everyone he can from making the choice to submit to God through Jesus in hopes of thwarting the eternal plan of God for their lives. If he should lose them to the love Jesus provides, then he must at least minimize their commitment and weaken their presentation of His life, so that others will not see that love.

John 8:42-47 NIV   Jesus said to them, "If God were your Father, you would love me, for I came from God and now am here. I have not come on my own; but he sent me.

43) Why is my language not clear to you? Because you are unable to hear what I say.

44) You belong to your father, the devil, and you want to carry out your father's desire. He was a murderer from the beginning, not holding to the truth, for there is no truth in him. When he lies, he speaks his native language, for he is a liar and the father of lies.

45) Yet because I tell the truth, you do not believe me!

46) Can any of you prove me guilty of sin? If I am telling the truth, why don't you believe me?

47) He who belongs to God hears what God says. The reason you do not hear is that you do not belong to God."

Satan knows that if he loses his grip on someone because he or she chooses to embrace the life and Lordship of Jesus, he must settle for second best. He must lead them to accept compromise, any form of compromise, along with their acceptance of the nature of Jesus. Through all of the corrupt and even seemingly innocent means at his disposal, he must dim the light of the life of Jesus in those he has lost so that others will not be able to clearly see the nature of Jesus walking among them.

If Satan can minimize your passion to do the will of God, if he can somehow distort the image of the life of God that's supposed to be exhibited in you as a man who professes to serve Jesus, if he can in any way have you deny the character and power of Jesus in the life you present to others, he can minimize the number of those who will embrace the provision God has mercifully made available and all that it accomplishes.

Hebrews 12:1-3 NIV   Therefore, since we are surrounded by such a great cloud of witnesses, let us throw off everything that hinders and the sin that so easily entangles, and let us run with perseverance the race marked out for us.

2) Let us fix our eyes on Jesus, the author and perfecter of our faith, who for the joy set before him endured the cross, scorning its shame, and sat down at the right hand of the throne of God.

3) Consider him who endured such opposition from sinful men, so that you will not grow weary and lose heart.

Remaining Right Before God

Romans 14:12 NIV   So then, each of us will give an account of himself to God.

A man who has chosen to build an honorable legacy understands his accountability to God and overcomes the plans of the enemy. Most of us have never fully grasped the understanding that one day we will stand before the living God and be required to give an account of every breath we have been given by Him. This sovereign side of God is as real as the gracious, loving, all-forgiving ABBA God image taught in our churches today. He truly is the ABBA Father to those who are His through Jesus. This singular presentation of only the soft, merciful characteristics of God, however, has done a great disservice to the heart issues and plans God intends for His true church.

It seems as though the Righteous Judge side of God is rarely taught. It has been swept under the religious carpet of a gospel that teaches of deliverance from the fires of hell, grace, and mercy only. The elimination of the presentation of God as the Righteous Judge has left the church - and the men in the church in particular - free to function in a widely accepted attitude of independent living. It has fostered an ignorance of the need for accountability regarding the eternal impact of our actions and created an image of a God Who is there to serve us, rather than us serving Him, as it should be. Jesus deserves far more!

A Life Planned by God

Let's take a look at a life that has been planned by God, one that will pass His criteria for a life well-lived. The Bible calls all of those who follow Him to live the kind of life Jesus lived when He walked on this earth. Most of us have given lip service to those words, but far fewer have it functioning in our hearts and actions. The possibility of living that kind of life someday, somehow, may have occurred to us at one time; but days, months, and years of life challenges have dimmed any hope of actually making the needed changes to go there. "Anyway, no one around us is even mentioning that kind of life as necessary," so we think.

Any desire of actually following in the steps of Jesus - crucifying our worldly ways and functioning as a mirror of the heart of Jesus with His love for only God's ways- left most of us long ago. That kind of life is simply not our priority.

God's Word, however, hasn't changed. God's heart hasn't changed. God's promise of His judgment on our lives for how we've acted as followers of Christ hasn't changed. Ignorance on our part will not be a justifiable excuse when we stand before Him. Living the on-fire life of Jesus is the criteria and pattern to which we are called. The choice to live any less is called a lukewarm existence.

[Men, I believe that God is talking to the church of today and specifically to those men who have relinquished their offices of husband, father, and leader in their sphere of influence. We have adopted the spiritual influences of the world and its ways to one degree or another. The Laodicean spirit is the spirit we are of if we function within priorities that are not God's priorities for us.]

What is a True Follower of the Life of Jesus as God Sees It?

Jesus did and said nothing unless it was ordained and said by His Father in heaven. Jesus had no desires that He determined to be above the desires of His Father. Jesus owned nothing of the world in His heart, even His own life. Jesus lived only for others. He loved without limitations. Jesus held His reputation in low esteem, cared only what His Father thought of Him; and lived only for His Father's desires over His own. Jesus understood His life was not His own, but was owned by the Father for the specific purpose of doing the Father's will. Jesus dedicated every moment of His days to the plan God had for Him. Nothing else mattered except fulfilling the purpose Father God had for His life.

The Life of Jesus is the Benchmark to Follow if We Say We Are in Him

I John 2:3-7 AMP And this is how we may discern [daily, by experience] that we are coming to know Him [to perceive, recognize, understand, and become better acquainted with Him]: if we keep (bear in mind, observe, practice) His teachings (precepts, commandments).

4) Whoever says, I know Him [I perceive, recognize, understand, and am acquainted with Him] but fails to keep and obey His commandments (teachings) is a liar, and the Truth [of the Gospel] is not in him.

5) But he who keeps (treasures) His Word [who bears in mind His precepts, who observes His message in its entirety], truly in him has the love of and for God been perfected (completed, reached maturity). By this we may perceive (know, recognize, and be sure) that we are in Him:

6) Whoever says he abides in Him ought [as a personal debt] to walk and conduct himself in the same way in which He walked and conducted Himself.

7) Beloved, I am writing you no new commandment, but an old commandment which you have had from the beginning; the old commandment is the message which you have heard [the doctrine of salvation through Christ].

Line up your life with the life of Jesus. With all of the mercy you may give yourself, with all of the excuses you may present, with all of the possibilities of your good intentions, how does your life really compare to the life Jesus lived? If you closed your eyes for the last time in the next minute, how would your life compare to the standard God requires of you since you have claimed to be His, namely the life of Jesus?

Now place yourself before the Righteous Judge and the inescapable, exposing light of absolute truth. In that light, how close were your desires to those of Jesus - toward His Father, toward sinners, toward brothers and sisters in Christ, toward the things of this world, toward following His commands, toward those who don't know God, etc. etc. If God took one segment of your heart at a time, one precept, one truth as you saw it, one real love of your heart compared to His loves and exposed them in the light of His truth, more than likely you would have little confidence in saying that you truly followed the life of Jesus, the One you claimed to serve.

We will all stand before God one day with no excuses. The fact is that if we don't change our ways and submit to His ways, you and I will find that we have lied to God. We have lied to Jesus and deceived ourselves into believing we are true followers of the ways and life of Jesus. There is no question that we have been lukewarm at best. In reality, most of us have served only ourselves and called it serving God in so many areas that we little resemble who Jesus is to others. Is it any wonder the world has negated the witness we have tried to present of Him?

[We can become stumbling blocks to those in the world and to other Christians. See Romans 14.]

We Need to Own a Proper Perspective

If the full and complete understanding that our life on this earth has an eternal impact is not clear to us, even the most ardent of us will fall short in seeing the importance of our lives in God's eyes. His desire that we have a significant legacy to present to Him must be part of our daily decision-making process, so that we can move in the direction of being obedient to do only His will. His standards for the lives of those who say they follow Jesus must become our standards, if we are going to stand pleasing before Him at the time He judges our lives.

Each of us, especially us men, needs to fall on our face before God, asking for mercy for our illicit love affair with the world and its ways if we call ourselves Christians. We need to repent to God of our rebellious hearts,

62

understanding that we have not really considered living up to the expectations He set for our lives. Most of us have not even entertained the idea that we should be building an eternal legacy and a heritage that is significant in God's eyes, if we say we are His through Jesus. We need to humble ourselves in the presence of the Lord and allow Him to impart to us how to live a life that has eternal significance.

Once that is done in our hearts and we own it through the power of the Holy Spirit, we need to implement whatever changes are necessary to please the Lord and do His will, no matter what the cost might be. If that means changing our job, selling a home that is too large, cutting back on our lifestyle, intervening in the life of our rebellious teenager, making things right with others, focusing on rebuilding our marriage, or moving to another community, we must do it. We need to get back on track with the Lord and never leave His will again.

What Is a Significant Heritage as God Sees It?

If your defense to the Lord on the day you stand before Him has anything to do with what you have acquired in the life He gave you, it is as worthless as a bucket full of holes. To think that anything attained from the world is important to God would nullify part of the significance of the life of Jesus. He owned nothing.

Oh, the wonder of God's way of looking at things! To Him, the life of Jesus - the slaughtered Lamb, the King of all kings, the Lord of everything that has and ever will exist - is the most significant life ever lived. To Father God, His worth is immeasurable, His heritage worth proclaiming throughout the heavens for all of eternity. In the eyes of God, His legacy is the standard for all of human creation to follow. Jesus raised the bar and set the criteria for a life considered significant in God's eyes. His life is the perfect example for all to follow until the end of time, and it has been given to you!

As you read the Word and the best accounts of His life, Jesus appeared to be a vagrant, an itinerant preacher. His sole possession, the garment He wore throughout His visible life, was first of all given to Him and then destroyed at His death. By carnal standards, His legacy was insignificant, even nonexistent, to the "important" men who lived at that time. Submitting to the harshest treatment of His day by allowing Himself to be hung bloodied and naked on a cross, with most of His followers scattered, He was cursed, ridiculed, and spat upon, as if He were a despicable human being. Even to one of the sinners on a cross next to Him, His life was deemed worthless and a joke, His credible heritage scorned.

Most witnesses to His death probably walked away from that event thinking that His life had been a mockery of the things of God. Compared to the pompously arrogant who crucified Him and the religious leaders who in the crowd's eyes were certainly worthy of God's blessing, His life was a dismal failure, something not worth sharing with their children as testimony of an honorable life, one worth emulating.

How Did Jesus Do It?

In studying the pattern of the life of Jesus, we must come to realize that every aspect of His life pleased His Father. Several glaring examples stand out and should be applied to our own lives. They are attainable only through the power of the Holy Spirit.

Jesus was obedient to the will of His Father even to the point of His death. All of His heart determination fell in line with His Father's desires. What the Father wanted, He did without question. Jesus considered nothing His own, even His life. Everything belonged to His Father. Jesus did nothing by His own reasoning or the logic of the day. Everything was done of His Father in heaven. Do you see the pattern that is acceptable and significant to God and the one we are to follow?

We have been bought with the blood of Jesus. We are owned by God. Everything we have is owned by God. Every breath we take is given to us by God. Every thought, action, dream, and desire is to be confirmed by God before it is determined valid enough to act upon. In this life and beyond, we are to be empty vessels, conduits so that the life of Jesus can be lived through us and the plans of God can be implemented through us, as seen through Jesus' example.

Our true legacy is to impart the importance of leading a significant life for the glory of God to everyone with whom we come in contact throughout our time on earth. By the power of the Holy Spirit, this honorable legacy, then, is the impartation of the character and integrity of Jesus to everyone we meet through the way we live our lives, teaching them by our words and actions who He is and how He lived as an example for their lives. This continues the plans of God. This is important to God. This makes our lives significant to Him. This is our honorable legacy, which will continue uninterrupted through those who knew us and saw Jesus enough in us through word and deed, so they, too, had the opportunity to choose and follow Him when He called.

Ps. 16:5-6 AMP The Lord is my chosen and assigned portion, my cup; You hold and maintain my lot.

6 The lines have fallen for me in pleasant places; yes, I have a good heritage.

Chapter 4
MASH icu Study Questions

1) Do you really believe you can live the kind of life Jesus did?   Y/N

2) Do you even want the kind of intimacy Jesus had with His Father?
Y/N

3) Does your perspective line up with God's Word?   Y/N

4) How do you see your heritage with God?

[Living a significant life is not living a life of perfection. We are all in the process of being perfected. Living a significant life is making the necessary changes and modifications to our lives and our attitudes that please God as we become aware of them, the attitude we adopt as we address the things that are out of line in our lives. As we get our lives in order with God's order, the power of God is free to move in us and in those around us because of our testimony of the cross.]

Father,

I ask You to line my heart up with Your Word. Teach me to see my worth and my legacy from Your point of view. Teach me how to live as You desire me to live. Thank You, Lord!

Chapter 5

Theft – How to Rip God Off Without Really Trying

How much of what you own is really yours according to God?

Matt. 6:24 NIV "No one can serve two masters. Either he will hate the one and love the other, or he will be devoted to the one and despise the other. You cannot serve both God and Money."

Luke 12:48b NIV "...From everyone who has been given much, much will be demanded; and from the one who has been entrusted with much, much more will be asked."

Over the years, Peter Wilson had numerous conversations with his neighbor John Cornell, a retired naval officer, regarding his desire that Peter take over his charitable work and the care of his niece upon his death. Peter weighed his decision carefully and eventually agreed to see that John's legacy continued under his supervision and even beyond.

When the time came, Peter sat in the lawyer's office, dumbfounded at the magnitude of John's assets, most of which took the form of vast real estate holdings. In the estate document, there were few directions, stipulations, or requirements pertaining to the use of the holdings except for a long history of charitable giving and a request that Peter see to a few heart missions on which John had spent a good deal of time and energy.

The technicalities of the law and the task of perusing long, legal documents were something for which John had no time, so the testament was pretty much wide open and available for interpretation to the chagrin of John's lawyer, who had often tried to convince John to modify and strengthen the document. John, however, trusted Peter. To him, that was much more important than any legal piece of paper with a bunch of do's and don'ts, so the will was more a documentation of a few simple heart requests than it was one of legally demanding responsibilities.

John's niece was an invalid from birth and when her parents were killed in a plane crash when she was in her teens, he had her moved to a luxury suite in the highest-rated, most costly care-giving facility on the West coast. Very dear to his heart, he felt compelled to get her the best care, especially considering how God had blessed him.

John asked Peter to disperse the majority of his wealth over a period of years to those facilities that cared for people who were hurting, such as dope, alcohol, and emotional treatment centers. He had set up several foundations that dispersed a generous amount of money to these facilities every month. It was his desire that Peter continue doing the same work, using the Cornell family name. Charitable work was extremely important to John and he wanted his legacy to continue. He asked Peter to pass this same arrangement on to someone Peter trusted when he made out his own will.

Finally, John stipulated that Peter was to pay himself a monthly maintenance fee, one that he felt was reasonable to cover his costs for overseeing John's desires. There was no suggested amount indicated because once again, John said he trusted Peter.

As he waited for everything to be transferred into his name, sky high greed began to rise up in Peter (something he didn't anticipate and even worse, didn't seem to mind) and over time he modified every one of the requests John had made to benefit himself. Eventually, he took a very large salary for himself, eliminated most of the charitable donations, sold the properties; and placed John's niece in a government home, which was glaringly inferior to the place in which she'd lived for most of her life. He never visited her and sent only a small burial donation for her funeral when she passed away.

Peter lived a very expensive life, using almost all of the money with which he had been entrusted to appease every wish he had ever had, every dream he had ever dreamed. To compound his violation of John's wishes, Peter married a very high maintenance woman and had two children, who grew up unaware of the stewardship of money and spent everything they could get their hands on for their own comfort.

After Peter and his wife died, their two sons fought over their now relatively small inheritance. They spent what they won from each other on themselves just as they had done all of their lives. In the end, they each died almost broke and their children had to pay their funeral expenses.

[OK. Take a breath and think of how much better you would have handled this opportunity.]

There are many spiritual and life lessons to be learned from this tragic account of incredible selfishness. The most important lesson may appear to be the stewardship of money, but one of the more obvious lessons we could point to at this juncture would be the violation of John's wishes and the stewardship of his desires.

Once Peter had received his inheritance, he gradually gave no thought to John's desires. All he could see was how he could benefit from John's wealth. As far as he was concerned, he owned everything he was asked to steward. The fact that John had intended to keep his plan of charitable giving alive after he was gone meant nothing to Peter. Peter really did not have the heart of John functioning within him. Anyone in need meant so little to him that he could walk past them on the street every day and not feel a thing. The welfare of John's niece became burdensome and was seen as a financial drain rather than an opportunity to be a benefactor to someone who had no ability to help herself.

All in all, Peter robbed John of everything for which he stood, everything for which he cared. He also robbed others of what had been intended for them. In a very real way, Peter ripped off John, violating everything John had entrusted to him.

[The spiritually impotent man is unaware that he is supposed to care if his life is significant to God or not. He will rip off God without a thought.]

From Our Father's Heart

*Many of you have been entrusted with much
that is to be used for My work during the short life I have given you.
You have, however,
consumed most of what you have been given —
whether that be money,
talent, influence, education, or any other gifting—
upon your own lusts.
Your gifts are not really gifts, as you suppose,
but simply the returning to Me of what was never really yours.
All was rightfully Mine in the first place.
You have been put in charge of what I have given you,
as hired shepherds of sheep would be;
but you have sold My property for your own gain.
You have been found out and now are being called to account.
This day you must make a choice:
serve the Lord Jesus Christ alone
and be part of the great harvest
or serve the world and its materialism.*

If you have given your life to Jesus, you are no longer your own in the economy of God. You and everything you own have been bought with the precious blood of Jesus. If you fully understand covenant, you know that you transferred everything you are and will ever claim to be over to the Lord and He gave you all of Himself. He has given you Himself as a mighty inheritance, which makes you wealthy far beyond your greatest hope.

[Unless each of us has spiritual eyes and a spiritual heart, we can easily lose our ability to walk in God's purpose for giving us such an inheritance. We will squander the wealth we have been given in Him on ourselves in the same way Peter squandered John's wealth.]

69

Let's back up. In the story, the real issue was not the material wealth given to Peter. The real heartbreak was not how he squandered it. If you analyze the issues through the eyes of absolute integrity, the real tragedy was the flagrant disregard for the intended use John had in mind when he made Peter the inheritor of his wealth.

John had a burning desire that his wealth be used to meet the needs of others. He had a heart for those who could not help themselves. He cared very much for his niece and her portion in life. As his days were drawing to a close, he thought he had selected someone he could trust to carry on his mission, to facilitate his desires.

John asked Peter to continue on with his wishes, but Peter was incapable of doing so even if that were his intent. The character of John simply was not in Peter. Peter could no more think and act like John than an animal living in the wild on his own instincts.

Sure, there were many violations. Sure, the story is tragic. However, unthinking, uncaring Peter was simply doing the best he could. In his ignorance, selfishness, and greed, all he was capable of doing was violating everything for which John stood, blissfully unaware of how far he was from the heart of John.

I see this story as a snapshot of a great portion of our own hearts in regard to the heart and wishes of God. Holding untold wealth, Father God has given us a spiritual inheritance far beyond our wildest imagination. With it, He has given us a stewardship of dispersing that wealth in the Name of Jesus.

If we are in Christ, his life was placed in us when we acknowledged His saving power and declared Him Lord over our lives. We are, in actuality, containers of His life so that generation upon generation might have the presence of Jesus, complete with all of His character traits, visible to those around us. It is the desire of Father God for people to see Jesus and embrace Him unto salvation and Lordship. They are to see Him in us. If we do not have the ability to exhibit Jesus to our generation - either because of our ignorance to do so or our unwillingness to do whatever it takes to become more like Him by becoming less - are we not robbing God of His desires in the same way Peter robbed John of his?

John cared very much for the welfare of his niece. He sought and found someone he thought would take care of her. Peter violated his wishes. Peter had no capability of caring for John's niece.

In the same way, Jesus died so that everyone could have the opportunity to be cared for by Father God. It is the wish of Father God that none should perish. Most of us could care less if our neighbors burn in hell for eternity. We may say we care; but if we really did, there would be no price too high to pay for them to know Jesus. We would do whatever it took to find a way for them to hear of the wonder of the cross and what it has provided for them.

If we really had the heart for them that Father God does, we would share Jesus every time an opportunity came our way, even to the point of seeking others out every available moment. If we really had His heart and really desired to fulfill His wishes, we would not be able to stop sharing the love of Jesus.

Peter had been given the freedom to take whatever finances he needed for himself in order to be able to focus on dispersing the wealth he had been given to others. Instead, he consumed it all upon himself and his own desires, sharing only a very small portion with those for whom it was intended.

We supposedly gave God everything when we gave our lives over to the Lordship of Jesus Christ. We supposedly agree wholeheartedly with the Bible verse that tells us that God gives us the power to gain wealth; that He is the source for all that's given to us. Then, we are very proud of ourselves if we give even ten percent back to His work, consuming the rest upon our own comfort and so-called needs. The wage we give ourselves is as much a theft of God's property as the wage Peter took for himself.

From Our Father's Heart

How trustworthy are you?
At what price do you feel that you would deny Me?
When would you deny My Word?
Never, you say!
You are doing it every day!
Each time you place your own interests above Mine,
you are opposing My Word.
Stop and ponder that truth.
I have called you to be like Jesus in your world.
He lived a life of sacrifice and service,
owning nothing for Himself and caring only for others.
He gave up everything so that you could be at peace eternally.
Caring nothing about His own well-being,
He hung on a cross so that you could be forgiven.
Even though He was part of your creation process,
He gave up total control of His life
so that you could learn obedience.
That is the kind of attitude that I desire to be in you.
You daily deny Me simply by attempting
to be in control of your life in any way.
It is the opposite of the character of Jesus.
Why would your remaining in control of any area of your life
not be a denial of My Word?
I know that you don't see it that way,

71

but it is one of the main reasons that I can't trust you.
It is the very basis for all My dealings with sin.
It is called rebellion.
You need to turn from the ownership of your life
and surrender fully to the understanding
that you have been purchased at a very great price.
You no longer own your life or anything that is associated with it.
You need to consider obedience to My will
to be your only reason for living.
Surrender fully to Me now.
Repent of your rebellion.
Submit totally to My will.
Become trustworthy so that We can walk closely together.
I desire to tell you the intimacies of My heart.
I am waiting!

II Cor. 5:14-15 AMP For the love of Christ controls and urges and impels us, because we are of the opinion and conviction that [if] One died for all, then all died;
15) And He died for all, so that all those who live might live no longer to and for themselves, but to and for Him Who died and was raised again for their sake.

I Cor. 6:19b-20a NIV ...You are not your own;
20a) you were bought at a price...

Could it be that we, as men, are impotent to even desire the heart of God, much less function in it? Let's revisit the idea that Satan has a plan to spiritually make all of mankind impotent, so that they have no natural desires to fulfill the plan of God and honor His wishes for their lives. Let's consider the possibility that he has so completely succeeded at his plan, that society and even the church in general no longer really see their distance from God's desires as something even remotely out of line.

Does Father God really expect us as believers to make our daily priority the salvation of those who don't know Jesus? Is He really asking us to care about the welfare of others in the same way He does, the same way Jesus does? Has God really entrusted us with His financial prosperity along with the accompanying mindset that it's not about how much we give back to Him, but how much we are allowed to keep for ourselves? If we study the Word thoroughly, if we find the Lord really does want us to function in the same way Jesus functioned, if we call ourselves His followers, then many of the teachings we have been under are laced with deceit and have rendered us impotent to even desire to do things God's way.

Col. 2:6 AMP As you have therefore received Christ, [even] Jesus the Lord, [so] walk (regulate your lives and conduct yourselves) in union with and conformity to Him.

Let's take the example of the most sacred cow in the church - money. In most churches, if a pastor stood up and taught the idea that everything was owned by God and people had a right to only a small portion of what they earned, he would be preaching to the trees and bushes in the woods very soon. Not only would his flock desert him, he would lose his building along with all the pews where his people used to sit.

The lie that only one-tenth of "your" money is God's is in violation of every covenant principle He established. Nowhere in any covenant document does it say that only a portion of one party's assets are available to the other person in the covenant. Each partner has 100% access to the other person's assets when the need arises.

John 16:23 AMP And when that time comes, you will ask nothing of Me [you will need to ask Me no questions]. I assure you, most solemnly I tell you, that My Father will grant you whatever you ask in My Name [as presenting all that I AM].

The covenant God has made with us through Jesus is the backbone of the Gospel. You are in covenant with God through Jesus. You can come to Him in the Name of Jesus to withdraw anything you need from Him. It's called prayer. Why do you think you end your prayers with "in Jesus' Name"? You are coming to God, your covenant partner, to request of Him in the Name of Jesus, the One who is upholding your end of the covenant (something God proved in the Old Testament that we could never do ourselves)! It is as if Jesus Himself is making your request. God is literally keeping both sides of the covenant in play.

We tend to be very good at grasping that 100% of who God is and what He has available is ours, at least in theory. However, we tend to forget that God, at least in theory, has 100% access to us and all that concerns us. How is it possible that He would make an exception to His covenant agreement with you when it concerns your most hazardous lust, your most focused possession, your most fertile soil for greed, your most treasured, worldly god - money? It makes no sense. It's no surprise that the impotent hearts of the men in the church have no desire to be right with God in this area. Most choose not to even discuss it. Most would rather rob from God than be subject to His right to whatever they earn and consider theirs for the keeping. The act of ripping off God is rampant in the world and vibrantly alive in His church as well.

Matt. 6:24 AMP No one can serve two masters; for either he will hate the one and love the other, or he will stand by and be devoted to the one and despise and be against the other. You cannot serve God and mammon (deceitful riches, money, possessions, or whatever is trusted in).

(For more information on covenant, our books - <u>The Overcoming Life</u> (starting on page 141) and <u>God's Final Frontier</u> - can be of help.)

Chapter 5
MASH icu Study Questions

1) Do you see yourself in Peter in the beginning of this chapter concerning God's desires for the wealth He has given you?

Journal or discuss your answer.

God gave you the power to rise above your old life when He made you a new creature capable of thinking and acting like Jesus did. Considering the spiritual wealth and power He has bestowed upon you as His child, what steps will you take to no longer live in your old ways concerning the material things the Lord has given you?

Father,

I am so sorry for stealing from You. Please teach me Your ways concerning Your things and cause me to walk in them. Thank You, Lord!

Chapter 6

What's the Bottom Line?

Bottom line – God, you, and wood, hay, and stubble

John 7: 38-39 AMP He who believes in Me [who cleaves to and trusts in and relies on Me] as the Scripture has said, From his innermost being shall flow [continuously] springs and rivers of living water.

39) But He was speaking here of the Spirit, Whom those who believed (trusted, had faith) in Him were afterward to receive. For the [Holy] Spirit had not yet been given, because Jesus was not yet glorified (raised to honor).

II Cor. 4:10-16 AMP Always carrying about in the body the liability and exposure to the same putting to death that the Lord Jesus suffered, so that the [resurrection] life of Jesus also may be shown forth by and in our bodies.

11) For we who live are constantly [experiencing] being handed over to death for Jesus' sake, that the [resurrection] life of Jesus also may be evidenced through our flesh which is liable to death.

12) Thus death is actively at work in us, but [it is in order that our] life [may be actively at work] in you.

13) Yet we have the same spirit of faith as he had who wrote, I have believed, and therefore have I spoken. We too believe, and therefore we speak,

14) Assured that He Who raised up the Lord Jesus will raise us up also with Jesus and bring us [along] with you into His presence.

15) For all [these] things are [taking place] for your sake, so that the more grace (divine favor and spiritual blessing) extends to more and more people and multiplies through the many, the more thanksgiving may increase [and redound] to the glory of God.

16) Therefore we do not become discouraged (utterly spiritless, exhausted, and wearied out through fear). Though our outer man is [progressively] decaying and wasting away, yet our inner self is being [progressively] renewed day after day.

While I was growing up, I was incredibly naive about spiritual things. It never occurred to me that they even mattered. They were beyond my scope of reasoning, so I had nothing to do with them.

I did, however, understand cars. They made sense to me. I knew what wheels did; I comprehended the concept of the internal combustion engine, the transmission, the differential, and how they functioned together to transfer the power from the engine through the driveshaft to make the wheels turn. When the wheels turned, the car went forward. It was all pretty cool to me.

With the grasp of that basic concept, everything else about cars was just parsley, something added to make it look better or go faster. There was no mystery with cars. I understood the concept and easily and joyfully navigated in the world of cars with my friends.

For us men, the ability to grasp the basics of any concept is vital to our ability to function in any area. Life is a series of repeating, "Just give me the basics. Show me how it works and I'll be OK. I can take it from there." We understand that practically and figuratively 1+1=2. We deal with everything this way. Just give us a formula and we're set to go in any area of our lives.

Depending on the generation in which you grew up, your particular version of 1+1=2 (your formula) allows you to function within your circle of influence. In my dad's generation, it was farming. He understood farming and everything connected with it. In my generation, it was cars. I understood cars. In the next generation, it was electronic equipment. Then came computers. Presently, it's technology. For future generations, only the Lord knows what form 1+1=2 will take.

When we, as guys, can make 1+1 equal 2, whether that equation is pertinent to a horse pulling a wagon, a transmission, a computer chip, a powerful receiver with big speakers, or internet marketing, everything else is simple. If we can continue to use 1+1=2 in whatever form necessary to function in any given situation, we can get a job done or be comfortable in our knowledge of how it works. Once we know how anything works, we can keep it running.

Any man who grasps what 1+1=2 is in any set of circumstances is well on his way to accomplishing his given task. In business, the 2 is the bottom line. In horses, it's the blood-line; in cars, it's the performance, etc. Grabbing hold of and understanding the 2 changes everything. It transfers things from the abstract and nebulous to the concrete. It gets us to the finish line, the goal. We get that!

For most men, the spiritual realm and the concept of actually living and loving as Jesus does have never become the goal and purpose of our lives! It's something abstract, out there. We have never really desired to find a spiritual 2. Therefore, we have never really seen the value of functioning in it properly. Sure we get the idea of sin, the need for salvation, heaven, hell, good, bad, etc.; but any more than that takes us places we literally don't understand, so we pass it off and declare it women's territory. They comprehend things like love, servanthood, caring, and all that emotional stuff.

The Incredible Power of Finding the Spiritual 1+1=2 for Men

John 3:5-8 NIV Jesus answered, "I tell you the truth, no one can enter the kingdom of God unless he is born of water and the Spirit.

6) Flesh gives birth to flesh, but the Spirit gives birth to spirit.

7) You should not be surprised at my saying, 'You must be born again.'

8) The wind blows wherever it pleases. You hear its sound, but you cannot tell where it comes from or where it is going. So it is with everyone born of the Spirit."

Romans 3:22 NIV This righteousness from God comes through faith in Jesus Christ to all who believe.

Romans 10:9-10 NIV That if you confess with your mouth, "Jesus is Lord," and believe in your heart that God raised him from the dead, you will be saved.

10) For it is with your heart that you believe and are justified, and it is with your mouth that you confess and are saved.

Mankind acquired a real problem due to the deception and subsequent rebellion against God's ways in the Garden of Eden. Since both Adam and Eve chose to fall in line with Satan's plan, he became their leader. From that time until Jesus died on the cross, mankind could only function under the world's system, one chosen by Adam and Eve. God's spiritual realm and the way His kingdom worked did not register with them. They could not understand the things of God, especially the deep things, nor did they desire them. God had to create laws for them to obey and a heavy-handed way of enforcing those laws so they would submit to them.

[Someone who is highly educated can be a spiritual fool!]

Except for the small number of earnest men that God could use - such as David, Moses, Abraham, and Noah - mankind in general was spiritually impotent, deaf to the words of God, blind to His ways, and helpless against the workings of Satan from the time of the deception in the Garden of Eden. They were unable to reproduce anything spiritual because they had a carnal nature, one that could only produce carnal, fleshly thoughts and ways. Since the whole human race had come under the influence of this system, which was under the leadership of Satan, his plan was the predominant factor in their lives rather than the plan of God. They were outside of the kingdom of God, wallowing in fleshly things and ignorant of the spiritual.

New Ground Rules

Father God changed all the ground rules established by Satan through the life, death, and resurrection of Jesus Christ, so that man could live His way and prosper. He created a new playing field and a new way of competing in the game, so to speak- a spiritual way.

God established a new covenant, or agreement, one that moved everyone who entered into it with Him into the spiritual realm. It gave mankind a choice once again, this time initiated and directed by God. In John 6:44a KJV, Jesus tells us: *"No man can come to me, except the Father which hath sent me draw him..."* Fulfilling Father God's desire that "none should perish," the Holy Spirit initiates situations throughout the lifetime of every individual in which he or she has the opportunity to personally accept Jesus and the work of the cross.

Once a person does accept Jesus as Savior and Lord by the confession of his mouth and the belief in his heart that God raised Him from the dead, he becomes born of the Spirit of God and enters into the new covenant with all of its promises and rewards. His eternal "inner man," or "inner being," - that spirit which is designed to function spiritually and spend eternity with God - is born, brought to spiritual life by the Holy Spirit.

[Here's where most men lose it and let the women do all of that "spiritual stuff."]

This is the area where Satan focuses so that men become spiritually impotent. He tells us the spiritual world is difficult to understand and is not pertinent to daily living – marriage, raising kids, jobs, cars, horses, computers, sports, etc. He loves to separate spiritual stuff from the "important" stuff men love to do. If he can keep the spiritual from affecting the daily routine or if he can make God's plan appear religious and cold, he can convince men to never really enter in to fully grasp the plan of God and desire it as their priority in life.

The Concept of Action and Reaction

In the physical world, when you hit a nail with a hammer, there is a reaction; the nail is driven into a piece of wood. Men readily understand the action- reaction concept. In the spiritual world, there is an equally simple action-reaction concept. An example would be the changing of one's inner nature.

The plan of the cross and the covenant promise created an action-reaction eternal law. If a person confesses with his mouth that Jesus is Lord and believes in his heart that God raised Him from the dead (action,) he will be saved (reaction or result.) This confession is the "hammer" that is used by God to fulfill the words Jesus spoke to Nicodemus when He told him that a person must be born again of the Spirit.

When a person performs this heartfelt act, the Holy Spirit, the Spirit of Christ, comes to dwell inside him - the driving of the nail in the coffin of our old life. That person now becomes the container for the life of Jesus to be lived through him. His inner being, the eternal being or spirit that is designed to be with God and fully surrendered to His ways, has been made alive.

II Cor. 5:17 AMP Therefore, if any person is [ingrafted] in Christ (the Messiah) he is a new creation (a new creature altogether); the old [previous moral and spiritual condition] has passed away. Behold, the fresh and new has come!

Gal. 2:20 AMP I have been crucified with Christ [in Him I have shared His crucifixion]; it is no longer I who live, but Christ (the Messiah) lives in me; and the life I now live in the body I live by faith in (by adherence to and reliance on and complete trust in) the Son of God, Who loved me and gave Himself up for me.

A new creation has been established in the surrendered man - a creation that will be completely trustworthy to follow only the ways of God, just as Jesus did, when brought to fullness by the power of the Holy Spirit. For us motor-heads, a brand new model of car just rolled off the assembly lines.

Chapter 6
MASH icu Study Questions

1) Do you fully understand the 1+1=2 spiritual concept?   Y/N

(This concept is pivotal to all of your thinking as you draw close to God. Go back and pray through this premise and ask the Holy Spirit to reveal it to you.)

2) Do you fully understand the spiritual rebirth, the concept of being born of the spirit?   Y/N

(You may want to prayerfully study the story of Nicodemus in John Chapter 3 for greater understanding.)

3) Can you list those things in your life that you have not included as part of your spiritual life?   Y/N

4) How do you think your life, your marriage, your family, your job, your life with your buddies would be different if you fully placed everything you are and everything you own under the Lordship of Jesus Christ and the Spirit of God was at the very core of everything?

Father,

Teach me Your ground rules for living. I need to know what is important to You and how to apply it to my life. Show me every 1+1=2 in the spiritual realm. Teach me to start thinking your thoughts and living in Your power to fulfill them for Your glory. Thank You, Lord. Amen.

Chapter 7

Trusting That Your Inner Being Follows After Truth

Your example of Christ's life to the world shows the power of the cross in overcoming death. It brings honor to the life, death, and resurrection of Jesus. Do you really care?

Eph. 3:16-19 AMP May He grant you out of the rich treasury of His glory to be strengthened and reinforced with mighty power in the inner man by the [Holy] Spirit [Himself indwelling your innermost being and personality].

17) May Christ through your faith [actually] dwell (settle down, abide, make His permanent home) in your hearts! May you be rooted deep in love and founded securely on love,

18) That you may have the power and be strong to apprehend and grasp with all the saints [God's devoted people, the experience of that love] what is the breadth and length and height and depth [of it];

19) [That you may really come] to know [practically, through experience for yourselves] the love of Christ, which far surpasses mere knowledge [without experience]; that you may be filled [through all your being] unto all the fullness of God [may have the richest measure of the divine Presence, and become a body wholly filled and flooded with God Himself]!

Gal. 4:19 NIV My dear children, for whom I am again in the pains of childbirth until Christ is formed in you, ...

Phil. 2:12-13 NIV Therefore, my dear friends, as you have always obeyed – not only in my presence, but now much more in my absence – continue to work out your salvation with fear and trembling,

13) for it is God who works in you to will and to act according to his good purpose.

Phil. 2:12-13 AMP Therefore, my dear ones, as you have always obeyed [my suggestions], so now, not only [with the enthusiasm you would show] in my presence but much more because I am absent, work out (cultivate, carry out to the goal, and fully complete) your own salvation with reverence and awe and trembling (self-distrust, with serious caution, tenderness of conscience, watchfulness against temptation, timidly shrinking from whatever might offend God and discredit the name of Christ).

13) [Not in your own strength] for it is God Who is all the while effectually at work in you [energizing and creating in you the power and desire], both to will and to work for His good pleasure and satisfaction and delight.

About This Inner Being

Paul saw a problem developing within his fledgling churches. He saw they were deviating from the pattern set for them, which was displayed in the life of Jesus Christ.

Over the course of establishing and maintaining these churches, there was a proper time to instruct followers, inform them of truth, teach them of the ways of God, and chastise them when they were acting foolishly. This, however, was different. This was a situation ripe for instilling ways of overcoming and helping them to overcome their spiritual problems in a spiritual way.

The churches already knew what was right in the eyes of God. They had been told how to function. They knew what did and did not please God. The previous Bible verses - letters to each of the churches at that time - were, on one hand, a guiding light to the path of healing as they identified the power of the Holy Spirit as the solution. They were also a lesson in submission to His power as the only antidote for sin.

Spiritual problems could only be overcome by the spiritual power of God. Paul knew it, and he knew it had to be taught to them (and to us) by example, if we were all to survive and prosper in Christ.

He called upon the power of the Holy Spirit to change the people inwardly from his knees, rather than asking them to change in their own strength. He was equipping them, so they would not fall apart when their worlds were challenged as he knew they soon would be. He was also teaching them how to help others become strong enough to overcome the challenges of those days. That's also some mighty good information for today's Christians in today's perilous world.

[Because of the life, death, and resurrection of Jesus and because of His covenant, we are no longer human beings having a spiritual experience, we are eternal, spiritual beings having a temporary human experience.]

Our Inner Being is Spiritual, Not Carnal

The inner being or inner spirit of a born again child of God is a spiritual being that only accepts, desires, and is nurtured by the things of God, the same as in the life of Jesus. We actually house the full and complete nature of Jesus in our earthly body. (Of course, allowing the full and complete nature of Jesus to freely function in us is another story.)

This inner being, in which dwells the very Spirit and character of Christ even while housed in these earthly containers of ours, has no taste buds for anything that is not of His Father in heaven. It craves the things of God and performs only in line with Jesus' character and the benchmark life He lived. It is nourished solely on the Word, which is at work in us through the Holy Spirit Who is in line with the truth of the Word. It is empowered only by the power and might of the Holy Spirit. The inner being receives, contains, and functions only according to the nature of Jesus Christ. It desires only the things that are important to the very heart of God, the same things Jesus desired. It can never be defeated because it embodies Jesus Himself, Who already won over Satan and the world almost two thousand years ago.

[God never intended for us to get better; He is helping us to get empty of ourselves!]

Since the inner being has been given life as a spirit by the Holy Spirit, it has no alliance whatsoever with carnal or fleshly ideas, concepts, matters, and concerns that may present themselves. It is designed to fulfill only the plan of God. Because it is the very nature of Jesus, the inner being is not moved by anything other than what moved Jesus. It only understands being absolutely obedient to the Father's will and fulfilling the Father's desires. It only responds and functions in conjunction with those elements that are under the Lordship of Jesus.

Everything else remains under the jurisdiction of the carnal nature and is only able to produce, understand, and accept carnal things. That is one of the main reasons there is so much weakness in the church and so much impotence in the men who claim to know Jesus as their Lord.

Since the spiritual inner being is ignited within someone upon the confession of and submission to the Lordship of Jesus Christ, any area of that human being not fully submitted to the Lordship of Jesus Christ remains in a carnal state until Lordship is honestly declared over it. (It would be very good to read the previous sentence over and over until it is fully understood. It is pivotal to the plan of God becoming our goal, a "2," in our lives as men.)

Flesh Births Flesh

II Cor.4:16 AMP Therefore we do not become discouraged (utterly spiritless, exhausted, and wearied out through fear). Though our outer man is [progressively] decaying and wasting away, yet our inner self is being [progressively] renewed day after day.

Flesh can only give birth to flesh, no matter how seemingly spiritual the disguise. Flesh can only birth fleshly activities, religion, laws, or man-made doctrines, no matter how spiritual they may sound or how zealously they may be enforced. Any attempt to function spiritually with the carnal nature will only birth religious activities, not God-ordained eternal wealth. Your new inner being can only give birth to or be renewed by spiritual things that are accepted by God and a part of His plan.

Commitments to Christ for Salvation vs. His Complete Lordship

I believe the Holy Spirit is grieved when people commit their lives to Jesus only unto salvation, instead of also putting everything under His Lordship. With that kind of incomplete commitment, most people make Jesus the rightful Lord over their salvation and trust Him as their only access to the Father for eternity. However they have missed the intended opportunity to submit every area of their lives to His Lordship and therefore remain weak, and vulnerable to the ways of the world.

I can't even count the number of times over the years when people, especially men, would counsel with me regarding the sin in their lives, sin that would overwhelm them to the point that they gave up on a God they considered powerless, uncaring, and unreachable in prayer. When questioned about this issue of Jesus being the Lord over every area of their lives, most of them said they'd never even heard of that concept. They had said what is called the "sinner's prayer," but did not understand the power of Lordship. No one had ever told them of their need to establish Lordship, even though the confession of Lordship leads to salvation - not the confession of their sins, as they were led to believe.

Romans 10:9-10 NIV That if you confess with your mouth, "Jesus is Lord," and believe in your heart that God raised him from the dead, you will be saved.
10) For it is with your heart that you believe and are justified, and it is with your mouth that you confess and are saved.

[Satan loves to keep the truth of absolute Lordship from anyone in Christ. He may lose an individual to Almighty God, but if he can hide the reality of Jesus' complete Lordship over everything, that person will likely remain powerless and impotent and incapable of being used to help bring about change in others. It's time we no longer submit to his plans and live in God's plans]

88

Once Jesus is fully acknowledged as Lord in every area of life, mighty and wonderful spiritual growth can occur. I've seen it often. As people submit to the complete Lordship of Jesus Christ, the Holy Spirit is free to guide, direct, and make lasting changes in their lives. There is no longer the constant fight between the new nature and Satan's incessant efforts to cause people to revert back to their old, worldly ways, something of which the sold-out inner being wants no part. The regenerated inner being, infused with the life of Christ, is totally opposed to useless carnal, fleshly religion, even though the flesh would gladly settle for it.

The Holy Spirit is jealous over us, longing to equip our inner man to flow freely in all that Jesus is as He works out our declaration of Lordship in our daily lives. This is what Father God provided for us through His covenant with us, which was accomplished at the cross of Christ – both now and forever. It solidifies our place and function in all of eternity as we present the very character of Christ back to God on the day we stand before Him. This is what will elicit "Well done, good and faithful servant" and cause our lives to be of significance in Father God's eyes.

To attempt to nourish, build up, make strong, make more "spiritual," or equip the inner man in any carnal way – things done in our own strength - is outright deception. All that results is foolish religious activity, which is pretty much useless in the kingdom of God. These dead, uninspiring works are distasteful to men who are concerned with the things that are truly important to their Father in heaven.

Let's Get Back to Those 1+1=2's

Satan doesn't want us to see those 1+1=2's in our lives. He wants us to remain impotent and uninterested in deep spiritual commitments. If you are trying to be spiritual when all that you are and think is not fully under the Lordship of Jesus Christ, please stop. It will only frustrate you as you try to be the husband, father, church attendee, and community leader of your own making, believing you have what it takes to make it through life and into eternity. It's all a dog and pony show. Your religious activities are not truly significant to God and have little bearing on His lasting, eternal plan.

Focus on Lordship. It is the spiritual hammer that causes all of the other God-pleasing elements of spirituality to fall firmly in place for eternity. From this moment on, choose to place everything you can think of under the Lordship of Jesus Christ. Make Him the undisputed Lord over everything, even over who you are not. Get your hands off of your life.

[Pray something like this if you really want to get right with God. "Father, I believe that Jesus is the Lord over all. Jesus, I ask You to be the

Lord over every area of my life. I take my life and make it Yours. I submit fully to Your Lordship.]

As you continue chapter by chapter in this book, you will have the opportunity to focus on the areas that need to be placed under the Lordship of Jesus Christ, so that His life can flow through you unhindered in a manner that pleases Father God. You will be shown several "2's" that will bring your life into proper focus. Allow the Holy Spirit to show you one by one those areas which still need to be surrendered, either for the first time or once again as He reveals what is truly involved in surrendering a specific area. Make your daily life an act of surrender as the Holy Spirit prompts you. If you find yourself trying to put yourself back in the driver's seat in some area, surrender it again immediately!

Use the hammer God has given you, not one you have made up yourself or one you have been told will make you more spiritual. It all begins and ends with Jesus, the author and finisher of your faith. Allow Him to tear you loose from the impotence and deception in which Satan has had you and desires to keep you. Determine to walk in the fullness of what He has provided for you!

Heb.12:2 AMP Looking away [from all that will distract] to Jesus, Who is the Leader and the Source of our faith [giving the first incentive for our belief] and is also its Finisher [bringing it to maturity and perfection].

Remember, it's not how much you do, but to whom you surrender everything that determines how much your inner being will thrive and how much you will understand, desire, and function in the wonderful life the Lord has for you. As you prayerfully read on and become aware of the all-encompassing life God intends you to live, do not attempt to achieve it any other way than by repenting of your old ways and surrendering them to the Lordship of Jesus Christ, allowing the Holy Spirit to strengthen and empower your inner being with His power. One way or another, it will be stated many times throughout these pages that anything else is foolish, useless, religious activity, which will result in continued spiritual impotence and the horrific prospect of presenting an insignificant life to Father God on the day you stand before Him.

Spiritual 1 + Spiritual 1 = Spiritual 2

The "1 + 1" of your spiritual "formula" is, first, your submission to the Lordship of Jesus Christ over every area of your life (which affords you access to all of the covenant promises the cross provides); while the spiritual "2" stands for whatever it is God wants to impart to you or requires

90

of you. All of this is courtesy of His power and might so that you become a reflection of Jesus for all to see.

The Lordship of Jesus Christ over everything is the single corridor God has provided to remove your spiritual impotence. It is the spiritual equivalent to the mechanical "How does it work?" of the natural realm. It is the only "action-reaction" provided by God to overcome useless, unacceptable works of the flesh.

If you need to do so, introduce yourself to Jesus all over again. Open your heart up to the Lord in prayer. Rediscover His overwhelming love for you. Pursue first love with Him once again and recapture the wonder of His mighty works. Ask Him to show you which areas you have surrendered to the absolute Lordship of Jesus Christ and those you haven't. Write them down. Don't push this aside with the usual "I've already given everything over to Him," as you may have done for many years, all the while being deceived and remaining spiritually impotent. Don't be fooled into believing everything is under His Lordship when it probably isn't. Your spiritual life depends on it!

Take the time to list everything you can think of in your world, your marriage, your children, your ministry, your career, your relationships, etc., that is or is not under His Lordship. Come clean. Cover everything and include it in the following prayer when you can mean it from the bottom of your heart, because the Lord is waiting eagerly to answer your prayer and transform you through the power of His Word and His Spirit – the Holy Spirit. It's a win-win situation!

Chapter 7
MASH icu Study Questions

1) What changes do you need to make so that Father God will call you a true follower of Jesus on the day you see Him face to face?

2) What steps do you need to take so that God can make those changes in you?

Lord,

I place everything in my life (read your list) under Your complete Lordship. I am tired of trying to complete in the flesh what was begun in the Spirit. Teach me to understand Your ways and then give me the power to continually walk in them. Thank You, Lord!

Signed _____

Real answers come when we make Jesus the Lord over every challenge, every idea, every thought, every piece of property, every right we feel we have, every plan, every penny we make, and every relationship we enter, moment by moment, day by day.

When we are no longer lord over anything and everything we can think of, our new life—full of hope, wisdom, and power—can begin.

Intensive Care Unit II

ABBA-initiated Intimacy

The Oneness of a Loving Father God with His Adoring Child

Romans 8:1-4 NIV   Therefore, there is now no condemnation for those who are in Christ Jesus,
²⁾because through Christ Jesus the law of the Spirit who gives life has set you free from the law of sin and death.
³⁾ For what the law was powerless to do because it was weakened by the flesh, God did by sending his own Son in the likeness of sinful flesh to be a sin offering. And so he condemned sin in the flesh
⁴⁾ in order that the righteous requirement of the law might be fully met in us, who do not live according to the flesh but according to the Spirit.

Our loving Father God is always calling His children to Himself. In His presence is the place we belong, the place Jesus won for us at the cross. Only as we spend intimate moments with our Papa God, only as He reveals His heart to us as a loving Father to his adoring child, are we able to face the challenges we will encounter on the road to serving Him as the priority of our lives. As God reveals His mercy and our true motives are exposed in these times, we can be assured His revelation is an act of love.

As we progress toward restoring our marriages and families, we must continually seek intimacy with the Lord. It is our time spent with Him that will allow us to know His will and act in accordance with it, empowered by His love and His presence, all for His glory.

[Intimacy with God is always found by the quiet, resting soul. Is it any wonder the enemy has plans to keep men busy?]

Chapter 8

Beginning Steps Toward a Significant Life

God is not through with you yet.

"I didn't know that sitting on the lap of my Father God and being tucked into the folds of His garment was the highest form of warfare," Terry said. "I never saw intimacy with God as the backbone of my faith and my real life in Him."

Jack took a few seconds before responding to the man in front of him, knowing that Terry had reached a monumental point in his relationship with Jesus. Jack's next words could set the direction for his friend's life for many years to come. "Lord, please give me truth for my friend," he prayed silently.

"Terry," Jack began slowly, "warfare is not really something you do; it is what the Lord does for you. Jesus has earned for you the right to enter into the presence of God for your every need and for every desire He wants to share with you. Everything you'll ever require, all you'll ever become, begins in the lap of your loving Father. Your intimacy with Him is not only the restoration of the relationship Adam lost in the Garden, it's also the most powerful weapon you have in overcoming the enemy and his attempt to hinder the plans of God in your life. If the enemy can keep you from developing an intimate relationship with Jesus, he wins. He knows you'll never be a real threat to him. That's the real battlefield and most often it's fought in your mind."

Jack stopped for a moment to let his statements sink into Terry's spirit, knowing that for so long, Terry had been fighting battles that were not his to fight.

"When you make intimacy with the Lord your priority in life," he continued, "your focus and your delight becomes the Lord Himself. Your eyes no longer focus on all of your challenges, all of your needs, and all of the enemy's tactics. You see only God and how big He really is and how much He loves you. You are obedient to Him and love Him because of His great love for you. You may not have thought about this before, but your obedience is a mighty weapon. When you walk in obedience, you are telling God that you are depending upon Him and He delights in fighting our battles for us.

"When you appreciate over time Who He really is and how much He loves you, you will be drawn to Him and the ways and cares of the world will continually fall away. The plan of God concerning the souls of men will become central to your life in Christ. In actuality, all of the wars and challenges you will ever face have already been won on the cross. Your life is a working out of what happened at Calvary. Every day, the work of the cross is at work in you. When you placed your life under the Lordship of Jesus, your old life died and your new life began in Him. That allows Him to live His life through you and you don't have to fight your own battles. "

Terry stood silently, asking God to help him absorb what Jack had shared.

Ephesians 3:10-12 AMP [The purpose is] that through the church the complicated, many-sided wisdom of God in all its infinite variety and innumerable aspects might now be made known to the angelic rulers and authorities (principalities and powers) in the heavenly sphere.

11) This is in accordance with the terms of the eternal and timeless purpose which He has realized and carried into effect in [the person of] Christ Jesus our Lord.

12) In Whom, because of our faith in Him, we dare to have the boldness (courage and confidence) of free access (an unreserved approach to God with freedom and without fear).

I Cor. 4:2 AMP Moreover, it is [essentially] required of stewards that a man should be found faithful [proving himself worthy of trust].

II Cor. 5:20a NIV We are therefore Christ's ambassadors, as though God were making his appeal through us.

In any battle plan, there must first be a definitive course of action and then there must absolute dedication to its execution if a battle is to be won. Any independent thinking creates an atmosphere of chaos and positions every other participant in harm's way. One deviation from the plan of the leaders could potentially nullify contingency options and back-up strategies; and most importantly, create a weakness in the unified front. Any seemingly small digression from the original content of the plan could change the tide of the battle, and possibly even have a devastating impact on the outcome of the war.

History resounds with ill-fated battle plans, wrong decisions that changed the course of nations, and thinking that was ignorant of the overall battle plan, which caused untold havoc in the rank and file. Although slightly different from the standpoint that the outcome has been foretold, the spiritual battle that's been set in place by God to purify the hearts of men and propel them to call others to respond to His plan is of utmost importance to our well being. Whether we walk in obedience or disobedience regarding God's plan will result in either blessing or harm in our lives and in the lives of others.

98

God's Plan for Mankind

The plan for mankind has been laid out and predicted in God's Word. There will be no deviation from it. In the end of times, there will be a one world government ruled with an iron hand by an anti-Christ figure. He will set himself up as god, violating the sanctuary of the Lord with His blasphemies. All nations will gather against Israel and will eventually be defeated by God Himself in His perfect timing. That scenario is cut in stone by God and will not be changed by anyone or anything.

Leading up to this climactic promised scenario, there will be a great falling away from the plans of God as people harden their hearts toward Him. False gods will rise up and many who claim to know the Lord will follow their deceptions. As the world migrates toward a one world government, wars will be initiated, nations will rise and fall, and societies will grow more and more dangerous so more and more control can be instituted. There will be a great falling away from the truth, all in line with the promised outcome. To attempt to hinder this process or try to stop it from happening is to set oneself up against the plans of God. Not highly recommended!

It is very sad to say, however, that this is precisely what many in the body of Christ - especially in these United States - are looking for and attempting to do in their own reasoning, worldly passions, and fears. Many want their comfortable world to remain comfortable. They would rather fight for their personal well-being than fight for the plan on the heart of God to be fulfilled.

Many contingents of the church today see their commission as one of changing society or fighting for rights. Although the Lord may initiate short-term solutions to address the onslaught of woes we see today as an extension of His mercy, the ultimate plan of God will prevail.

Granted, the Lord may call some of His workers to initiate programs to temporarily pause, delay, or redirect things that are not in line with His desires; but His inevitable plan will prevail without a hitch. Any continued effort to change society that goes against the plan of God, especially in these closing hours of God's timetable, would appear to be a misuse of desperately needed time, resources, and Christ-like people.

The Plan of God

God's plan is that none should perish, but have life – both now and forever – through Jesus Christ. This opportunity is available to all within the timeframe He's established for their lives on this earth.

It's that simple and that direct. You would do well to read and meditate on that objective until the Lord shows you the truth of it. It needs to be planted firmly in your spirit and encompasses far more than the limited concept of an individual gaining access to heaven as the only reason for the cross.

As stated before, Satan wants to distract, redirect, and eventually immobilize those who are pursuing the Great Commission. He hates to see others not only brought into the kingdom of God now and for eternity, but he hates to see God helping them to become all they can be in Jesus Christ. He wants men to be impotent, so that there is no desire to see Jesus reproduced in others. He wants families to be disjointed, so that their members will not be instrumental in the development of the character of Jesus in their circle of influence. He wants whole societies to have no idea what the plan of God is, so that many will never hear and surrender to the opportunity God has provided for them through Jesus.

Masterful and cunning, Satan delights to see those he has lost for eternity involved in an array of very good-looking, supposedly important activities, which are designed to cure social ills without an emphasis on the souls of men. In doing so, he has divided the front God wants to use to bring souls into the kingdom. The workers are being diverted. I know this is blasphemous talk in some circles of the body of Christ, but I believe it's time to say out loud what many surrendered hearts are hearing in their prayer closets and what Father God is imparting to the open hearts of those who will listen.

From Our Father's Heart

The world is again attempting to draw the line of contention.
They have categorized everything into either political
or moral issues
and have baited you, My people, to submit to their categories.
Jesus did neither.
He did not become a part of any worldly categories.
He came to give dead people life.
Finger-pointing morality has nothing to do with Christianity.
Why should you fall into the trap of contention?
It is all vain attempts for temporary change.
Real change can only occur
when My Holy Spirit controls a life and changes it for eternity.

Let's Talk About Issues

Any activity that does not have souls as its ultimate goal has no real eternal value in the overall plan of God and will be judged as wood, hay, and stubble on the day God judges your works. It would be good to take the time to evaluate why you do the things you do. Were they God's idea or yours? He's good about letting us know these things if we take the time to ask and then truly wait to hear His answer.

Changing society for the sake of having a better society or curing its ills is not of paramount importance to Father God. It not only falls pale in light of the plan God has for society; it could actually be working against the plan of God. If it was on God's heart to change society and make it better, then Jesus would've involved Himself in all kinds of issues and activities. He lived in a society where dead men were seen hanging on crosses that lined the streets, children were killed at the whim of a king, and even His friend John was beheaded and no one was brought to trial. In fact, He never even protested the beheading.

As a Christian, demanding that your kind of morality be the benchmark for any society is nothing more than foolish thinking and an incredible waste of God's resources. At its worst, it is working against the plan of God, Who has told us the love of many will grow cold amidst lawlessness and wickedness. There will be no desire for goodness and no desire to serve God, especially in the last days before Jesus returns.

Trying to force morality on society is religious gymnastics designed by the enemy to distract those who are designated to win the lost for Jesus. It is part of the impotence tactics that Satan is using to nullify important God-ordained, soul winning works within the body of Christ. You are deceived if you think that God has any part in religious activity, those efforts that are not born of His Spirit. You are concentrating on the nice little doggy that's wagging his tail on the other side of the street, intent on rescuing and protecting him from harm as you dart across the road, oblivious to the speeding traffic bearing down on you.

OK, calm down. Before you print up a sign with a derogatory statement and my name on it and attach it to the nearest pole, please hear me out. Put the magic marker down and let's talk. If you still feel the same after I'm through, you are free to continue making picketing and protesting a way of life, showing those who need to see Jesus how angry and unloving He is. The only Jesus they will more than likely remember will be the one you show them, until a merciful God can place them in front of one of His children who will love them and allow them to see who Jesus really is.

Consider this! If you see all of the wrongs in government and choose to affect change by working in government yourself as a true representative of Jesus, you impact people. You do know that if you lead other officials to the Lord, they will begin to make proper decisions, don't you? By honoring the plan of God that none should perish, He remains in charge of the rise and fall of governments and you get to flow in the wonder of the plan of God with a peace that you are in the direct center of His will for your life.

If you are outraged at the number of babies being killed every day, did you know that if you pray for an abortionist and live a spiritually sanctified life in his midst, you invoke the power of God on his behalf so that he may come to Jesus? If he does, he'll stop killing babies because the Spirit of Christ now lives within him. You have entered into the plan of God that none should perish and God has placed an issue on your heart that allows you to grow in the heart of Jesus while trusting Him to change other hearts. Your life of love allows God the freedom to use circumstances, whether good or bad, as He desires. What a great way to touch the heart of God!

Anyway, doesn't it seem a little ridiculous to carry a sign about God's love while harboring hatred for others in your heart or to hit someone over the head with a sign that contains the Bible verse: *"If My people who are called by My Name, will humble themselves, and pray and seek My face, and turn from their wicked ways, I will hear them from heaven, I will forgive their sins and heal their land,"* on it? (By the way, I have a good friend who went to a secular event to share the love of Jesus where a fellow Christian, who was there to protest, actually smacked him on the head with her sign when he questioned her motives and methods.)

Maybe it's time you read your own sign, either the one you carry or the one you harbor in your heart, if you desire to see society change. Humbling oneself, praying, seeking the face of God, and turning from your own wicked ways to heal a land seems a far cry from picketing evil, godless places and inflicting your moral outrage on those who are just as convinced that they're right as you're convinced that you're right. It's all the same spiritual impotence, no matter what side of the issue you support. You are needed in the real battle zone of winning souls and helping your family by the exhibition of Jesus through your life.

Did you know that the followers of the ways of Christ miss you while you're off doing your own thing? I believe Satan loves to involve undiscerning Christians in arguments over issues. He loves to thin the ranks of those who are leading others to Christ by deceiving them into thinking they must right the wrongs, losing sight of those who are perishing in the process. Just a thought: aren't all of those really bad people who are doing all those really wrong things just about as far gone as you and I were before Jesus cleaned us up?

The Mature Heart

The mature or covenant heart of Jesus is being prepared in God's people at this present time in preparation for the moment of His return and for the work that is to be accomplished in the last days before His return. The mature heart is a heart identical to the heart of Jesus. It pumps with the blood of the cross.

Jesus will not come back for a church that has passions and desires that differ from His. He will not marry a bride with whorish longings, someone who wishes to be satisfied by the world or any of its ways. He will not align Himself with anyone who does not share His desire to please His Father and complete the Father's plans both now and through eternity.

To be part of the work the Lord is doing in these days, your carnal life must be crucified and your fleshly desires must be purposefully put to death. The Holy Spirit is wooing those who will hear to surrender everything that does not line up with the Word and heart of God for its destruction – for the Lord's sake and yours. If you haven't heard Him in the past, hopefully you will hear Him soon for time appears to be running out. It's your choice.

This call, to have a heart identical to the heart of Jesus, is the highest call anyone who claims to follow Him can receive. It's a call of separation unto Jesus and Him alone, a call of consecration, a call to absolute holiness. It's a call which can be answered in only one way, by agreeing to the total elimination of anything that's of the world and its ways and by embracing only those things Jesus embraces. It's a call to the men of God who are designated to be leaders of the true church of Jesus Christ in the coming times, guiding and directing others to the heart of Jesus and overcoming the ways of the world, just as Jesus did, under His full and complete Lordship.

It's Your Time

I am convinced you're reading this book because your loving Father God desires a radical heart change in you that will allow you to modify your motives for living and wake up to the plan the Lord has for your life. He's asking you this very moment to take account of the people and resources with which He has entrusted you and then dedicate them to Him so that He can make all things significant in His eyes. I am convinced the Lord is making His men aware of what a significant, overcoming life truly is from His perspective, so that while you prepare for the coming of Jesus, you can honor Him with the rest of your days and influence the next generations to do the same should He tarry.

You need to respond to the heralding of the Holy Spirit during this late hour in God's timetable. No matter what choices you make, His plan will go forth with or without you. If you don't choose to change your ways, and you don't choose to respond to the call of total separation unto His ways, others will take your place and accomplish your assignments, while you remain distracted and sniff at the air for pleasures and projects that are not part of the overall plan of God. They will honor the Lord with the crowns you sidestepped in your impotence.

Chapter 8
MASH icu Study Questions

1) Do you know for certain the direction God intends for your life? Y/N

2) Is God's desire that none should perish at the heart of your relationships with family, those around you, in your business?   Y/N

3) Are you willing to completely change direction in any area of your life, if the Holy Spirit convicts you that you have been walking in deception? Y/N

4) Do you need to repent to anyone for the way you've been acting- whether in family, church, business, or social situations - for the times you thought you were serving Jesus, but now see you were functioning in another spirit? Y/N

5) Do you need to repent to God for being so gullible and blind, oblivious to His desires for your life? Y/N

6) Do you desire to gain and walk in the identical heart toward God and others that Jesus has? Y/N

7) Are you willing to pay the price to gain that heart? Y/N

Father,

  Please create in me the heart of Jesus, so that I am just like Him when He comes. Do whatever it takes to conform me to Your Word and the character of Jesus. Thank You, Lord. Amen.

Chapter 9

How Far Off? Wow!

The fruits of your life should nourish a God-given hunger in others.

Exodus 33:14-16 AMP   And the Lord said, My Presence shall go with you, and I will give you rest.

15) And Moses said to the Lord, If Your Presence does not go with me, do not carry us up from here!

16) For by what shall it be known that I and Your people have found favor in Your sight? Is it not in Your going with us so that we are distinguished, I and Your people, from all the other people upon the face of the earth?

A very good friend of mine presided as the head of a board in the church he attended. Knowing this man, his absolute integrity, and his great love for the Lord, I would imagine many spiritual feathers were ruffled with great zeal through some of the decision-making processes. Board members are generally chosen for their business savvy rather than their spirituality. His direct approach, uncompromising spiritual integrity, and great love for Jesus are a rarity in most fellowship board rooms, where the norm is not to offend anyone to the point where he or she won't come back. It is generally accepted to be more important to have a well-run business with a goodly amount of lifeless sheep than it is to have a smaller, on-fire group of sheep with less business aplomb but a heart sold out to the Lord. I don't believe God sees it that way at all.

Anyway, at one of the meetings, a broken and bereaved woman– whose husband was cheating on her with another woman, drinking to excess, and openly committing all sorts of ungodly stuff while participating in church activities - came to them to ask for church discipline, stating that her children needed to be protected from him and his ways, especially since he still proclaimed to be in Christ. She very definitely needed their support and her husband needed an opportunity to wake up.

After much discussion, the members decided that church discipline was in order. However, when the vote was taken, none of the members voted to do so. My friend was aghast. Inquiring why the vote had gone south, he was reminded of the very prominent church in the news at that time that had just been sued over a very similar issue.

"Do you realize we could be sued?" one of the members began.

"So?" my friend countered.

"We could lose everything as a church," the member continued and others chimed in with their opinions.

"What does that have to do with our biblical mandate?" my friend responded in the midst of the heated discussion.

Another obviously concerned member brought up a point. "We could all be sued individually. I think the lawsuit we talked about not only concerned the church but every member of the board also. I don't know about you, but I can't afford to lose my house and everything I have."

"You've got to be kidding me," my friend replied.

After several more minutes of discussion, my friend asked all of the members of the committee to stand up. Reluctantly, each member rose to his feet. Pointing to his loins, he asked each of them the question, "When did we become so spiritually impotent?" As his words had their desired impact, he continued. "We call ourselves men of God. When did we lose the ability to mirror the character and the integrity of Jesus? Do you realize that by fearing to offend someone under our stewardship, who is violating the principles of the Word of God, actually mocking God as he flaunts his sin openly within our church and in front of his family, we are offending God Himself?"

Again, he waited for a moment for the words to settle in.

"Gentlemen, are you really willing to offend God because you fear what someone might do to you? Are you really willing to stand before Him some day and say that the risk was too high, when He asks you why you chose not to do what you know you are told to do in His Word? I, for one, am much more afraid of offending God than I am of offending anyone down here."

Each man sat down. The vote was taken and the proper discipline was applied.

The story may seem like a weak example to illustrate an offense to God. I'm sure that there are many, many more powerful examples of offending God that I could've used to get the point of compromise across. Upon further inquiry with my friend regarding this situation, he couldn't even remember what happened after the disciplinary meeting took place. There is some recollection that the man went to another church, but nothing earthshaking happened. There was no happy ending, no restoration. There was no reconciliation between the man and his wife that he could remember. In fact, the whole situation went mostly unnoticed, except by God.

Upon further consideration, the story is probably one of the best examples that I could give, simply because of its outward minimal impact. It was just a bunch of men in a board room in some nameless church, who voted on a relatively common issue, probably the same issue or one similar to those that have arisen countless times in countless rooms over many years. How important could something so seemingly small be anyway? At least that's what a lot of people would be thinking.

The real issue, however, is how God feels about it. The real question concerning you and me is how many times in our lifetimes have we compromised ourselves and our spiritual integrity without ever giving a thought as to how we have offended the heart of God? (A heartfelt "I'm sorry, Lord" would be a good thing to do right about now.) As a man who claims to follow Jesus, how many times in the past have you really given thought to whether or not you grieve His heart? How many seemingly small instances have passed through your spiritually compromised life, instances you never even noticed?

From Our Father's Heart

My church and most of its leaders
are now paying the price for rejecting My ways
for hundreds of years.
What is called My church
has gone through a metamorphic change,
from basking in My presence
to becoming places where My Spirit is not really welcome.
Now I will do what I have always done in the past.
I will raise up a people who are truly Mine,
who have My heart and My love for others.
Those of you who have finally admitted that all is not well
have now become free to know
that I am moving you closer to Me,
even when those around you do not desire to do so.
Church games are over.
You will not find Me
where there is a mixture of flesh and traditions.
Do not be afraid to discern when I have left your fellowships.
Become familiar with My presence by spending time with Me.
Then you will know where I am and where I am not.
Flee from where I am not.
I will show you where to go and how to get there.
Trust the Spirit of My Son.
He will identify with His Spirit in others.
That's where I want you.
You who are hearing are My people.
I am delighted with you.

Earlier, we stated that spiritual impotence occurs through compromise upon compromise which causes a spiritual dullness to set in, a spiritual impotence so complete that compromise finally goes unnoticed. In that state, although most of us would never desire to openly offend God in a big way, we violate Him moment by moment and never even consider the impact of our actions.

Let's go back to the plumb line, the heart of Jesus, the One we say we are emulating and showing to the world. Having lived with the Father for all of time, walking in and fully understanding things like integrity, true love, union of spirit, holiness, obedience, and submission in their purest form, the most horrific action He could ever imagine would be to offend His Father in even the smallest, seemingly insignificant way.

The Word says that we live under the mercy of God if we are in Jesus and that is good enough for us. We are concerned that our sins are covered and they are when we ask forgiveness for them because of what the blood of Jesus has accomplished. What doesn't cross our minds very often is whether or not our actions grieve the heart of God, the One we say we love, especially those supposed little actions that don't mean very much to us, like the example at the beginning of this chapter.

Men, leaders of a church, stewards of the sheep who are sent to them, are willing to discard the needs of a desperately hurting individual seeking help because they fear a loss of their own material possessions. This should be grounds for dismissal and personal church reprimand. As an observer, wouldn't you think Father God might be concerned about the representation of Jesus their actions would show the family involved? (Even if the young men never heard of the incident in the board room, the heart attitude of the men would still be on display in other situations to which the teens would be privy.) Wouldn't you think He might consider the teens' spiritual growth and development a little more important than the safety of the board's material possessions? In the light of eternity, what do you believe the Lord will hold up for scrutiny in that situation? What do you think He held as significant in His heart?

Carrying the questions a little further, when did we lose the understanding of what exactly is held in high esteem by God? Maybe more succinctly, when did we determine we could pick and choose what does or doesn't mean something to Him? What made us think we had the wisdom to determine what God considers significant?

I believe all of these questions relate back to the idea of spiritual impotence and the effect it has had over the years. The concept that we have possibly offended the heart of our Father God, Jesus, or the Holy Spirit does not move us to repentance any more. We don't even consider it important enough to make it part of our communication with God, much less grieve over how many times we have offended Him, whether we knew it or not.

When a stud horse is in his corral, he is continually sniffing the wind for a brood mare. When he sees her, he is very excited to get to her and satisfy his natural instincts, even to the point where it becomes dangerous for his handler to be around him. His focus is so intense he desires nothing else but to be fulfilled.

If that same stud were to be made impotent, all of his natural instincts would no longer exist. He could be very near to a mare and never have any inclination to breed. He is also incapable of producing any offspring.

In Christ, we are to be singularly focused. We are to be passionately in love with Jesus and passionate about the plans God has so that none should perish. We should be "sniffing the wind" for the next opportunity to present Him to anyone and everyone that comes along. When people do cross our paths, we should be spiritually driven with excitement to flow in our God-given, Christ-like characteristics and show them the love of the Father. Our only purpose should be to have the life of Christ flowing through us. Sad to say, most of us are so impotent we have little desire to do so.

We have been living in a state of spiritual impotence, unable to even care about the things our loving Father cares about, fearful of what the world would do to us if we were as passionate as Jesus was when He walked the earth. How can we be so deceived that we believe we are following His example for living?

The same verse, one more time:

I John 2:5b-6 AMP By this we may perceive (know, recognize, and be sure) that we are in Him:

6) Whoever says he abides in Him ought [as a personal debt] to walk and conduct himself in the same way in which He walked and conducted Himself.

Chapter 9
MASH icu Study Questions

1) Are you afraid of offending God at all?   Y/N

2) Is honoring God the priority of your life?   Y/N

3) Are your reputation and your standing before others more important than your reputation and standing before God?   Y/N

You really need to address this issue before we go on to deal with other critical areas in your life. Take whatever time you need to present your heart position to God. Wait until He shows you the true position of your heart based on your actual past actions, rather than on your well-rehearsed ability to temper the impact and darkness of your sin in your own mind.

Father,

Teach me to never offend you again. Thank You for Your mercy upon me, Lord!

Chapter 10

Whatever It Takes, Lord!

What price is too high to pay to please Jesus?

For most of my walk with the Lord, I've been in full-time faith outreach, living only on whatever the Lord provides for my family and me. In that time frame, many people observed my life and knew for sure I had lost my mind. In the early years, I would see friends with good intentions arrive on my doorstep with Bible in hand and a "word" from the Lord in their hearts. The "word," of course, was that God never intended His people to trust Him completely with their lives, especially in the area of physical provisions. They would emphatically express to me that the reason I was in need for sometimes even the barest of life's essentials was that I was out of line with the Word of God. All I knew was that after much time in prayer and seeking the counsel of those I trusted, I had been called to learn what it means to trust God for everything. Doing anything else would have been disobedience.

"Man is supposed to work for a living, not just pray and trust God when there is need." It didn't matter that I spent hours and hours in prayer to find the will of God for myself and cry out on behalf of others, or that I put my hand to whatever the Lord gave me to do with diligence many hours each week; that didn't count. I am convinced those hours in prayer birthed many of the outreaches we have had over the years and account for the global outreach in which my wife Merry and I participate today.

As I reflect back, there were several times when these same "messengers" had the means to provide for my need so I could be somewhat relieved from my outward distress, financial and otherwise. When asked why they felt they should not be used by God as His instrument of provision, their response was that they were - by coming and "straightening me out" so I would no longer continue in the sin of being a "burden" on the body of Christ. Funny thing was, I rarely allowed my financial need to be known, especially to those who had the means to help.

Wearing one often-washed pair of jeans and one shirt or jacket to a wealthy church told others of my need without me ever saying a word. Walking when I had no car was interpreted by some of those observing my life as I was out of line and needed to be chastised in some way. Spending my days and weeks helping wherever there was need was foolishness as far as some were concerned. That should only be done when the other important things, such as real work at a real job, had been completed. I believe that by just living in their midst on faith, they were convicted of their own lack of faith, so much so they had to come against what the Lord was doing in my life.

Backing up a bit, I gave my life to the Lord in a cemetery in a local town one day before I planned to end it by driving off a bridge in my Corvette. I was living the life of a money-hungry, lusting, dope-alcohol-pornography-addicted fool, and my wife of twelve years finally had had enough of my idiocy. She severed herself from my stupidity and left with our six-year-old daughter. Wise lady!

I was a builder of very large homes at the time. Everything I did professionally was geared so I could take on enough building jobs to make me a very wealthy man. Just prior to the most crucial time in my life - meeting Jesus - it seemed like my dream was coming true. Then, the hand of God intervened and changed the course of my life forever.

Each of the building jobs I had on my desk, which were in different phases of completion and would finally allow me to realize my dream of becoming a millionaire by the time I was thirty-five, mysteriously fell away. Some of them were signed contracts, some were nearly completed plans, some were promises to build. None-the-less, I lost every single one of them within a week or so for what appeared in the natural to be no good reason. My literal house of cards had gone from the astounding certainty of financial fulfillment to no hope at all within an incredibly short period of time. Crash and burn!

Financially leveraged to the hilt, emotionally distracted by my sin, dealing with the fact my wife and daughter left me and now the prospect of financial ruin was more than my pride could bear. I was about to be exposed for the mess I knew I was all along. As a thirty-five year old man, I would find myself sitting in a fetal position at the head of my bed with my thumb in my mouth, my leather sport coat in the closet and my Corvette parked outside, afraid to answer the phone or run into anyone who might be after me for the money I owed him.

Reinforcing my gigantic ego by smoking something powerful or drinking something strong, I would work myself into a macho lather and face another day of make believe. However, I was quickly unraveling and I thought I could beat the inevitable by ending it all - flying off that bridge in my fiberglass coffin - before someone else ended it for me.

Then Jesus, in His endless mercy, came to me in a cemetery near my grandfather's grave.

The day was sunny, the "T" top was off, and I found myself frantically driving my Corvette from church to church for some reason. I hadn't been to church for many years except for Christmas and Easter in a show of spirituality, but now it seemed as if I needed a church more than

116

life itself. I even recall some moments of being almost separate from myself, as though observing my actions from a distance as I watched myself trying to kick in a window of one of the churches I'd attended, desperate to get inside.

Finding nothing open, I went to the cemetery where my grandfather was buried. In the center of the cemetery was a traffic roundabout that circled some trees and a large wooden cross, which were bordered by a stone perimeter about two feet tall. The sun went behind the clouds for a few minutes as I sat weeping uncontrollably on that stone wall, my back to the cross.

After several long minutes the sun reappeared, casting a shadow of the cross on the pavement in front of me. Remembering that someone, someplace, sometime in the past had told me that Jesus loved me, I looked at the shadow and cried out, "Jesus, if you want my miserable life, you can have it." He did! He took it and replaced it with His own. I am the only person I know that went into a cemetery dead and came out alive.

For the next years, the Lord took the time to clean up the mess I had made of my life. I did lose my wife. I did lose my daughter, but only temporarily. I did lose my business. I did lose my cars, the model homes, and the lake property I had purchased for my own dream home. What I gained, however, was something I had never had before. I had peace! I had hope even in the most hopeless situation. I also had a promise. Most of all, I had a knowing way down deep inside that I was loved and that everything was going to work out regardless of how it appeared.

To digress for a moment, I remember one time during those two years when the Lord gave me a short term job. I was hired by my brother-in-law to clean about one hundred and fifty toilets on a large construction site. I needed money so badly at the time that I took the job. (Pride not only goes before a fall. It is dealt with on a life-long basis!)

If you know anything about construction sites, you know this was not the ideal job. Toilet cleaners and construction clean up crews are pretty much on the bottom rung on the construction site. Most of the time, they are ignored completely, not because of their task but because of their reputations as being less than honorable. In that day, things had a general habit of mysteriously disappearing when they were around.

I remember telling the Lord while I was scrubbing one of the toilets, "Lord, I'm a builder."

He told my heart, "Jim, you're a toilet cleaner." Several times in the next few days this dialog continued until I finally understood what He was attempting to get through to the block of concrete between my shoulders.

Looking up I could finally say, "Lord, I'm a toilet cleaner!" I had finally learned what He needed me to know. I don't remember the exact time frame involved, but I do know it was one hundred fifty very filthy toilets later.

When I was completely comfortable with the loss of everything, the Lord restored my construction business through someone who admired some of the homes I had built and needed a business investment. He provided the financial means for me to have a small office and some living expenses so I could begin designing and building again. Almost immediately, I started my first building job. Everything seemed to be going right, but there was unrest somewhere in my heart even though the Lord appeared to be restoring what I had destroyed.

From Our Father's Heart

What is your part in My plan?
Do you even know?
I'm not talking about how much you go to church
or how much is required of you to maintain your lifestyle.
I am asking you if you really have spent enough time with Me
to know why I have called you into being.
What is the purpose for your life?
In the seasons ahead,
those in the world will have to adapt themselves
to the changing times.
They will have to modify their direction
and rethink their lifestyles
to adapt to the dictates of their circumstances.
Many of their hearts will fail them because of fear.
What they have valued and coveted as their god
will have vanished.
All of the times they worshipped and served that god
will have been in vain and absolutely fruitless.
There will be no evidence of their life's work.
Will you be the same?
Will there be a need for what you do in the near future?
If there is not, what will you do?
How will you respond to the changes that take place?
How will you bear up under the pressure?
Better still, will you prosper because you flow easily
from what is viable at present
directly into what is needed at that time?
Have you sought out your anointing
and are you honing your gifts so that they are sharp and fruitful
when you are called upon to use them?
Do you have the souls of people constantly in mind now

and are you actively doing something about them?
Do you care about the needs of others at present?
Do you care about the calling that I have for you,
or are you so caught up in your own needs
that you can't even take time to find what that calling is?
What if I needed you tomorrow
and allowed your world to change overnight?
Will you be able to hear My directions
or will you be cowering in fear just as the world will be?
You need to be in training and listen even now.
Flow in My anointing now so that you will be ready then.

Being a designer in demand, but also being an ambassador for Christ in my heart, I would seek out opportunities to tell whoever came in my path about the incredible life that was available in Jesus and how it had changed my life. I was sitting at my drawing table at about three o' clock one morning. I had been chastised the previous day for sharing Jesus with a client who was only interested in my home designing capabilities. I broke down. Here I was, back in the building business, jobs were coming in at a nice pace, people recognized my designing and building talents and wanted me to help them achieve their dreams; but I was becoming increasingly dissatisfied moment by moment.

I wanted to tell everyone about what happened to me and no one would listen. The words, "I hired you to design my house, not preach at me," from the day before rang in my ears. I began to cry out to the Lord for direction.

I don't know if the Lord spoke to me or if He just ministered to my heart, but I heard the words, "You can stay in the building business and I will bless you, or you can turn to Me in faith and you will know Me."

There were no options as far as I was concerned. I wanted to intimately and thoroughly know the One Who had given this dead man life, no matter what it would cost me.

Houston (Actually Pewaukee, Wisconsin) We Have a Problem

There was one small glitch, however. The man who invested in my fledgling company held about sixty thousand dollars of stock options in it. Over the course of several hours that early morning, the Lord showed me how the biblical characters, Shadrach, Meshach, and Abednego had been delivered from the fiery furnace without the smell of smoke on their bodies.

"I will deliver you in the same way," He told my heart.

Around ten o'clock that morning, after I crashed on my office couch for a couple of hours, the phone rang and woke me up. It was the man who held my stock options. He wanted to see me immediately.

Denying my request to go home and get cleaned up, he told me to meet him in his office in about twenty minutes. Twenty minutes later I was standing in front of his desk.

"I don't want you to say a word or try to convince me to change my mind," he told me immediately as I walked into his office. Then he proceeded to tell me of something in which he'd become involved. "I know that my actions will not allow you to remain in business with me because you want to serve the Lord, so here."

Sliding the signed stock papers across his desk to me, he continued, "Now leave. Turn around and walk out that door without saying anything."

I was free! I no longer owed anyone anything. I was free to make the choice that had been offered to me by the Lord earlier that morning. It was a miracle!

The next day I turned the design job on which I had been working over to someone else. Within the next week, I sold all of my equipment, closed the doors of my office, and never looked back. I left the building business to pursue knowing my Lord without even a hint of the smell of smoke on my body.

Over the next years the Lord worked incessantly at killing my fleshly desires. Over those same years, however, I saw the wonder of His mighty hand over and over between visits of those well-meaning people who could not understand my life. In the proper time, I met and married my incredible helpmate Merry, an accomplished pianist who had the same desire to get to know the Lord as I did. Together we navigated the untried waters of a faith outreach, dodging unwarranted chastisements, avoiding pitfalls of fear; and violating every principle of life that seemed logical and proper, according to those who couldn't understand why we would throw away so much in exchange for what seemed to them to be so little.

In addition to the visits of those who had a "word" for us, there were several honest hearts who had observed our lives from afar and chose to come closer to see if being completely sold out to the Lord and living on faith was for them. They felt a calling to do so, but the counsel they had received was very typical of the counsel of those who had little faith in God themselves. "It is not for today. It is not in line with the real Word of God. Paul was a tentmaker while he did the work of God," etc. etc. Then they met us; we talked differently to them about God and how big He really is.

One very specific instance that broke our hearts happened during one of the most stressful times in our walk. I'll call them Tom and Nicole. Tom knew he had a call on his life, that he had been called into the ministry through many separate personal revelations, convictions, and prophetic words given to him over several years; and most of all, through his diligent study of the Bible and the many examples of those who had been called to

120

serve the Lord in faith. He was willing to do anything, give up anything; and go anywhere the Lord wanted him to go.

Nicole had the same call. We knew it, she knew it and she said so. However, Nicole needed things. Nicole needed security. She loved God with all of her heart, but she was afraid of committing everything to Him and relayed this to Tom often and with much conviction. Both of them would come to our home, asking many questions and observing many things. They knew of the miracles we had experienced (that's for another time or another chapter) - the faithfulness of God and the wonder of His provision for us. They also observed the sparse lifestyle that we lived and the pressures we often faced before the Lord moved on our behalf.

Eventually, the fear in Nicole caused Tom to turn from the calling he was convinced they had together. He said "no" to God.

I remember the day it happened. He knew what he had done and he was never the same afterwards. He had refused the offer God had given him for a significant life and settled for less than the best. The price was simply too high.

Over the years, we observed their lives, which were filled with religious activities, spiritual programs, and a myriad of meetings, services, and leadership positions, as they attempted to satisfy the emptiness they both felt. They prospered physically, but there was always a longing in their hearts for something they couldn't put a finger on. Tom had difficulty looking me in the eye when we talked about his decision.

Without knowing what actually happened at the time of their decision, they knew that something was lost forever. They had submitted themselves to a spiritual impotence. They longed to be able to feel what they had once felt and no longer could - to have the desires they once had and live the passion they once lived while the Lord was wooing them to Himself.

The spiritual drive, which was natural to the life of Jesus lived in them, had been quenched by fear. No matter how much they attempted to feel it again, they were impotent to flowing in His full nature. The price was too high for them and they refused to pay it. God continued to love them and prosper them outwardly and they continued to love Him back, but something was always missing and they knew it.

Psalm 106:12-15 AMP Then [Israel] believed His words [trusting in, relying on them]; they sang His praise.

13) But they hastily forgot His works; they did not [earnestly] wait for His plans [to develop] regarding them,

14) But lusted exceedingly in the wilderness and tempted and tried to restrain God [with their insistent desires] in the desert.

15) And He gave them their request, but sent leanness into their souls and [thinned their numbers by] disease and death.

Verse 15a scares the living daylights out of me - _And He gave them their request, but sent leanness into their souls_... Do you have any idea what it means to have leanness of soul? (Maybe you do. Maybe you are living in that leanness even now.) It means you have an unquenchable desire you can't put a finger on and it's never fulfilled. Most of the time a person doesn't even know it's there, he or she is so spiritually impotent. Leanness of soul comes from petitioning God with insistent desires that are intended to make your life more comfortable or continually asking to be blessed.

[The spiritually impotent debate over how much of their lives, and how much of what they have is supposed to be given back to God. Significant hearts ask how much they are allowed to keep.]

Don't get me wrong! God delights in blessing those He can trust with His blessing, no matter what form it takes. Prosperity in Christ is part of the heritage that was provided at the cross. His character is to flow provision to His stewards as tools to accomplish His will, not consume it upon themselves.

Often God will give those who are weakest in Him their selfish desires for personal gain, prospering them, even though He knows it's going to allow them to remain out of His overall plan and His perfect will for their lives. Even though they are so spiritually impotent He can no longer reach them and they will consume what He gives them upon themselves and their own lusts, He can still use them in His own way. He will hold up their greed and selfishness as examples to those who choose to function with the heart of Jesus and not squander God's resources.

You don't ever want to go there! If you are already there, you need to remember the concept of Lordship over that area and request that the Lord make some serious heart changes in you before you find yourself standing before Him with all of your stuff burning in a pile off to the side.

Jeremiah 12:5 AMP [But the Lord rebukes Jeremiah's impatience, saying] If you have raced with men on foot and they have tired you out, then how can you compete with horses? And if [you take to flight] in a land of peace where you feel secure, then what will you do [when you tread the tangled maze of jungle haunted by lions] in the swelling and flooding of the Jordan?

God is looking for valiant men, who have been refined in the fiery trials sent their way and are now consecrated solely unto Him through Jesus. He is looking for those who are willing to stand with Him in this end-time generation by the power of the Holy Spirit. He is going to use anybody and everybody who submits fully to Him - men, women, and children; but

122

He is looking among His men for leaders who will be powerful through their submission to the Lordship of Jesus Christ and unbeatable in their service within the plan of God.

Today's men, those who call themselves men of God and followers of Jesus, are for the most part incapable of winning the race set before them in a society of relative safety. Lean of soul, selfish of heart, they are impotent. They have nothing worthwhile to offer their families, their fellowship, or society when things get rough. They are a mere shadow of who Jesus desires them to be, who He meant for them to be. When they are called upon to do mighty acts of heavenly valor and eternal wealth for the One they say they serve, they will have nothing of consequence to share, for they have rejected the true wealth that's available to them.

If you are part of that impotent group, what are you going to do when things unfold as prophesied in the Bible during the coming perilous times? How will you stand against and overcome raging darkness as Jesus did when you have been blind and impotent while maneuvering through relative light?

If you fail to glorify God with your life by continually fulfilling your own desires in times of relative safety, how do you think you will do when really dark times come? How will you lead others to an overcoming life in Jesus when you are overcome yourself?

[What price is too high to pay to honor the work of the cross?]

Men of God, it is time for you to remove yourself from the league of the impotent and submit yourself completely to the Lordship of Jesus Christ so His character can be formed in you. Search your heart and decide if you even care to compete in the race that honors God.

Chapter 10
MASH icu Study Questions

1) Will you pay whatever price necessary to find the heart of God for your life?   Y/N

2) Do you care at all that you are offending God by not seeking Him regarding His plan for you?   Y/N

3) Will you do whatever He asks you to do even if others think you have lost your mind?   Y/N

4) Is pleasing yourself or other people more important to you than pleasing God?   Y/N

Father,

   Please remove the leanness of soul I have gained because of my selfish requests. I am sorry for my incessant prayers of asking You to make my life comfortable. Thank You for forgiving me!

Chapter 11

Thinking We Belong

As Christians, we have forgotten that we are actually different than the people in the world!

II Cor. 5:17 NIV Therefore, if anyone is in Christ, he is a new creation...

As part of our outreach, we periodically join with a brother in Christ who has built an astounding panel truck called "Born Again." The truck is a marvel of automotive engineering. More than 2700 horsepower pushes this unique demonstration vehicle down the track with the front wheels raised at a 30 degree angle off the ground. My friend Terry, the builder and designer, looks past the engine through the floor boards and steers the raw power by using the right and left brake as it screams past astounded fans. The truck body is wild enough, but the engine is really amazing. It is big and bright and full blown. When you fire that baby up, it literally sucks the air out of your lungs with its power and volume. (For you ladies who may be reading this, that's a good thing.)

What is really fascinating is the response to the truck when it runs. Even though "Born Again" is much more powerful than any other vehicle at the tractor pulling contests, (more than double the horsepower in some instances,) and even though it is designed as a demonstration vehicle and is not a part of the actual competition, some of the fans in the stands don't understand its purpose. When it is hooked to the sled, they judge it as though it's on the same level as the other vehicles. Because of its raw power, it can get no traction in the loose dirt, so the running times recorded are sometimes not as good as the times of the vehicles which are actually competing. It has even been booed after a run by those who have no inkling as to the magnificence of the machine and what it is made to do.

"Born Again" is not meant to run with the other vehicles. It has been designed to display a different form of power and has a different purpose for running. Even though it may be included in the group called "vehicles" in the events throughout the day, it is nothing at all like the other vehicles. Its purpose for existing is not even remotely close to that of the other vehicles.

From Our Father's Heart

Do you know that you are different?
Really, really different?
First of all, in My eyes,
there is no resemblance between you
and anyone who has not chosen the Lord as his Master.
Since I see in the spiritual realm,
I can easily distinguish between those who have chosen Me
as their Father
and those who still belong to the father of lies.
Both of you are designed to live for eternity with your fathers and are
custom-designed to be there.
You adapt easily to your new homes when it is time.
Of course, these homes are as different
as you, their inhabitants, are.
Yours is more magnificent than you can now imagine.
Theirs is horrible beyond belief.
Because you have been designed to live among others like you,
I desire you to be with each other now.
Do you know that by interacting with each other as My children,
it is making your inner being strong?
You need to draw upon My Spirit
whenever your interactions with those like you
bring challenges your way.
Each of you has the seed of My Spirit within you,
so as you choose to act like My Son toward each other,
you will grow.
When you don't choose to act like Him,
there are setbacks in your spiritual wealth.
To you, these setbacks seem inconsequential.
I, however, observe the great harm that is done to My plan.
You also further the kingdom of darkness
by remaining far from My light.
It is time to realize how different you really are
and then walk in that wonderful difference with Me.
Start now.
Let My Word and its promises inhabit you.
I will then inhabit the praises that rise from you who are Mine
as you help each other grow toward Me.

To me this scenario very much describes us as Christian men. If our lives were compared to the event of the tractor pull, those of us who know Jesus as the absolute Lord over everything in our lives are participating in society right alongside those who have not been born of the Spirit, as Jesus told Nicodemus we must be. Our lives are judged by outsiders with the same criteria they use to measure all others in the race, even though we are absolutely different, carrying in our inner being the very nature of Christ. This critical distinction should give us a vastly different reason for running in the race; namely, to fulfill the Great Commission and be used of God to help bring in as many who will come before time runs out, not to achieve worldly success.

Most of the time, unfortunately, our goals are very similar to those of the world. Even more horrifying, we are often so unlike Jesus that others can't seem to see the difference between those born of the Spirit, as we are, and those who are not.

As men, we have believed the lie that our success is measured in the same way as the success of others. Even though we are spiritually nothing like those around us, we follow the same spirit of the world in our business practices and our social activities except, of course, those that cause us to sin openly.

Even though we have been given different directions for participating in the race, we tend to compete to achieve the same outcome as those around us as we head for the finish line. We strive for success, carnal wealth, popular social standing, recognition for what we have accomplished, etc, etc. We classify those things significant as if they define our legacy. God calls those achievements insignificant. Men can accomplish those things in their own strength and cunning; and they do, most of the time never even considering God.

Are We Supposed to Even Be There?

Are we as Christians supposed to go to the typical workplace with those who don't know the Lord to provide for our families? Unless we are called to a specific type of ministry or mission field, of course we are. Are we supposed to practice stellar work habits, initiated and implemented by the power of the Holy Spirit? Can we have nice homes in which to live and raise our families? Of course! Problems arise with God when we make those things our gods, displacing Him in our hearts from His proper #1 position. We, as followers of Jesus, are not supposed to become workaholics, losing our spiritual perspective, our marriages, and our families in order to maintain the things we have acquired through our impotence.

There are only two reasons any Christian man is to be in the workplace at any level. One is to provide for the real needs of our families

129

as husbands and fathers. The second is for the people in our circle of influence to see Jesus large enough in us so they will desire to accept Him as their Savior and Lord. We are to get involved in the workplace and participate in work-related activities right alongside of others, but our goals and reasons for doing so must be of God, not of our own making. Any other motive for participating limits the ability for God to move us when and where He pleases.

Think of it; if things own us, if our mortgage is so high that both husband and wife need to work, how do the children fare? The question is not whether or not they are OK as far as you're concerned, but how are they really doing in God's eyes? If we "need" more toys, better this, and bigger that, how can we hear Him when He has a plan to move us down the road or possibly even to another country? If our personal recognition is a priority for us, how can we serve others with the heart Jesus has?

If our life, with all of its entanglements, clouds our eyes to the overall plan God has for mankind and for us in particular, we have been rendered impotent and will not hear what He really has planned for us. We can't even be motivated to desire the things that are important to God. We are not only in the world; but we are of it, rather than being separate from it as He commanded.

Chapter 11
MASH icu Study Questions

1) Are you exactly where God designed you to be even though you may not fit?   Y/N

Journal or discuss how you know your answer to be truth.

Father,

Please show me how to act as someone who is changing because of my submission to the cross of Christ. Thank You, Lord. Amen.

Chapter 12

We're Just Not Like the Other Guys Anymore

You are a spiritual being that has direct access to a spiritual God.

The spiritually impotent man demands that his power and authority be recognized by others. The spiritually healthy man submits his whole being to Lordship and serves everyone so the authority and power of Jesus is recognized through Him.

John 16:23 AMP And when that time comes, you will ask nothing of Me [you will need to ask Me no questions]. I assure you, most solemnly I tell you, that My Father will grant you whatever you ask in My Name [as presenting all that I AM].

Eph. 1:21 AMP ...Far above all rule and authority and power and dominion and every name that is named [above every title that can be conferred], not only in this age and in this world, but also in the age and the world which are to come.

Phil. 2:9 AMP Therefore [because He stooped so low] God has highly exalted Him and has freely bestowed on Him the name that is above every name.

Col. 2:9-10a AMP For in Him the whole fullness of Deity (the Godhead) continues to dwell in bodily form [giving complete expression of the divine nature].
10a) And you are in Him, made full and having come to fullness of life [in Christ you too are filled with the Godhead – Father, Son and Holy Spirit – and reach full spiritual stature].

Eph. 4:6 AMP One God and Father of [us] all, Who is above all [Sovereign over all], pervading all and [living] in [us] all.

For many years, I have studied many books pertaining to our life in Christ and took most of the opportunities that came my way in an attempt to learn exactly who we really are in Christ and what kind of power we've been given because of the covenant the Father established with us through Jesus. In my travels, I have seen so much that has been labeled the power of God, things supposedly done in the Name of Jesus and claimed to be His manifest presence, when what actually transpired was nothing more than

133

spiritual slight of hand and a glorified dog and pony show. On the other hand, I have been witness to some amazing things done through humble servants of Jesus that have no explanation other than our merciful God showed up and some mighty wonderful spiritual things happened.

July 17, 2006 was quite an eventful day for our family both spiritually and physically. Let's back up to Sunday, July 16, when an interesting topic of conversation cropped up.

Merry, Jubilee, and I were having one of our home fellowship services. The three of us had just spent some time in the Word and were discussing what part God actually wanted us to play in the area of spiritual warfare. In addition to agreeing that obedience was a key weapon, we concluded as a family that as far as we were concerned, the real power of God was manifested when two factors were present.

First, God seemed to delight in showing up on behalf of His children when they practiced getting out of the way. His real presence came when there was no hope in the hearts of the participants other than the hope of Jesus, the power of the cross, and the promises given in the Word. God simply doesn't desire to share His glory with anything fleshly, especially human egos. When we increase, He seems to decrease in our midst. When we consistently choose to decrease, He delights in being God for us. I am quite frightened for those TV evangelists who take glory for what God has done; or worse yet, call godly what has been done in the flesh.

Second, after the flesh is completely out of the way, we are to walk in humble obedience as His directions unfold. We simply do whatever we are told to do, resting in the fact that whatever happens is up to God. It is not our place to help Him determine the outcome or define the process. We simply obey and trust in God.

In His mercy, the Lord ministered to us on Sunday what we would need to implement the very next day. That Monday evening, I had just concluded a counseling session at a local restaurant about twenty minutes from our home and began to feel a little ill. Worsening by the minute, I said good-bye to the man I was with and asked him to pray for me as I left. I began the drive toward our house via the freeway. About two or three minutes into the drive, my chest began to feel as if a truck had parked on it, and I experienced an incredible pain from shoulder to shoulder and down each arm. Something was drastically wrong.

In too much pain to continue, I cried out to the Lord and asked if I should pull over, head for home (which was the next turn off,) or proceed on to the following turn off, which led to the local hospital. To my surprise, I felt He was telling me to head for home. Immediately, the pain stopped. I was assured I could make it there.

Upon arriving home, I walked in the door from our garage and called out, asking Merry to dial 911. She asked who needed help, thinking

134

one of the neighbors was in trouble. I told her it was for me, that I believed I was having a heart attack. She quickly accomplished the call and then knelt down beside me to pray. By that time, I was lying on the living room floor, breathing with great difficulty. I heard her say, "Oh, Jesus, help us," which was natural for my wife because of her love and dependence upon Him for everything. It was also Step 1 of what we had learned the day before – getting out of the way. It wasn't a conscious effort on her part, but the Spirit of God orchestrating this particular time frame.

As I lay on the floor, my eyes uncontrollably began to roll upward and things became somewhat surreal. I knew others were on the way and Merry was there; but it all seemed as if I were watching it from a distance.

Suddenly I saw a large black cloud forming off to my left above my head. It seemed as if it was about a thousand miles away, but it headed in my direction at a tremendous rate of speed. I knew it wasn't good. The thought of death came to my mind. I had a great peace because of my commitment to the Lordship of Jesus, but something just wasn't right. I didn't know what it was, but something about the black cloud was not of God.

Then, as if she was speaking through a gigantic bull horn, I heard Merry say, "Spirit of death, I command you to leave and spirit of life, I command you to come back into him in the Name of Jesus."

The Lord was showing me on my end the effect of her prayer and His power. Her voice resonated in the spiritual realm and in my ears with absolute authority and uncompromising power. As soon as her words were spoken, the black cloud - which was now extremely close – exploded, as if an atomic bomb had been detonated in its center.

I remember my eyes immediately returned to their usual position and I became aware of my surroundings once again. A neighbor, who just happened to be a paramedic, was kneeling next to me asking if I was OK. Just about that time, the ambulance arrived and I was taken to the hospital, where it was confirmed I'd had a heart attack. A stent was immediately placed in one of the arteries near my heart and I went to the recovery room. As incredible as that all was and as grateful as I am to the Lord for what I just explained to you, I believe the next part of the story is even more powerful and more encouraging than the miracle of the intervention of God on my behalf.

While in the recovery room, I began to relate what had happened to me while I was on the floor, mentioning to Merry her bellowing voice and absolute authority. I said to her that I never knew she had that kind of power in the spiritual realm. It was all so unlike the quiet, unassuming person I knew her to be. She looked at me with an expression of surprise.

"Jim," she said, "I wasn't yelling. I was whispering helplessly to Jesus with my hand on your chest. I just said what I said without even thinking. It had to be the Holy Spirit prompting me. He just told me what to say, I guess."

After that she told me she never sensed anything but an utter dependence on the Lord, knowing the outcome was entirely up to Him. She had no formula, just great need and her only hope was Jesus. Without knowing it, she was walking in Step 2 of what we had learned the morning before in our church service, simply doing what He asked us to do, whether we knew it or not!

The fact that Merry is who she is and could only be who she is, while the Lord showed Himself to be who He is and always will be, is one of the most exciting lessons I have ever learned. Relaying that story has also been an astounding gift of encouragement to everyone who hears it.

From Our Father's Heart

You have been given access to Me in the Name of Jesus.
It is the only name that is powerful enough
to accomplish that access.
I send you to others in the Name of Jesus.
It is the only name powerful enough
to break down all of the barriers
that would hinder your representation
of truth to them.
Jesus!
The single Name that spans all time.
The Name from eternity past to all of eternity future.
Your world was changed by it.
You even count down the time of waiting for His return to you
by events that He has established.
Jesus, the Name that is above every name ever given.
Jesus: whisper it, speak it, shout it from the roof tops,
and weep in praise when it passes your lips.
Jesus!
Your very soon coming King!

How blind we are to understanding the complete access we have to our Father in heaven that has been provided through the cross of Christ! How blind we are to the power of simple prayer that comes from a humble heart! Could it possibly be because we have considered our own prayers to be so ineffective we have consequently negated the tremendous power available in communicating with God? Have we minimized the incredible gift we were given as symbolized by the veil of the temple that was torn from top to bottom – complete access to the throne room of God?

136

If our prayers are impotent, we are impotent. No wonder most of us have little desire to flow in more of God. Who really wants to pay the price to get close to a God that he or she perceives as powerless, ineffective, and distant? Satan has done a marvelous job of lying to us, which we then embraced and allowed it to minimize in our eyes who we actually are in Christ and what has been provided for us in His covenant with us.

Isaiah 8:11-13 AMP   For the Lord spoke thus to me with His strong hand [upon me], and warned and instructed me not to walk in the way of this people, saying,

12) Do not call conspiracy [or hard, or holy] all that this people will call conspiracy [or hard, or holy]; neither be in fear of what they fear, nor [make others afraid and] in dread.

13) The Lord of hosts – regard Him as holy and honor His holy name [by regarding Him as your only hope of safety], and let Him be your fear and let Him be your dread [lest you offend Him by your fear of man and distrust of Him].

Isaiah 31:1 AMP   Woe to those who go down to Egypt for help, who rely on horses and trust in chariots because they are many and in horsemen because they are very strong, but they look not to the Holy One of Israel, nor seek and consult the Lord!

We live in a church society that longs to see the power of God manifest. Most of us gravitate toward the loud voices, the glitzy programs, and the well-rehearsed, miraculous-appearing shows that supposedly demonstrate the power of God. In doing so, we have become undiscerning of those who really are of God and represent Him with honor and those who are building a following for themselves.

[When your life is reviewed and the fires burn away the wood, hay, and stubble, what if there is nothing left to give to Jesus except ashes?]

On one occasion, we happened upon yet one more telethon, which demonstrated our incredible ability to grieve God in a very unique way. Wanting the phones to ring with commitments of support, this particular "evangelist" began to pray for one of the hapless members of the studio audience. The "evangelist," resting her hand on the forehead of the victim, prayed with great fervency and then pressed on the forehead of the person until they fell to the floor. (I've experienced the real deal; this was fake.) As the camera followed the person to the floor, the "evangelist," with crocodile tears in her eyes, looked directly into the camera and said, "See, that's why you need to give to this ministry." I don't know what happened after that. I turned off the TV and dove into a prayer of repentance for

137

myself and asked forgiveness for the whorish heart that claimed to represent Jesus.

Can you imagine how that whole concept must grieve the heart of Father God? Can you imagine the accountability of that evangelist gone bad? Can you imagine the terrible witness that display is to the person who's searching for answers and observing such downright foolishness? Can you imagine the spiritual impotence of the person who needs to manufacture the power of God, because he or she does not flow in His real power?

Chapter 12
MASH icu Study Questions

It's Time for Some Hard Questions, Men of God.

1) Are you willing to put aside the foolish trappings you thought defined you as a man of God and gain the humble heart that exhibits who Jesus really is to those who observe your life?   Y/N

2) Are you willing to begin defending your God, no longer endorsing religious foolishness in yourself first and then in those who dishonor Him by using His holy Name to validate foolish things?   Y/N

3) Are you willing to spend your life fulfilling God's desires rather than your own as your priority?   Y/N?

Father,

I have dishonored Your Name more often than I realize. I have stood by when others have taken Your Name and made it a laughing stock. Please forgive me. Teach me to live for You, honor You, and defend You in the way Jesus did. Thank You, Lord, for Your great mercy upon me."

Chapter 13

Are You Exactly Where God Planned for You to Be?

Every step of our lives should be directed by God.

"I think this is it!" Randy stated in excited yet hushed tones, feeling a pronounced stirring from the Lord rather than any natural indication it was time to move. He shook Michelle, his wife of eleven years, out of a fitful sleep. For several days, they'd known this event was imminent.

Running to the other bedroom, and already dressed in anticipation of its occurrence except for their shoes, the young couple guided their now wide-awake and very frightened children from their small home to the back yard. Esther, the oldest, had her backpack in one hand and Hannah's little hand in the other. Two year old Deborah, sensing something was wrong, could only stare bug-eyed and alternate between whimpering and sucking her thumb. Full-blown wailing was on the horizon. Michelle scooped her up on the run, while Randy guided Esther and Hannah to the back door.

The volcano some forty miles away had steadily increased its threatening activity. Glowing rivers of unstoppable lava could be seen flowing unhindered from its rupturing crown in the dim morning light. The lava continued its journey down the sides of the immense mountain. The increasingly panicked cries of the local residents could be heard as they fled to the relative safety afforded by moving further away from the base of the volcano. The headlights of small ant-like vehicles seemingly inched their way down from the tree line toward the main highway close to the family's home.

"I'll get on the radio to rescue central," Randy said, as Michelle stood under a tree near the concrete cistern and wrapped the girls in the comfort of a cozy blanket.

Randy and Michelle, in answering the call of the Lord on their lives, had sold all they owned and moved to the remote island about four years ago. Establishing a small school for their tiny community, they taught children of all ages what they needed to know about the world around them and the wonder of the Gospel of Jesus Christ. Both received great acceptance and many were brought to salvation and equipped to function in their society and for eternity.

Returning from the only communication possible between the outside world and the small village, Randy began to direct some of the men who had already gathered near the school to implement the rescue operation instructions he had received from the helicopter base on the nearest, much larger island.

"Prepare the women and children first," he told Manny, a large, dark-skinned man and trusted friend. "It's about twenty minutes each way by chopper and about twelve people can fit in each load. They're calling in choppers from the charter services to help, but we don't know how many that will be. Try to keep families together."

Manny immediately gathered other willing hands to help him with his task. In short order, the first of many greatly anticipated choppers appeared above the palm trees to their left and arrived to the cheers and relief of the men, women, and children who held or stood near their meager belongings.

Throughout the day, choppers both large and small gathered frightened passengers and flew them to the safety of the nearby island. Based on what could be observed, the volcano was sure to explode sometime that day, so everyone worked with great purpose and efficiency to see that all made it out safely. On an island that size, it meant certain death for anyone who remained.

"How many more trips will be needed?" the operator from the helicopter base asked.

Randy, who had sent the children with Manny's family much earlier and Michelle on one of the latest flights, responded over the din of the now very active and out-of-control mountain. "It should take only one more to...," Randy stopped in mid sentence. A tremendous explosion ripped through the atmosphere and came across the radio speaker with great distortion. "Tell my family I love them."

The only communication that followed was the sound of static, which the radio operator quickly and mercifully tuned out.

From Our Father's Heart

Does anything really move you any more?
Do you care if people are going to be separated from Me
for their eternal lives?
When was the last time you wept for souls?
When did you give up any comfort
for the sake of someone hearing My Word?
I know some of you are fulfilling My plan for you,
but what about those of you
who have settled into a mundane spiritual existence?
Where is your fire?
Your time is considered your own.
Your money is yours!
My gifts to you make you proud rather than grateful!
What is it going to take to wake you up?
You are about to find out unless you wake up to My heart!

Old manna is no longer nourishing
and some of you are starving to death spiritually.
Repent now!

Earlier in this book, I shared a time when the Lord gave me a choice: to remain in the building business where He would prosper me or leave the business and come to know Him. If you recall, once I made the decision to know Him, He delivered me immediately from the business in a miraculous way by bringing the stocks of my corporation back into my possession.

Without knowing it at the time, the Lord was in the process of defining my life. From the moment I came to the Lord, I had a burning desire to find His direction for my life. I didn't know what it was called. I didn't know why it seemed so important to have His direction; but I knew somehow that until I did, I would never have any peace – which was something I wanted and desperately needed.

Until I met Jesus, most of my life was reactionary. I would simply gravitate to whatever I could do well or whatever seemed like a good opportunity at the time. Finding direction in life in this manner caused me to continually question whether I was in the will of God when things got rough or weren't working out. As I continued to bounce around, I discovered I was really good at designing homes and building, so that's where I landed.

When I met the Lord, I wanted to know exactly why He created me, not just find someplace where I fit in pretty well. When He delivered me from the building business, I didn't know I would be in a training program for the mission He had for me. Some twenty+ years later, my wife Merry and I are writing books, speaking at seminars, ministering one on one; and helping others find direction for their lives. I love to see people find their calling in life.

God has undoubtedly defined my life. I have no question in my mind about where I'm supposed to be, no matter what comes or where it may lead. I have no question regarding what I have been called to do. Over the years, when things got rough, there was never more than a brief period of reflection as to whether or not I was in the right place; I knew I was. The Lord confirmed it in my mind, my heart, and in my relationship with Him. He defined who I am and I endeavor to walk in it with His direction and power so He is honored.

No one or nothing can rob me of what He has placed in me so thoroughly. Because of what He's done, I can view hardships as refinement opportunities, rather than dismal circumstances that cause me to question my calling. Because of my Father God's incredible mercy and grace, I know who I am, who I have been created to be, and exactly what I am supposed to do that will be a pleasing offering to Him on the day I meet Him face to face.

After reading the story in the beginning of this chapter, there are those in the church who would question whether Randy and Michelle had really heard from God when they sought His direction for their lives. There are those who would question the integrity of a God who would fracture an obedient family that was only doing what they believed He had called them to do. Neither of these questions should be the focus. The point is we need to spend enough time with the Lord, so when things come our way that cause us to momentarily question if we're in the right place, we can go back to a time when He made things rock-solid in our hearts and continue on because of that remembrance.

What are you supposed to be doing in life? I'm not asking what are you doing or what would you like to do; but are you sure you're doing what the Lord planned for you to do even before you were born? Are you willing to find out what that is no matter what the consequences might be?

Once more, using Jesus' life as the benchmark, personal danger, personal scorn, personal loss, and even the loss of His life had no bearing on whether He was going to do what His Father ordained for His life. I'm sure He didn't relish the prospect of dying in the manner He did, but the outcome of His surrender to His Father's will and His actions brought Him unparalleled joy.

Heb. 12:2b AMP   He, for the joy [of obtaining the prize] that was set before Him, endured the cross, despising and ignoring the shame, and is now seated at the right hand of the throne of God.

Do you know that most men have spent more time choosing what car they're going to drive, what career they're going to have, or what home they're going to buy than they've spent with the Lord to find out the reason He's given them breath and how He'd like to use their lives? You may want to examine your own life to see if you fall in that category. As best you can, take some time to reflect on your past and present days. How much time do you spend in petitioning the Lord to find His perfect will for your life vs. the time you spend in petitioning Him for that which pertains to your job, house, or the next vehicle you plan to purchase?

[Assess your life to see how it can become a significant presentation to Him.]

Chapter 13
MASH icu Study Questions

1) Why are you doing what you do every day?

2) Do you love what you do?   Y/N

3) Do you know for sure you are doing what you're supposed to be doing?
Y/N

4) Does the Lord consider what you do significant?   Y/N

5) Have you ever asked the Lord what He would like you to do as your
life's calling?   Y/N

6) Are you willing to do whatever He gives you to do, no matter what it
may cost you, even if it's your life?   Y/N

Father,

Please make my priority in life the desire to fully understand Your plan for my life. Give me the strength to make the changes necessary to please You. Thank You, Lord!

Chapter 14

Decision Time

*People around you are supposed to say you
live like Jesus lives.*

OK, I'm a cheesehead! I don't care to put one of those things on my head and I've never seen a Packer game at Lambeau field, but I love it when they win. I'm a pretty fair weather fan, but I follow the Green Bay team as much as I can when I'm not doing something else. (These recent years have been pretty exciting to follow.) Although the thought of wearing a construction hat with two cans of soda attached to it along with two long tubes running from the cans to my mouth and standing shirtless within camera range in -30 degrees Fahrenheit with my belly painted green and gold is far beyond what I would do for the team, I am somewhat of a sports fan.

Anyway, when I was younger, I remember the dynasty the Packers enjoyed under the leadership of Vince Lombardi. He told them that if they obeyed his rules and used his methods, they would be a championship team.

It took three years, but that promise became a reality. In December of 1961, the Packers beat the Giants 37-0 to win the National Football League Championship.

The Packers went from being a weak, disorganized group of players to functioning as a dominant, cohesive team. Under his leadership, they won six division titles, five NFL championships, two Super Bowls (I and II) and acquired a record of 98-30-4. They became a benchmark for all other teams.

Those years were wonderful if you lived in Wisconsin. The team rose from obscurity to become an NFL leader for the years Vince Lombardi was with the team. It was a miraculous turnaround.

In view of the purpose of this book, this story is a testimony of the need to make a change in order to turn a losing team around. Something had to happen or the team would continue to lose and lose... Well, you get the picture. As exciting as this time was, as wonderful as the memories may be, the hard work, dedication, and involvement of thousands and thousands of people - whether fans, coaches, owners, or whatever - has no eternal impact and means nothing in that respect as far as God is concerned, unless somehow someone came to know the Lord in the process.

There is application for us as men, however. Let's use the sport scenario to deal with some eternal implications.

Fact 1: The team was in trouble. They were losing practically every game they played. Although the uniforms were similar, the team had little ranking with the other teams. They had no power so they were not considered a threat by any of them.

Fact 2: If the team were ever going to make a difference, someone had to make an assessment. Someone had to come to the realization that something was dreadfully wrong and say it out loud to others who would listen so something could be done about it. That had to happen before anything would change.

Once it was determined that change was needed, the ebb and flow of the battle began to shift in favor of the Packers. The winds of change had begun; the tide was beginning to turn. Much work would be required, the traditional way of doing things had to be modified, many decisions had to be implemented; but change was definitely in the works.

From Our Father's Heart

Do you know that I hold you in the highest regard?
You are My ministers of the eternal covenant
that I have established for the good of all mankind.
I hold you very dear to My heart.
For many reasons, I must train and refine you.
Never do I enjoy seeing you go through challenges
to your faith and your commitment, but they are necessary.
You have a great responsibility.
You are a steward of the most important event
in the history of mankind.
My covenant with you is what the life, death,
and resurrection of Jesus is all about.
Now you have the privilege of demonstrating it
to the world and to the angelic beings.
With that privilege comes the corresponding responsibility
of presenting it properly.
That is what My training is all about.
Submit to My hand.
Embrace My love.
As you grow, you will discover more wonders
than you could ever imagine.
The more I can trust you, the more I can reveal to you.
I delight in you.

Men, as representatives of the way Jesus lived His life, we are in trouble. We are losing every game we play. Our marriages are mediocre, but we think they are as good as anyone else's. Our families are being torn

148

apart, but we believe that is the way it is supposed to be, considering all of the influences in the world. Our churches are weak and ineffective as far as God is concerned, our businesses and our governments have lost the ethical standards for which they once strived; and our societies are in chaos because they are void of our Christ-like leadership.

The sad fact is, it is our fault. We as men have failed to follow the standards set by the One we say we follow, Jesus Christ, and it's time we said it out loud.

In the world, as we "play" alongside all of the other teams and players, we are not a threat or a challenge to their dark thinking. We certainly are not the threat Jesus was to their thinking. They crucified Him! As a matter of fact, we are so insignificant and ineffective that we are not even of much consequence. Our play has been nullified. The team we represent has little standing in the eyes of those around us and, therefore, garners little respect for the One we represent.

What is so amazing is that we are not even supposed to be playing the same game. Jesus established a new game, a totally different game with a new playing field and new rules. In Christ, our goals are supposed to be Jesus-oriented. The game plan to which we are supposed to adhere is nowhere near the same as the one utilized by anyone who is not in Christ. Our achievements and our successes are not measured with the same rating system. In fact, most of what we do outside of the overall plan of God will burn away as so much wood, hay, and stubble; that means nothing to those who are playing the games of the world.

Do you really understand what this means? Everything you worry about, everything that consumes your time, everything that takes your attention away from the plan of God for your life is eternally worthless. You could strive your whole life, pay whatever price necessary to achieve success as the world defines success; and, unfortunately, it will be more-or-less useless in God's eyes.

Throughout our travels, Merry, Jubilee, and I found ourselves in unique parts of the United States. Most communities have some area nearby that showcases someone's dream gone wrong. We would drive or walk past a dilapidated old farmhouse with its shabby, far past rundown out-buildings verging on collapse. Sometimes we would visit a "ghost town," some kind of community from the past that looked to a bright future for so many, yet was doomed to eventual failure.

My heart would break to think of the countless heartaches, the overwhelming worries, and the faded dreams that no doubt consumed the lives of those who once lived there. I would attempt to place myself in the shoes of the overworked farmer as he stood and stared at his failed, parched, or flooded crop, knowing his family had nothing for the cold winter ahead. I would grieve for the prospector who saw the mine shut down because it was played out. I would feel the astounding heartache as wagons were packed

149

with meager belongings and the owners had to leave their homes because a once thriving town had gone bust. How many scenarios, how many dreams, how many nightmares, how many shattered plans – all considered vitally important at the time – were truly of consequence?

In the light of eternity, when we stand before God and give an account for the breath He gave us, if our lives did not have the plan of God as their main focus, what good were they? Sadly, they could even be judged as something that interfered with the plan of God. I pray that understanding permeates your inner being and becomes alive to you as you turn more fully toward God!

OK, Men, So We Need to Change, but Where Do We Begin?

Rev.3:18-20 NIV "I counsel you to buy from me gold refined in the fire, so you can become rich; and white clothes to wear, so you can cover your shameful nakedness; and salve to put on your eyes, so you can see.

19) Those whom I love I rebuke and discipline. So be earnest and repent.

20) Here I am! I stand at the door and knock. If anyone hears my voice and opens the door, I will come in and eat with that person, and they with me. "

After bringing to light the need for change in the previous chapters, it is now time to initiate some strategic plans in specific areas that will carry over into all other areas of our lives, bringing them in line with the Word of God. There are four general areas that are very close to the heart of God, which once and for all need to be placed under His absolute Lordship. They are: your relationship with God, your marriage, your children, and your associations with others, in order of importance. In the final section of this book, we will address these four areas that need the Holy Spirit's intervention, if they are going to count for something in God's economy.

As these very crucial areas get in line with the plan and intent of Father God and the heart of Jesus, your life will be well on the way to becoming significant in the eyes of your Father. If you allow these areas to be inspected by the Holy Spirit and submit to any and every change that comes to light, you will experience the fullness of His power in those areas as the Holy Spirit makes those changes in your inner being. This new direction that pleases the heart of Father God will become part of your eternal legacy.

Significant changes will require the implementation of some drastic measures. As good as Vince Lombardi was in helping the Packers to achieve a turnaround, we have an infinitely better coach to ensure that our lives turn around – Jesus! He is the author and finisher of our faith. He will

150

keep us moving in the right direction until the day we are with Him in eternity.

Heb. 12:2a AMP Looking away [from all that will distract] to Jesus, Who is the Leader and the Source of our faith [giving the first incentive for our belief] and is also its Finisher [bringing it to maturity and perfection].

To see any real eternal change in your life, you must first realize that your "business as usual" way of dealing with your life will not be any more effective than it has been in the past. It's time for full and complete submission to the Lordship of Jesus Christ over every area of your life.

You now need to say out loud what you have begun to understand in your spirit. You know drastic changes need to be made and only the Lord can make them in you, if you are going to really influence your world as a representative of Jesus and stand before Him one day to present Him with a life of significance.

Chapter 14
MASH icu Study Questions

1) Do you now know it's time to address everything that offends God in every area of your life?   Y/N

2) Are you ready to submit everything you own, everything that owns you, everything you are, and everything you are not to the Lordship of Jesus Christ as the only cure for your impotence?   Y/N

3) Are you willing to get the job done through the power of the Holy Spirit even if it gets very personal and comes against the sacred cows in your life? Y/N

4) Are you willing to humble yourself before your wife and your children as the Holy Spirit convicts your heart of its impotence and starts initiating the changes for which you've asked?   Y/N

Good! (That's for if you said "yes.") Let's get on with the God-honoring steps that will allow you to present back to Him a significant life when you stand before Him. Taking these steps through the power of the Holy Spirit will lead you to address any area that is out of line with the plan God has for you - the life for which Jesus died so that you might live His to the fullest.

You will need to pray continually through these next chapters as they address steps for change in your relationship with God, your marriage, your family, and your present and future associations. Only God can implement the eternal changes that need to take place. You can't do it in your strength. You can't even do it by mixing your strength in with His. It would be foolish to try. Without continual prayer and submission to the Lord, you will be like the farmer who has nothing alive in his fields, but still expects to feed his family from his non-existent crop.

Father,

I ask that You give me the wisdom to see what changes are needed in my life in order to please You and Your strength to allow them to take place. Thank You, Lord!

Chapter 15

Preparing Your Heart for Change

The battle is the Lord's.

Phil closed his laptop, the vile images to which he'd just submitted himself still vivid in his mind. He began to feel disgust because of his sin. Once more, he had failed his Lord. This had to be what seemed like the thousandth time he had to come to God with the same filthy sin. How could He forgive him another time? There had to be an end to His mercy if he kept on hurting his loving Father over and over again. His own father gave up on him long ago; now he knew for sure he had reached the limit with God, no matter what the Word said. All he could do was moan with regret and attempt to shake off the filthy feelings that made him feel hopeless in light of his failures.

All of the success he had strived for and attained at any cost meant nothing. In his heart, he finally believed what he had been told all of his life - first by his father and then by everyone else he allowed near him. He was no good. He was worthless. Burying himself in the work at his desk, he once more placed all of his promises to God aside, knowing he could never live up to the life Jesus had for him.

Whether in the Spirit or in the flesh, Phil did not know. Suddenly he was caught up into a realm he did not recognize. "Could this be happening?" he thought to himself. "I must be dreaming," he assured himself. "If I'm not dreaming, this is the scariest place I've ever been."

Phil's fears were extinguished immediately upon the entrance of his Lord and Master. The radiance of Jesus was overwhelming; His countenance brilliant beyond words. Phil stood and stared, unable to move. Jesus looked lovingly at him and grasped his hand, placing his other hand on Phil's shoulder. "I love you enough to die for you again if I had to," He said, looking deep into his eyes. Phil was amazed he had no desire to run and hide as he thought he would so soon after sinning. He had no sense of guilt, fear, or any emotion other than unfathomable love toward his Lord. He could feel only the love Jesus had for him, too. There was no hint of unforgiveness or condemnation. In fact, there was not the slightest trace of remembrance of his sin. He didn't know how he knew this; he just did. Phil also knew Jesus had come to him for a specific task. This was not the time for the adoration, praise, or worship that welled up in his heart. Somehow, he knew there would be time for that in the future. For now, he was simply supposed to listen as Jesus spoke.

"Phil, you've been listening to a lie about your sin. You've come to believe that it's your job to try to overcome your flesh and the spirits that

155

wooed you to sin before you came to Me. That is impossible for you to do, so you must stop trying. I overcame them all with My death and resurrection. Your job now is to trust in that completed work to make you who I desire you to be. I will complete the work I started in you. You have My Word on it." Jesus smiled a brilliant smile at His pun. He spoke again with compassion toward His beloved. "You spend so much time focusing on your sins that you've lost the joy of Our time together. I miss you."

With those words, the Lord of All gestured to one of the angels that suddenly became available to Him. Working silently, the angel went about its task. All of the controlling spirits that had been "friends" to Phil for so long were forced from their hiding places by the radiance of the glorified Lamb that had been slain. Removed from their deceptive coverings and exposed for what they really were, each was ordered by the Master to remain still until they were told to move. They could do nothing but obey.

"Phil, what you are about to witness has already been accomplished two thousand years ago by My work. My Father's altar is the cross. At that definitive time, He nailed every controlling spirit in your life to that cross forever through My sacrifice. That cross is an altar of life for you and an altar of death for them. My work was complete for your salvation. The cross is empty; the grave is empty. You now have the freedom to call upon the power of My completed work to destroy all of your enemies forever should they attempt to harm you. My life brought death to your flesh, but you must trust in that completed work or you will continually struggle in your own strength to try to overcome your flesh. The enemy is a liar and desires you to believe he still has some power over you. All of his power has been broken because of My cross. For your benefit, I would like to demonstrate what happened at the cross. It will show you how free you really are, OK?"

Phil nodded his head in approval, a combination of wonder and anticipation filling his heart.

"Do you desire to have these vile spirits removed from your life forever?" Jesus asked, anticipating the answer, knowing a positive response would allow Him to demonstrate the freedom that had been won for His friend long ago.

Stunned once again by His radiance, Phil could only answer after the Lord gave him the strength to respond. "Wow, Lord, I do," was all he could voice. "I do," he said again, reflecting on all the prayers of helplessness that had brought him to this incredible event. Jesus smiled and placed His hand on Phil's back.

"I am delighted to do this for you," He said with enthusiasm and a smile that conveyed His overwhelming love for Phil. "I don't want these vile passions from your past harming you anymore. They only get in the way of you heading toward a significant, overcoming life." With that, He turned to the revolting forms that had been immobilized by His command.

156

A simple wave of His hand moved massive angelic creations into position behind each of the four dominant spirits Phil didn't realize were still a stronghold in his life, even after he'd established his relationship with Christ.

The first form was called out by the angel in charge. "Lack of love for the Word of God, come forth." The angel behind the repulsive, oozing green mass moved it forward.

Jesus turned to Phil, "This has been the gatekeeper, which has allowed all of the other blasphemies to enter in and harm you. It's like rotten yeast that inflates improperly and permeates all of your being. It is in charge of the spirit of laziness during prayer, which makes it easy for you to eliminate time with Me in favor of other activities, like work and entertainment. It also emits a selfishness that makes you care little about what I really care about. Would you like it to be removed from your life?" He asked, already knowing the answer.

"Yes, Lord," Phil responded again. "Please take it away."

Jesus raised His hand. The angel immediately moved the being over to what appeared to be the cross on which Jesus shed His precious blood once and for all eternity. "Let's apply My blood to this spirit, shall we?" When the gruesome, formless green mass heard what Jesus said, it spewed a sulfur-like substance from all of its pores and sputtered a gurgling invitation to Phil to join it even while gasping for its very existence. The sticky, mastic-like substance - the very addictive nature of the spirit - that had held this spirit to him for so long dissolved at the mention of Jesus' blood as it lost its life. Phil felt a weight of what seemed like a hundred pounds leave him as it ceased to exist.

The next spirit to be dealt with was the spirit of faithlessness. It was brought forth attached to a tether. Looking like a loathsome, hard-crusted gnat with its insect legs continually in motion as it scurried nowhere, it made a continual buzzing sound as it ran blindly into everything. Wide-eyed and drooling in fear, it had no direction for its movements other than self-preservation. The incessant buzzing increased to a fevered pitch as it was faced with its judgment. This increase in noise was used to draw attention to itself and away from the things of God whenever proper choices needed to be made.

Jesus continued. "This spirit uses fear and distrust to control. It instills the fear of loss of any kind, which leads to worrisome self-preservation and self-serving attitudes. It causes you to desire to remain in your comfort zone, unwilling to exhaust yourself for Our work. It is ignorant, having no fear of My Father and Me. It is unwilling to learn of Our ways and will not ally itself with anyone except to serve its own purposes. Untrusting and conniving, it is unthinking, infecting, remorseless, unteachable, full of adulteries, whorish, aimless, hopeless, and without any hint of truth. It thrives on the wounds you have received

157

throughout your lifetime. It has used all of these against you to stop you from growing." Then He again asked Phil if he wanted to be free from this bondage.

"Please, loose me, Lord," he responded. "I'm helpless without Your power."

"My blood is sufficient," Jesus replied as He looked in the direction of the gnat and it instantly ceased to exist. Then Jesus commanded, "Bring forth the spirit of lust."

As the angel did so, Phil understood how much of a hold this spirit had over him. For an instant, he didn't want Jesus to deal with this one. "Maybe later," he thought.

Jesus, well aware of the turmoil in Phil's heart, looked at him intently. His eyes were full of pain. "I'm sorry, Lord," was all Phil could say. Jesus touched Phil on the shoulder once again, filling him with a love that eliminated any desire for anything other than a true covenant relationship with the Lord. He knew instantly that any other direction was a lie he had listened to far too long. He wanted it gone.

As Phil basked in the love of Jesus, the tentacled, lust-filled creature slithered forward, dripping pus and making grotesque, gurgling noises of overindulgence as it did. It moved unwillingly, its powerful tentacles grasping feverishly in every direction, as it attempted to hold onto something, anything, to save itself. Everything about this hideous, haughty, bloated creature with its devilish, wandering, adulterous eyes emitted a hatred for the Lord. Phil knew only the presence of Jesus prevented this clammy, foul-smelling spirit from grabbing hold of him again.

"The job of this spirit is to blind your eyes to everything that is really important, making useless desires a priority," Jesus said quietly. "Each tentacle has a specific purpose. As they are allowed to attach themselves to you by your willingness to listen to the deceits that come from its mouth, you become more and more entangled each time you give in. If you submit enough times, you will become immobilized and unable to do Our work."

As Jesus was talking, the foul blob spewed vomit and putrid substances in every direction, attempting to stain the angelic beings in the room. Its efforts were in vain as the substances fell harmlessly to the ground, disappearing as soon as they landed.

"When these tentacles are removed, they will continually attempt to reattach themselves. Once you repent, they must fall away. Because the nature of this spirit is so insidious and relentless, you must be close to Me to keep it away. You need the power of My blood to sever every attachment. I will destroy the strongholds and heal the wounds they leave. The ultimate purpose of this spirit is to desecrate and destroy My temple." Phil knew Jesus meant he was that temple. "You must never be enticed by even the smallest deviations from My Word. They are simple traps to entangle you and cause you to plunge deeper and deeper into sin."

Jesus stopped and turned in the direction of the spirit of lust. With a slight movement of His hand, its tentacles slipped away from Phil, froze in place, detached from its body; and shattered in tiny little pieces upon impact with the ground. The torso of the creature immediately began to fly uncontrollably around the room, deflating like a balloon before it came to rest at the feet of the attending angel. The angel picked up the squealing mass and awaited Jesus' orders. He spoke reassuringly again to Phil of the blood He shed on the cross and as He did so, the foul spirit released curses, disease, and rebellion in Phil's direction, which proved to be an exercise in futility. Each assignment abruptly dropped away with a resounding thud and died. For several, seemingly very long moments, Phil watched the life ooze from the entity that was destroyed by the work of the cross.

Jesus then drew Phil's attention to the last form that stood there, awaiting its demise. It had a vicious, vindictive smile on its almost beautiful face. As he looked closer, however, he noticed the epitome of evil behind that smile. It scared him. If it hadn't been for the presence of Jesus, he would have run blindly to get away from that evil presence. Phil wondered how that being could look so calm and in control, having observed the fate of each of its predecessors.

"This is pride," Jesus said, never taking His eyes off the trim, well-kept figure that stared with ice-cold, uncaring eyes that transmitted hatred and defiance even to the living Christ. "It is so full of its own strength that even now it will not submit to the fact that its time is over in your life. Look how it remains aloof and confident. If I would allow it, it would try to barter with Me as an equal for some lesser fate than it deserves. It has an iron will and would even attempt to try to control the time and place of its execution. It is truly the shadow of its master, the one who is most prideful. Turning His back to the spirit and facing Phil once again, Jesus gave the command to put the pride in Phil's life to death, after Phil acknowledged he truly wanted to commit his entire life to Jesus' Lordship.

While Jesus was talking to Phil, he could hear the confident, contemptuous spirit bargaining for position and an audience with the Lord to defend its case. After realizing this effort was in vain, the spirit of pride turned all of its attention to the angel that was leading it purposefully to the cross. Finally, after presenting its lofty credentials over and over and exhausting all ploys to achieve vindication, it turned to other demands. It attempted to direct the unhearing angel on how it should be put to death, where it was to be placed after it was gone, and how long it wanted to be able to talk before it was all over. It even demanded to have a say in the process of the completed act. When it realized that even these tactics proved unproductive, the spirit of pride began to whine pitifully. It let out a squeal of contempt and hatred that sounded similar to the call of a hog being slaughtered as it was literally nailed to the cross. Jesus Himself threw the carcass into the abyss. Never before had Phil witnessed such a crystal clear picture of living for self vs. living for Christ.

After watching the form fall into a place Phil could not see, Jesus turned to him. His countenance was one of true joy. "I submitted Myself to what had to be done, so you might be free from them," He said, referring to the now non-existent spirits. "I took great joy in knowing what the cross would provide for you. You must remember that the power and love flowing out from the work that was accomplished at the cross are far more powerful than anything that controls your flesh. Everything needed was fulfilled so you and My Father and I could have constant fellowship.

"When you surrender fully to that final work, you will never again submit to anything that will harm you. Study what has been done for you in My Word. Learn what your provision is. Repent whenever you lose your way. You will be amazed at how free you are as soon as you ask for forgiveness and reaffirm My Lordship in your life each time you fall. Your repentance, your turning from your sin, puts into effect the benefits of the work I have done for you. When I forgive you each time you come, your sin is as far from Me as the east is from the west. I no longer remember it. I do not have a bad memory; it simply is forgotten because I have covenanted to forget it. Each time you come, it is as though it's the very first time, not the thousandth. I forgive you forever and love you for eternity." With those words, Jesus put His arm around Phil's shoulder and told him things too wonderful to express, even if he could have found the words.

Whether in the Spirit or in the flesh, he did not know. Phil was caught up into a realm he did not recognize. He did know, however, that he had a new desire to praise his Lord and Savior, Jesus Christ. Somehow Phil knew the way he perceived his relationship with Jesus was changed forever. His time with his Lord would never be hindered by his failings. It simply was not his job to remove the sin from his life. Only the Lord could do that! What he needed to do was keep coming back to the One who loved him unconditionally. What peace!!!

Accompanying Bible Verses, New International Version

Colossians 3:1-5 " Since, then, you have been raised with Christ, set your hearts on things above, where Christ is seated at the right hand of God.

2) Set your minds on things above, not on earthly things.

3) For you died, and your life is now hidden with Christ in God.

4) When Christ, who is your life, appears, then you also will appear with him in glory.

5) Put to death, therefore, whatever belongs to your earthly nature: sexual immorality, impurity, lust, evil desires and greed, which is idolatry.

Galatians 2:20 I have been crucified with Christ and I no longer live, but Christ lives in me. The life I live in the body, I live by faith in the Son of God, who loved me and gave himself for me.

Galatians 3:3 Are you so foolish? After beginning with the Spirit, are you now trying to attain your goal by human effort?

Ephesians 6:12 For our struggle is not against flesh and blood, but against the rulers, against the authorities, against the powers of this dark world and against the spiritual forces of evil in the heavenly realms.

Revelation 1:10 On the Lord's Day I was in the Spirit, and I heard behind me a loud voice like a trumpet...

You Are Valuable to Jesus!!!

Everything God initiates has love as its motivation. The revival call that is stirring in your heart this very moment is motivated not only by His love for you, but also by His love for others. The heart that desires that none should perish, so they can spend eternity with God, pumps with love and causes our loving God to continually move on our behalf so we can honor His plan that none should perish in whatever capacity He wishes, no matter how much we fail Him presently.

2 Samuel 14:14b NIV But God does not take away life; instead, he devises ways so that a banished person may not remain estranged from him.

I am convinced the Lord has one word as a solution for all that has been said and all that is missing in your life. That word is repentance, a turning away from your sin – deep, honest, and heartfelt.

The world can't hear anything from God. They are impotent to accomplish anything for God. They can't follow Him. They don't understand Him. They have no desire to even get to know Him.

Rom. 8:5-11 NIV Those who live according to the sinful nature have their minds set on what that nature desires; but those who live in accordance with the Spirit have their minds set on what the Spirit desires.

6) The mind of sinful man is death, but the mind controlled by the Spirit is life and peace;

7) the sinful mind is hostile to God. It does not submit to God's law, nor can it do so.

8) Those controlled by the sinful nature cannot please God.

9) You, however, are controlled not by the sinful nature but by the Spirit, if the Spirit of God lives in you. And if anyone does not have the Spirit of Christ, he does not belong to Christ.

10) But if Christ is in you, your body is dead because of sin, yet your spirit is alive because of righteousness.

11) And if the Spirit of him who raised Jesus from the dead is living in you, he who raised Christ from the dead will also give life to your mortal bodies through his Spirit, who lives in you.

The end of everyone who does not know God through Jesus Christ is revealed in the Bible. This outcome can be avoided if they repent of their rebellion against God and submit to what Jesus has done on the cross. Using the Word of God as our source, this is our only option. The choice is ours.

As stated before, the plan of God will reach its conclusion in the way He said it would as foretold in His Word. The one world government, the antichrist, the mark of the beast, the battle of Armageddon, all of it, every last detail will be fulfilled just the way God said it would happen. Nothing can change it. Nothing can stop it from happening.

As you are now well aware, Satan has a plan to spiritually emasculate society. Since he can't change the plan of God and couldn't stop his defeat at the cross, he is attempting to make society completely impotent regarding the things of God. He has done a magnificent job of rendering the world useless to the plans of God and he has the church well on its way to joining them.

But God!

I love that phrase. *But God!* But the Magnificent, Sovereign, Almighty, All-Powerful God is at work! He is waking up the hearts of men like you and desires with every fiber of His being that you come wholeheartedly back to Him to lead a life of significance. He wants to instill in you the very covenant heart of Jesus, one that will turn you into a true, powerful, valiant, significant man of God, a man He can use in these closing days as you wait for and focus on Jesus.

A True Covenant Heart

The men who are most powerful in God's eyes function in the covenant heart of Christ. Someone with a true covenant heart seeks to please the one with whom he is in covenant as a priority. We are in

162

covenant with God. The covenant heart that God is in the process of restoring in men who will submit to His call is one that is passionate for the life of Christ to be fully formed in the inward parts, then exhibited openly to the world; and one that looks longingly at all times for Jesus to be honored and glorified.

Please take time to reflect on the previous sentence. This is where God desires to take you. Is it your desire to go there even if you have trouble believing it's possible?

Valiant men, who renew their covenant with God and with each other, must be the catalyst in their circle of influence; so those they influence can see the need for and the wonder and power of this kind of heart and desire it themselves. God is stirring the hearts of men at this very moment to desire the covenant heart, to surrender completely to Jesus and then walk in His life as the new creation they are.

God is rebuilding His truth in the hearts of those who are seeking truth, infusing them with a new desire to be all they can be in Jesus Christ. He is restoring the offices of husband and father in His church. He is reversing the spiritual deadness and revitalizing open hearts with a new love for Jesus. He is causing those who repent of their spiritual deadness to once again live and act as Jesus would toward Him, His Word, His desires, and His promises - all for the fulfillment of His plans during this season in time.

If we liken this time to the rebuilding of a football team, God Himself is in the process of building a team that will never lose another game. It is a team that has so embraced His will there is nothing that can sway them from perfectly executing every task with the flawlessness Jesus did. This team will have immersed itself in the plans of God and the ways of Jesus so thoroughly, they will know how to love as He does, serve as He serves, submit to the Father's plans as He does, and win according to the Father's game plan.

Honest men of God are putting their swords away, no longer attempting to change the world or live in its ways. They are putting their desires away and submitting to the desires of Father God, just as Jesus does. They are putting their passions away and taking on the passions of Jesus. They are putting their own roadmaps for life away and submitting to the Father's will for their lives, determined to establish a significant legacy in His eyes. They are embracing the mind of Christ and implementing His heart in their circle of influence.

From Our Father's Heart

Delight in Me
and I will bring to you the desires of your heart
as they line up with My heart.

163

As you restore your relationship with Me as your priority,
I will show you how to restore all of your other relationships.
I will focus your life for you.
I will reinstate your proper priorities.
I will hold you close while you are being refined.
You delight My heart
whenever you respond to the call of My Holy Spirit.
Prepare to be overwhelmed by My power
and My majesty working through you.
Let's move together now.
Time is short.
Much is to be accomplished.
As I accomplish My Word
in your very inner being,
you will be amazed at how free you become
to follow the ways of Jesus.

Your Moment in Time

Everyone who follows Jesus has very specific moments in their lives that are pivotal to their relationship with Him and the direction they take in life. This specific instant may very well be one of those moments for you. If you have followed the theme of this writing, you were initially given the opportunity to understand how far away you may be from the plan of God. You quite possibly have progressed toward assessing those things in your life that are out of line with that plan, and more than likely have understood there is nothing you can do to bring about real, eternal change in your own strength. Having done all of that, this timeframe of preparing your heart for change and counting the cost of those changes may be the most important timeframe of your life. Don't take this time lightly! Don't let this moment slip away, allowing you to remain spiritually impotent - possibly for the rest of your days.

You need to ask yourself if this is your timeframe to stop offending God through living a lackluster spiritual life even though you say you follow Jesus and His ways. Is this your time to fully realize who you really are supposed to be in Christ and then determine to live that way?

God Has a Map That Will Lead You Back to Him

The roadmap back to God is always through a turning from your old ways to follow the ways of God. It is the full understanding that your old man is dead and making the choice to never again resurrect him. This moment for you is very much like the moment when Vince Lombardi walked into the Green Bay Packers' dressing room - only infinitely more

164

important. The players had choices to make if they wanted to be part of a winning team. They had to do it Lombardi's way. Lombardi came with a new game plan, a plan some of them had never experienced before. He came with and demanded from them a new attitude, one that had few options other than winning. He came with a new idea of allegiance, one that considered his ways and the good of the team as the reason for participating. He came with a new standard. In order to participate, the players paid the high price of dying to their old ways, but the success along the way and the final outcome would be worth it.

You have a choice this very moment. You can choose God's way or continue on the sidelines in your own strength with the dismal possibility of not becoming part of the vibrant, powerful team the Lord is building.

Acts 21: 10-14 "After we had been there a number of days, a prophet named Agabus came down from Judea.

11) Coming over to us, he took Paul's belt, tied his own hands and feet with it and said, "The Holy Spirit says, 'In this way the Jewish leaders in Jerusalem will bind the owner of this belt and will hand him over to the Gentiles.'"

12) When we heard this, we and the people there pleaded with Paul not to go up to Jerusalem.

13) Then Paul answered, "Why are you weeping and breaking my heart? I am ready not only to be bound, but also to die in Jerusalem for the name of the Lord Jesus."

14) When he would not be dissuaded, we gave up and said, "The Lord's will be done."

Just as the Packers had to change their heart attitudes and allegiances, Paul had to change from being a person who rested on his heritage and his standing in the community to a person who was completely sold out to the plan of God. He had to turn from his old ways to the ways of Jesus and His allegiance to His Father God. If Paul was to become a trusted follower of Jesus, then he had to think, care, and function only as Jesus did, or else he was a hypocrite.

The position Paul first occupied was lofty. The position Jesus gave up to become like one of us has no earthly comparison. It's a sacrifice we cannot comprehend. The price Paul paid was high, but the price Jesus paid was higher. The road Paul was called to travel was rough, but the road Jesus chose to travel was strewn with the horrors of ridicule, persecution, and a death so spiritually horrible for Him, we can't even begin to appreciate the cost of His obedience.

To change from who you are at present to who the Lord desires you to be - one of His valiant leaders within His families and His church- is

165

not going to be a walk in the park any more than it was for the Packers under Lombardi, or Paul, or Jesus. Your decision to become the trustworthy person God wants and needs will cost you dearly. It may cost you everything, just like the first century Christians who lost everything to have significant lives. Nevertheless, Jesus deserves your commitment.

[This may be your time for the power of God to change you.]

As you are weighing your decision, keep in mind that nobody stood in the face of one of the Packers and called him a wimp after he had gone through the training that made him part of a winning team. Nobody in his right mind could call Paul a wimp after he had been used so mightily by the Lord. Certainly nobody of any consequence called Jesus a wimp after He bore the price He had to pay and won the fiercest battle in all of eternity, the battle to win mankind back to His Father in heaven. All that ultimately matters is that Father God calls your life significant and your legacy honorable in relation to the cross of Jesus.

Count the Cost

You need to take the time to count the cost now. Are you content to stay on the sidelines of the plan of God or are you willing to pay the price it will take to play in the game, the eternal plan of God? The decision is simple. However, the walk will be challenging and possibly extremely rough, depending on how the Lord allows His enemies to play their hands. Turning from your own ways to the ways of God is the death of whatever is not of Him. Death is never easy.

God's Step by Step Process Back to Him

Just like society, the Christian church and specifically men have step by step and rebellion by rebellion allowed themselves to be rendered impotent. That ground can be reclaimed and restored step by step. Men can come back in line with the true nature God intended for His creation if they submit to what the Holy Spirit is doing. The playing field was changed at the cross. Every victory was already won at the cross. All history pivots around the cross. All of everything yet to happen refers back to the cross. The only possible way to get in line with God and His Word stems from the cross. It's time to go back there before you can go forward.

If you've read anything in these pages that moved you to understand how far your ways are from the ways God has planned for you, repent, turn away from the sins you've been shown, and allow God to change you. Then take the next area you are shown by the Holy Spirit and let Him deal with that. Stay the course! Keep on repenting of every area the Holy Spirit shows you is in need of change until you have a clear conscience before God and know for sure that every area of your life is completely and totally His. Step by step, you will walk in the new creation model won for you at the cross. The world may not like you, but your Father in Heaven will be pleased.

Important Spiritual Note!

As stated before, God wins! Jesus has already won all of the battles necessary to allow the plan of God to be completed. The Holy Spirit's power is more than enough to fulfill all that has been established through the cross of Christ everywhere and in anyone. There are going to be no surprises ever in the heavenly realms. It is God who is in charge and no one else. All of what we have been discussing has nothing to do with whether or not God is in charge, whether His plan will go forth, or whether Jesus is Lord. That is established fact.

Everything that has been discussed has to do with whether or not you choose to be part of what God is doing or whether you choose to remain in an impotent, atrophied bench warmer position on the sidelines as God is accomplishing a mighty and wonderful work in His men and in His end-time church. This study is really all about your decisions and your submission. It's about responding or not responding to what God is doing.

Chapter 15
MASH icu Study Questions

1) What personal changes will you need to make to be in line with what God asks of you?

Journal or discuss.

2) Are you committed enough to God to allow Him to make those changes? Y/N

3) Is this a no holds barred commitment?   Y/N

Just as God is relentless in His pursuit of making us like Jesus, you must become relentless in your pursuit of change.

4) If you are not committed enough to make the changes, why not?

Father,

I really need Your strength to be able to follow Jesus. Please do whatever work in me that's necessary. Thank You, Lord!

Chapter 16

Choosing God Above Everything Else

Christianity 101

Matthew 6:33 AMP   But seek (aim at and strive after) first of all His kingdom and His righteousness (His way of doing and being right), and then all these things taken together will be given you besides.

Chris stared at the needle tracks in his arm, a constant reminder of the choices he had made to bring himself to this point in his life. Once a successful businessman on his way to the top with a loving wife and family, he could only lament over the turns his life had taken because of his addictions. How could he have fallen so far? How could his needs mean more to him than those he once loved and need him?

He had to make a choice or he was going to die as one more hapless vagrant in some garbage-strewn alley. He had to choose either life or death. He knew it and he knew how difficult the road back would be. Picking up the filthy needle, he inserted it in his arm once again. As the drug flowed through his body, he resolved that maybe he would choose to love his wife more than his habit tomorrow. Maybe he could help his kids tomorrow. Maybe...Chris rolled into a smelly corner near a large dumpster and passed out.

Across town, Jerry turned the corner and drove into the parking lot of his club. Late for his meeting, he had shaken off the pleading look in his son's eyes that said, "Please, Daddy, stay here with Mommy and me." Business once again called. It was going to be one more late night, one more closed deal that allowed him to live the way he wanted. "Success has its price," he thought to himself. Anyway, to change direction in life now would be almost impossible. He was way too far down the corporate road to give his family the amount of personal time with him they seemed to need.

Maybe one day his wife and family would realize he was doing this all for them. It was a time in life to set them up, so they wouldn't have to grow up in poverty as he did. They needed to realize that. He was sure God knew that.

"Why don't I have peace in my heart, Lord? Why can't I shake off the look Joey gave me? Why do I feel so bad when I'm doing so much for them?"

As he locked his car and headed for the club entrance, Jerry resolved to spend more time at home tomorrow. Tomorrow he would give some special time to his wife, Susan. Tomorrow, he would really focus on her insistent need to be with him and make some changes he knew were necessary to be the husband and father she and Tommy wanted. Oh wait, tomorrow was that conference in Detroit...

Whatever vehicle Satan uses to hinder the work of God, whether dismal failure, monumental success, or anything in between, the results are always the same - an insignificant life standing before Father God one day. His entrapment is so diabolical that the road back is impossible to embrace without God's involvement and intervention.

When I first started writing this book, I spoke to a man from another part of the country over the phone about the book's concept. As he began to understand the idea of spiritual impotence, he relayed to me that he had a mare and two geldings in his pasture. Then he said something to this effect. "I could give those gelded horses all the training and care in the world, but it will never compensate for the loss of their testicles and the desires they bring. He was absolutely right. Applying that insight to the spiritual realm, knowledge or wisdom in itself will never cause a spiritual change or reinstate spiritual desires.

Paying the high price of a change in life direction for the good of others and for the honor of God is gargantuan if you are spiritually impotent. In fact, it is impossible to do alone. Only if you choose to love God above the other gods you serve will you walk the necessary road of repentance combined with action. Only if you choose to begin a life of seeking God and His right way of living as your priority every day and submitting to His power to change you, will you have any spiritual success in building a life of eternal significance.

If you are content to remain spiritually impotent, the road back will appear as something simply not worth the effort. If you really don't care if your life pleases God, you need to have a heart change. If you are bound with fear for whatever reason, do it afraid, at first, if you must. The Lord is working both His end and yours. Trust Him! If your thoughts are "It'll take too long" or "It's too costly" or "I'm too weak to do it," then your days will continue to be relatively useless to God, days of compounded spiritual atrophy. Go to God! He will come to you with His power as you do.

Exodus 33:13-16 NIV "If you are pleased with me, teach me your ways so I may know you and continue to find favor with you. Remember that this nation is your people."

14) The Lord replied, "My Presence will go with you, and I will give you rest."

15) Then Moses said to him, "If your Presence does not go with us, do not send us up from here.

172

16) How will anyone know that you are pleased with me and with your people unless you go with us? What else will distinguish me and your people from all the other people on the face of the earth?"

It is imperative you understand that the reversal of your spiritual impotence as a man is definitely possible. In fact, it is the endtime call for men who are destined to be used during the perilous times ahead. However, because the deception is spiritual and, therefore, the only road out of the deception must be spiritual, true healing can only occur through the supernatural, intervening power of the Holy Spirit, the Word, and true repentance. It is not a matter of knowledge. It will not go away with more study. It cannot be removed by doing good things. You must be restored spiritually so your only purpose in life is to please God. You need to know God in an intimate way, basking in His presence and functioning only from being with Him as your priority every moment of your journey. You must also be endowed with the spiritual tools to get the job done.

In these final chapters, there are steps that need to be taken so the Lord can impart significance to your life. These steps, if done in the flesh, will be nothing more than religious exercises in futility if they are not initiated by God, directed by God, and implemented by God. You will need Holy Spirit wisdom and power far beyond your own ability to implement these steps on a long term basis or you will tear apart the lives you encounter, leaving a legacy of death instead of life. You will need all of the fruits of the Holy Spirit functioning through you to affect others properly. These spiritual fruits can only come from a great work done in you by the Lord Himself through your full submission to Him in your time spent with Him for the rest of your life. In actuality, you will need to completely get out of the way and allow the Lord to live His life through your every moment.

[If you attempt to change your life with fleshly wisdom and power, you will cause much harm to those around you and bring dishonor to Jesus by your weak, carnal actions and useless, religious activities.]

Getting to Know God All Over Again

Ephesians 5:1- 2 AMP Therefore be imitators of God [copy Him and follow His example], as well-beloved children [imitate their father].
2) And walk in love, [esteeming and delighting in one another] as Christ loved us and gave Himself up for us, a slain offering and sacrifice to God [for you, so that it became] a sweet fragrance.

The eternal placement of God as one's priority, number one friend and confidant is the most important action anyone can take if he or she desires to build a significant, overcoming life in Christ. It is vital that God becomes your only purpose and is behind your every purpose in life. You and I are to be imitators of Him, thoroughly immersed in Him, walking in the love of Jesus. To move from the place you are to being able to submit fully to the Lordship of Jesus Christ and experience the absolute presence of God in your life, you first need a working knowledge of Who God really is and who you really are to Him. There needs to be an awakening of His great love for others and for you in your heart. This work must be accomplished in you. You need to have a Holy Spirit directed revelation of the nature of God and His longing for you to come to Him as your ABBA (Papa God.)

[Pray continually for the Lord to reveal Himself to you in new and vibrant ways each day from now on.]

For God to become your best friend and the reason behind all you do, a spiritual transformation must take place in you as it did in Paul. He was changed inwardly from a man who was zealous to work for God to a man who was zealous to know God through knowing Jesus.

Phil. 3:10-11 AMP [For my determined purpose is] that I may know Him [that I may progressively become more deeply and intimately acquainted with Him, perceiving and recognizing and understanding the wonders of His Person more strongly and more clearly], and that I may in that same way come to know the power outflowing from His resurrection [which it exerts over believers], and that I may so share His sufferings as to be continually transformed [in spirit into His likeness even] to His death, [in the hope]
11) That if possible I may attain to the [spiritual and moral] resurrection [that lifts me] out from among the dead [even while in the body].

It took a God-imparted determination in Paul to know Jesus. Only God could reveal to Paul who Jesus is, what He had done and how it affected him; and then enable him to flow in His resurrection power to overcome his personal impotence. It took a supernatural revelation of Jesus and His heart, so Paul could be transformed inwardly to the point where he could rise above the lifeless ways of the world, mirror the ways of God, and implement His plans as a new creation in Christ.

Hebrews 1:3 AMP He is the sole expression of the glory of God [the Light-being, the out-raying or radiance of the divine], and He is the perfect imprint and very image of [God's] nature, upholding and

174

maintaining and guiding and propelling the universe by His mighty word of power. When He had by offering Himself accomplished our cleansing of sins and riddance of guilt, He sat down at the right hand of the divine Majesty on high...

Do you really know Who God is and what He desires? Have you ever taken the time to find out what grieves Him or makes Him rejoice? Have you ever even thought of God as having feelings or cares? Have you ever spent enough time quietly in His presence to allow Him to speak to your heart the deeper things of His heart?

If the above questions are not part of your daily intimate moments with your Father in heaven, how have you existed? How have you known what He desires of your life? How can you possibly claim to walk as a follower of Jesus if you have never heard personally where He desires for you to go or how you are to function when you get there? What kind of relationship do you really have with your God?

We Have Access to God so We Can Know Him and His Desires

Mark 15:37-38 AMP   And Jesus uttered a loud cry, and breathed out His life.

38) And the curtain [of the Holy of Holies] of the temple was torn in two from top to bottom.

If you've done any study at all about the temple, you know that the actual presence of God rested in the Holy of Holies behind a curtain. Only a consecrated High Priest was allowed to come into the presence of God. It was the highest honor available to man.

When the temple curtain was torn from top to bottom at the time of Jesus' crucifixion, it was meant to convey that God was making Himself directly available to everyone through Christ. The completed work of Jesus at the cross gave us access to the Father for our every need and to accomplish the privilege of passing on the influence of Jesus to others. As we come to the Father in Jesus' Name, we are accepted in the same way Jesus is accepted by the Father. In actuality, we now have the legal spiritual right to call God our Father because of Jesus.

Whenever we limit our access into the presence of God to the recitation of our laundry list of personal needs or complaints about our personal discomforts, we have severely limited Jesus' purpose for dying and earning our right to be in God's presence. When we properly use the access we have been given to be equipped and empowered to pass on our inheritance to others, the work and purpose of the cross is fully in effect for us and through us.

Everyone born of God through Jesus Christ has the commission to pass on the influence of Jesus to those who need to hear about Him. It is the call of every man and women in Christ. Pertaining to this study, however, we need to continue to address the role of a man and his role in God's plans.

As stated often throughout these pages, men have violated the principles of the dynamic role intended for their offices of husband, father, and community leader through their spiritual impotence. Because of this violation of trust, it is vitally important to God that we reclaim the ground each of us has lost. It is time to get serious about the life God intends for us.

Ephesians 6: 10-13 NIV "Finally, be strong in the Lord and in his mighty power.

11) Put on the full armor of God, so that you can take your stand against the devil's schemes.

12) For our struggle is not against flesh and blood, but against the rulers, against the authorities, against the powers of this dark world and against the spiritual forces of evil in the heavenly realms.

13) Therefore put on the full armor of God, so that when the day of evil comes, you may be able to stand your ground, and after you have done everything, to stand.

There are no shortcuts to knowing God and knowing what He desires for/from you. There is no way you can act as He desires you to act without a full understanding of Who He is and what matters to Him. That knowledge comes only from being in His presence and in His Word. He always imparts Himself whenever you are with Him. He gives Himself to you for your good and His delight.

There is no way you can share His love unless you experience it for yourself, and it is impossible to experience that love unless you spend time with Him, getting to know Him. You must make Him the priority of your days.

Making God the priority of your life is vastly different than reading a laundry list of needs to Him each morning or flipping a prayer His way when a challenge comes your way. It takes a complete heart reversal as to how and why you approach Him. You need to transfer the bulk of your time with Him from times of petitioning Him for your needs to times of finding out what His desires are.

To even be able to begin to implement the steps necessary to turn your impotence around, you need to completely revise your approach to God and structure your life with Him according to His desires. You need to determine to know Him as your first priority. You need to find out what His heart is. You need to know what His purpose for your life is and surrender to it with a passion as Paul did. You need to seek Him to empower you to accomplish everything you do for the rest of your life. Your association

176

with God must from this day forward replace any other reason you breathe or you will find yourself discouraged, distracted, and powerless to make any eternal changes in your life.

Romans 8:14-17a AMP For all who are led by the Spirit of God are sons of God.
15) For [the Spirit which] you have now received [is] not a spirit of slavery to put you once more in bondage to fear, but you have received the Spirit of adoption [the Spirit producing sonship] in [the bliss of] which we cry Abba (Father)! Father!
16) The Spirit Himself [thus] testifies together with our own spirit, [assuring us] that we are children of God.
17a) And if we are [His] children, then we are [His] heirs also; heirs of God and fellow heirs with Christ [sharing His inheritance with Him]...

In the covenant Jesus made with Father God for us, we have become heirs with an inheritance. We are truly new beings, formed in the likeness of Jesus to continue His work in His Name for His glory. He actually resides in each of us! Our goal for breathing then is to live in that inheritance as children of God, passing it on to others, continually and constantly expanding the influence of Jesus into our every day world. Those we influence through the power of the Holy Spirit are our legacy. Because our goal and purpose in life is ordained by God to continue the work of Jesus by imparting His heart to those to whom He calls us, their spiritual health and wealth make our lives significant to Him.

Chapter 16
MASH icu Study Questions

1) Are you willing to ask God for a complete heart reversal in your approach to Him?   Y/N

2) Are you willing to take whatever time necessary to really become a study of God and get to know Him?   Y/N

3) Do you understand the need to make God your priority in life?   Y/N

4) Are you willing to receive whatever is necessary so change can be accomplished in you?   Y/N

Father,

I admit You have never been my priority for living. I'm sorry! Please draw me near to You so I can begin to really know You and know Your heart for me. I submit to Your hand of change in my life. Thank You, Lord!

Chapter 17

You've Chosen Him, Now Get to Know Him

A most delightful opportunity

Hebrews 12:12,13 NLB "So take a new grip with your tired hands and stand firm on your shaky legs.
13) Mark out a straight path for your feet. Then those who follow you, though they are weak and lame, will not stumble and fall but will become strong."

From Our Father's Heart

My children, you do not really understand the wonders of repentance.
Most of you are afraid of humbling yourselves
in front of each other
to the point that you would rather keep an offense active
than aggressively pursue reconciliation.
It is the same way that you treat Me.
You come to Me with your offenses
only when I have broken your heart to the point
that you can no longer stand it.
Then you pour your remorse out for a moment
and walk away until the next time you feel you must come.
It is a vicious, unnecessary cycle.
Too much wonderful fellowship is missed
between times of cleansing.
True freedom is the wonder of living a life of repentance
before each other and with Me.
That kind of life is not weakness; it is true strength.
It is absolute, open fellowship without any hindrances.
As you come to Me instantly and often,
I have ample opportunity to impart Myself to you,
allow you to grow unfettered by sin;
and see that you remain in a humble position before Me.
You are allowed to continually benefit
from a flow of My grace, mercy, and forgiveness.
Because of the openness of this kind of interaction,
My Word rings clearly in your spirit,
My voice is unmistakable over the din of life;
and My direction is clear, quieting all of the opposing opinions.

I love to see you in a constant state of forgiveness.
I love to flow continuously with you through your life.
I love unbroken fellowship.
Keep a short account with Me concerning sin.
Come to Me freely and often.
You will be amazed at how your life changes.
You will be astounded at the power
I give you to overcome the world.
You will find the prosperity of continuous forgiveness
so rewarding that your life as it exists now
will seem dull and dreary
as you look back on it from a position of freedom.

Chapter 15 makes it very clear that the single road to really knowing God begins with repentance, actually a life of repentance. It's a repentant heart for who we are not when we flounder, but a walk of joy in who we are becoming. This road of repentance is the game plan that the other team has no defense against, so Satan has blinded us to the importance of it. It is the spiritually powerful road that those used mightily by God have discovered and delight in traveling often. There are no shortcuts available on this road. There is no other game plan if you desire to be fully in the game as the Lord calls the plays. It is not an easy road, but it is the only road that pleases God. It is an impossible road to travel unless you are empowered by the Holy Spirit, for it is the road that leads to the death of everything you hold dear that's not pleasing to God. It will be chosen by only the most valiant men who are on their way to truly honoring God and desiring to know Him. Others will remain on the broad road of deception in an apostate spiritual state.

These verses in James that will help guide you back to a significant life are so pertinent that they not only bear repeating, but are worth dissecting and fully digesting. They are truly the starting gun for the first steps to knowing God and walking you through the challenges of repairing your marriage and rescuing your children. They are the compass that will guide you through the twists and turns of implementing the plan of God for your life.

James 4:4-10 AMP You [are like] unfaithful wives [having illicit love affairs with the world and breaking your marriage vow to God]! Do you not know that being the world's friend is being God's enemy? So whoever chooses to be a friend of the world takes his stand as an enemy of God.

5) Or do you suppose that the Scripture is speaking to no purpose that says, The Spirit Whom He has caused to dwell in us yearns over us and He yearns for the Spirit [to be welcome] with a jealous love?

6) But He gives us more and more grace (power of the Holy Spirit, to meet this evil tendency and all others fully). That is why He says, God sets Himself against the proud and haughty, but gives grace [continually] to the lowly (those who are humble enough to receive it).

7) So be subject to God. Resist the devil [stand firm against him], and he will flee from you.

8) Come close to God and He will come close to you. [Recognize that you are] sinners, get your soiled hands clean; [realize that you have been disloyal] wavering individuals with divided interests, and purify your hearts [of your spiritual adultery].

9) [As you draw near to God] be deeply penitent and grieve, even weep [over your disloyalty]. Let your laughter be turned to grief and your mirth to dejection and heartfelt shame [for your sins].

10) Humble yourselves [feeling very insignificant] in the presence of the Lord, and He will exalt you [He will lift you up and make your lives significant].

Let's Go Step by Step – Verse by Verse

Step 1: Recognize that you need to change.

v. 4 You [are like] unfaithful wives [having illicit love affairs with the world and breaking your marriage vow to God]! Do you not know that being the world's friend is being God's enemy? So whoever chooses to be a friend of the world takes his stand as an enemy of God.

A wonderful friend of ours made the statement that there are normally two things that move people to change. They are pain and vision. I am convinced her words are quite accurate. When we experience enough pain, we become more ardent seekers of God, usually to deal with the pain. It's not difficult for the Lord to have our attention and lead us from there. Vision from the Lord, where He reveals either Himself or the truth of something we previously could not see in our lives, is also a great catalyst for change.

I would like to present another facet of pain and vision. An awareness of our dismal life, although we call ourselves followers of Christ, brings pain to the open hearted. If we use that awareness as a catalyst for repentance, we can receive a new vision of our life in Christ, one that is in line with God's perspective.

If you have been brave enough to answer any of the questions from the previous chapters truthfully, if you have been touched or moved by any of the stories and examples, you are well aware that your life to this point has been relatively insignificant and your relationship with God is out of line with His Word in certain areas. Up until the time you realize this and begin to do something about it, you have been offending God - not a very good place to remain. That knowledge should cause you enough pain to determine to do whatever it takes to change, unless you are completely hard of heart.

Maybe you have been dropped to your knees often as you've been reading these pages and the Holy Spirit has convicted you of your offenses and your spiritual impotence. That is very, very good!

James 4:4 talks about illicit love affairs. God compares your love affair with the world to that of an unfaithful wife, breaking your covenant vows to Him. This kind of relationship with Him is far from the relationship Jesus has with His Father. It is impossible to say you follow Jesus if you choose to remain with heart positions that are diametrically opposed to His heart position.

What is good, however, is you realize and acknowledge that His observations about where you really stand are accurate and pertain specifically to you. Knowing that a drastic, irreversible change is necessary is the first step back to His heart.

Step 2: Understand God's heartfelt desire is for you to change.

v. 5   Or do you suppose that the Scripture is speaking to no purpose that says, The Spirit Whom He has caused to dwell in us yearns over us and He yearns for the Spirit [to be welcome] with a jealous love?

Father God's goal for your life is that you become all you can be in Christ Jesus. So if your goal is to head toward becoming a pathetic, frail, atrophied, self-serving loser in this world, while claiming to be a follower of the ways of His glorious, all-powerful Son, don't look for Him to help you get there. There is no more important mission on His heart than the mission Jesus has for you. There is no more powerful way for Jesus to be glorified than to have valiant spiritual warriors, who are unwilling to compromise, unwilling to turn away until the battle for souls has been won and the last enemy of the cross experiences the eternal consequences of his choices.

The Lord is cheering you on and doing everything in His power so you can come to a full realization of who He created you to be both now and in eternity. His great desire is that you walk in the fullness of the overcoming, victorious life in Christ that's available to you.

184

Step 3: Understand also that no change can come from your own desires, your own strength, your own wisdom, or your own flesh. You can't do it! It's impossible! Don't try this at home! The good news is: with God, all things are possible. The work must be done in you by the power of the Holy Spirit.

v. 6 But He gives us more and more grace (power of the Holy Spirit, to meet this evil tendency and all others fully). That is why He says, God sets Himself against the proud and haughty, but gives grace [continually] to the lowly (those who are humble enough to receive it).

Your complete submission to God's will is a death knell to your will. Your thorough understanding that nothing spiritual can be accomplished through carnal or religious ways is mandatory and must permeate your inner being. This is heart knowledge, not head knowledge. You cannot complete in the flesh what has begun in the spiritual realm or you will be a foolish Galatian (See Gal.3.) It is going to take the mighty power of God to overcome your spiritual impotence and restore your potency, so the character of Jesus can be formed in you, which in turn will be the living example to others of who Jesus is. Then you can legitimately say along with Paul, "Follow me as I follow Christ." Because of the power of the Holy Spirit in your life, you will not only talk the talk, you'll be able to walk the walk of Jesus and represent Him properly.

Step 4: Turn away from all that has rendered you powerless and submit to the power of the Holy Spirit to work the character of Jesus Christ in you. Consider all the ways of your old man dead, actually dead.

v. 7 So be subject to God. Resist the devil [stand firm against him], and he will flee from you.

Too often in verse 7, we separate the first sentence from the second sentence, thinking they are two different things. Actually, the way you resist the devil is by being subject to God. Too many people try to resist him without being subject to God and it only leads to disaster. Obedience is a vital key to living a victorious life in Christ, a life where you no longer live, but He lives His life through you. When the life of Christ flows through you, you have absolute power over the enemy. Satan is not going to stick around to experience the humiliation that results when Jesus is on the scene. He cannot withstand Jesus' presence.

Step 5: Draw close to God as your priority in life from this moment on.

v. 8   Come close to God and He will come close to you. [Recognize that you are] sinners, get your soiled hands clean; [realize that you have been disloyal] wavering individuals with divided interests, and purify your hearts [of your spiritual adultery].

Recognizing the very real possibility that it's been mostly your own motives behind what you do, where you go, and where you work is one of the first steps to spiritual healthiness. Have you ever been with people who have their own interests at heart in all they do, yet they continue to tell you what they're doing is for your best interest? Have you ever done that? That scenario breeds disloyalty. In the spiritual realm, it's called spiritual adultery. It is ineffective and distasteful to God. If you say you are a follower of Jesus, then you must have His interests at heart. You must resemble Him. How else can Father God use you and trust you to represent Him properly?

Step 6: Repent of everything the Holy Spirit shows you.

v. 9   [As you draw near to God] be deeply penitent and grieve, even weep [over your disloyalty]. Let your laughter be turned to grief and your mirth to dejection and heartfelt shame [for your sins].

Heartfelt weeping over one's disloyalty can only be a gift given by the Holy Spirit, one that should be sought after by followers of Christ. Grieving over your sin is admirable. It pleases the heart of God and facilitates the changes that need to be made in you.

Step 7: Choose to remain in a joyful, freeing, repentant state of mind and heart with every breath you take for the rest of your days by the power of the Holy Spirit.

v.10   Humble yourselves [feeling very insignificant] in the presence of the Lord, and He will exalt you [He will lift you up and make your lives significant].

Oh! To stand before your heavenly Father and have <u>Him</u> deem your life significant! If that thought doesn't stir you to action, you need to start this book all over again. You need to start repenting of where you are right at this very moment and request that the Lord soften your hardened

186

heart, giving you taste buds for the ways of God. Probably the easiest and safest place to start is to simply repent of your entire life. The Holy Spirit will orchestrate things from there and sort it out for you.

A Very Important Note!

Sometime in the near future, there will be a specific timeframe where you will transition from being a man who uses God to a man who lives only for God, if you turn your heart fully toward Him. It is what the Holy Spirit is doing in His men presently. However, that moment is not up to you. It can't be manufactured by you. It is not your call. That timeframe is totally up to God. It is planned, defined, implemented, and empowered by Him. It will be the timeframe that you'll actually dare to believe the Lord will use you beyond your wildest dreams, as you remain fully surrendered to Him. All of you and your limitations will be burned away in the light of His mercy, grace, power, and anointing. That includes your spiritual impotence.

More than likely, after fiery trials, many hours of prayer and repentance, and situation after situation where you are allowed to see your complete spiritual bankruptcy, you will finally come to the very end of yourself. Congratulations! You will never be the same. You will become a bondservant to Jesus Christ and cease to serve yourself or anything else other than Him. You will no longer "own" anything, desire anything, or give your allegiance to anything other than Him and His ways. That moment will define your life in Christ. You will care only about those things for which He cares. You will desire to no longer offend your Father in heaven.

Your heart will be on fire for souls and you will do anything, sell anything, and become everything Jesus is, all so you can please Father God. Nothing will be left of you to offend God any more. You will be a man after God's own heart and on your way to living a significant, overcoming life in His eyes. You will honor the gift of real life you've been given in Jesus Christ. It is your heritage! You can be absolutely confident the Lord will complete His work in you. Yes, you!

Have you ever taken the time to assess how much you really need in life? I'm sure the Lord will get His work accomplished regardless of your participation, but wouldn't you like to know you've used your time and resources wisely and properly before you stand before Him? Once you're there, it will be too late to remedy anything.

[Crowns at the feet of Jesus honor the work of the cross.]

Once you reach the point where your only desire is to glorify God, you will experience a love deeper than you can imagine, one that wants more than anything else to see others come into right relationship with Father God through Jesus and experience the blessed life you have found in Christ. No one will ever again be able to intimidate you into being less than all you can be in Christ. You will have counted the cost and found that the only thing that matters is the fact that your life pleases the Father, that He deems it significant.

Prepare to Be Overwhelmed

If you haven't seen the movie <u>Facing the Giants,</u> you should. I'm convinced this movie is anointed by the Lord to call His men forth from the schemes of the enemy that keep them spiritually impotent. The general story is very good, but there is one very important message within it that I believe the Lord wants to use to help us men prepare for our restored potency as true men of God.

In the movie, the head coach of a struggling high school football team is facing a crisis, both spiritually and in his physical surroundings. At his "moment in time," a word is given to him by a man of God. He tells the coach that he is to prepare for rain, a time when the Lord would move on his behalf. This word drives him to change his way of looking at his life and the way he functions. These changes were lasting. In the same way, I am convinced that at this very moment a "word" from the Lord is being given to you from these pages. You are to prepare to be the very man the Lord wants you to be, if you have repented of your life up to this point. You are to accept the fact that the Lord will use you.

Part of our spiritual impotence is the absence of the heart knowledge that the Lord has designed us through the new birth to be His vessels of wonderment. He has chosen to flow through each and every one of us with His power, might, and miracles. He desires that all the characteristics that are present in Jesus would flow freely in us on a daily basis – yes, you and me!

Our dilemma is that most of us don't really believe it can happen to us, that we can expect it to happen in us when we get in line with God's Word and His desires. We have settled for so much less than He intends that we don't believe, even if we allow our hearts to be turned around, He could possibly exhibit Himself through us.

We don't believe we can really love as Jesus loved. Up until now, it hasn't even been part of our thinking, much less our hope. We don't believe we will see our marriages turn around, or our children empowered by the Lord to become prophets for their generation, or young men and women used by God to take their school for Jesus as a testimony to the power of the cross. We don't believe the Lord will give us whatever it takes

188

to desire to spend every last cent we make to further His kingdom, keeping only enough for ourselves to cover the basics and actually rejoice in doing it. What's more, it's even harder to fathom that our families will be rejoicing with us as they, too, pour all they have into the work of God. Those kinds of things were incomprehensible before this moment in time.

I am at this very moment coming to you with this "word" as you read. I ask the Lord to make it yours in your inner man. As you move in the direction of repentance and change, allow the Holy Spirit to have His way and "Prepare to be overwhelmed by the goodness of your God."

Prepare to walk and function as you have never walked and functioned before. Prepare to be overwhelmed by the presence of the Lord working through you. Prepare to be overwhelmed as you find yourself loving as Jesus loves, honoring Father God as He does, and living before others with the integrity and holiness that characterizes Him. Prepare to be overwhelmed as you see your marriage turned into a brilliant example of the relationship between Christ and the church. Prepare to be overwhelmed as your children turn their hearts toward God and move in the power Jesus promised them. Prepare to be overwhelmed as you are used as a vessel of healing to many and a vessel of honor to the Lord. Prepare yourself and your heart to be overwhelmed as part of your new life in Christ.

Starting right now, are you prepared to be overwhelmed when you find yourself walking as Jesus walked - this day - in your generation? You need to prepare, if you have surrendered everything to Him. Will you just casually hope this might happen or are you really going to prepare to be seriously overwhelmed by the presence of God in your life? I urge you to prepare. It would bless God's heart.

Chapter 17
MASH icu Study Questions

1) Are you willing to spend your life anticipating the overwhelming presence of God?   Y/N

2) Are you willing to have God place a desire in your heart to please only Him?   Y/N

3) Have you counted the cost?   Y/N

4) Are you willing to learn how to die to yourself as Jesus did, so others might live?   Y/N

5) Are you willing to have the Holy Spirit guide you to a place where those around you may think you have gone off the deep end, maybe even ridicule you; but it is a place that pleases God?   Y/N

6) Are you willing to dare to believe the Lord might use you in a mighty way?   Y/N

7) Are you preparing to eventually be overwhelmed by the power, the majesty, and the presence of the Lord working through you, because you are now willing to be in line with His Word?   Y/N

Father,

I want it all! I desire You to make me like Jesus in every way You have provided because of the cross. Prepare my heart to be overwhelmed with Your goodness and love. Prepare my heart to be willing to give everything to You. Thank You, Lord!

Intensive Care Unit III

Advocate Action

Living Significant, Christ-centered Lives

Nothing can ever replace an honorable man who is fully submitted to the Lordship of Jesus as he fulfills his offices of husband and father with Christ-like wisdom, guidance, tenderness, and love.

James 4: 8-10 AMP Come close to God and He will come close to you. [Recognize that you are] sinners, get your soiled hands clean; [realize that you have been disloyal] wavering individuals with divided interests, and purify your hearts [of your spiritual adultery].

9) [As you draw near to God] be deeply penitent and grieve, even weep [over your disloyalty]. Let your laughter be turned to grief and your mirth to dejection and heartfelt shame [for your sins].

10) Humble yourselves [feeling very insignificant] in the presence of the Lord, and He will exalt you [He will lift you up and make your lives significant].

Once we are aware of our own need and have determined to flow in an intimacy with God and apply His heart of love in everything we do through humbling ourselves before God, only then can we implement what we have been called to do. We can have confidence in the fact that His presence is with us if we do whatever we are called to do for the good of God and the benefit of others. That will only happen if our flesh and all that goes with it are out of the way. Seeking God to eliminate anything and everything that does not glorify Him must be the first step we take toward restoring our lives. Bold moves and decisive actions accompanied by the love of Jesus accomplish much; the same actions done in the flesh cause untold havoc and produce an endless trail of wounded hearts.

Deep intimate moments with God allow Him to give us the grace and power to change, so that our lives and our actions have eternal significance. Because we are greatly loved and have the freedom to continually walk in an attitude of humility before God - recognizing our utter need for Him - the Holy Spirit empowers us to walk the path of righteousness and exhibit the life and love of Jesus Christ, which can be used by the Lord to draw others into a significant life in Christ for all eternity. We truly become advocates for God and for one another.

As you move in the direction of living significantly, it will be good to always remember that Jesus "covered" the sins of those who hung Him on the cross. He asked forgiveness for those who drove the nails in His hands and made His flesh like hamburger. Even though He was God and He was right, He humbled Himself to the very end. He gave up His right to be right so the eternal power of the cross would be flowing even to this very day.

That is the way we are expected to treat others. We are to "cover" their inability to see the things the Lord has shown us in our newfound intimacy with Him, so that the power of the cross can work in any situation that needs the presence of God. We are to take on the heart of Jesus on their behalf and for their good, praying for them rather than pointing out all of the ways in which they are wrong.

[Have you gone to God and petitioned Him to give you whatever is needed to help others live a significant life as God sees it, or are you only going to God to prove to Him and to others that you are right?]

Chapter 18

The Battle Plan for the War Against Your Old Life

Live for a cause greater than yourself.

II Cor. 10:3-5 AMP For though we walk (live) in the flesh, we are not carrying on our warfare according to the flesh and using mere human weapons.

4) For the weapons of our warfare are not physical [weapons of flesh and blood], but they are mighty before God for the overthrow and destruction of strongholds.

5) [Inasmuch as we] refute arguments and theories and reasonings and every proud and lofty thing that sets itself up against the [true] knowledge of God; and we lead every thought and purpose away captive into the obedience of Christ (the Messiah, the Anointed One),...

You are on the threshold of taking steps to reclaim your offices of husband, father, and community leader. You will not only be reestablishing an intimacy with God, you will be tearing down the spiritual strongholds that have kept you and your family in bondage up until this time. As these unseen spiritual changes take place, a corresponding action on your part will be needed to make physical changes, all of them causing you to interact with people involved in your world.

As you make changes in your life, it is paramount to remember that your warfare is never against people. All of the battlefields on which you are waging war are spiritual battlefields. The battle is, first and foremost, a battle against your own spiritual impotence. All of the battles you win will be won in the spirit first as you commune with God. Only after that has taken place will you see the results manifest in the physical realm as positive, everlasting changes.

It is vitally important that you exhibit the character of Christ to everyone you encounter on your way to rebuilding your life. Your words must come from your prayer closet, propelled by love. Take action only after you've spent time on the lap of your Father in heaven. Any changes you make in your physical world must be initiated after prayer, immersed in prayer, and implemented with the heart of Jesus. Your actions may be decisive, direct, and uncompromising; but every one of them must exhibit the love of Jesus toward those who are involved.

Never forget that you are in a spiritual war that begins in your heart and eventually affects those around you, as you redirect your life toward significance. The manner in which people are affected and respond to your new life depends in large part on how well you represent Jesus to them. How much the Holy Spirit moves in their hearts on your behalf depends on how much you welcome His presence in your daily life, as you endeavor to move only in His power.

You are in the process of reclaiming spiritual ground you've given to the enemy over the years through spiritual impotence. It is a battle against your old nature, never against others who are part of your life. If that is not extremely clear to you, please visit and revisit portions of this book before you even open your mouth or try to modify your life in any way. If you haven't already done so, immerse yourself in the Word and in fellowship with God so you won't cause irreparable harm to those around you and to the reputation of Jesus by foolish, fleshly actions.

You First - If Someone Would Only Say I'm Sorry!

Without knowing it, most people are walking around with a wounded spirit because of the harm someone has caused them in the past - maybe even you. A person may have extended forgiveness, which is the only way to bring about complete healing; but somehow the pain just doesn't go away. What we don't know is that our spirit, in essence, has a hole in it. It is as if we have been stabbed, possibly many times, by the words or actions of others. We are trying to function as if we're whole; but, in reality, we're attempting to cover our wounds with a tiny bandage to stop the bleeding, while continuing on with life. Spiritual wounds are very real and very debilitating.

When asked, I have found that most people who walk in woundedness have never had anyone who wounded them say "I'm sorry," either because the offender is unaware or incapable or the individual has passed away, leaving things unresolved. So, standing in for those who can't or won't repent to you, may I sincerely say, "I'm sorry. Would you please forgive me for all the harm I've caused you?" Can you find it in your heart to make the choice to forgive that person?

196

If you can accept that apology, and can truly choose to forgive the offender (whether man, woman, father, mother, family member, friend, etc.) as if he or she had said the words, you will be well on your way to discovering why you have led a powerless life as a man, or why you keep attempting to find something to fill the void you feel as a woman. Your healing has begun.

Predictable Challenges That Will Come Your Way

In my years of encouraging others to break loose from whatever bondages they may be in, I have noticed a strategy that's used over and over by the enemy to hinder any advancement. You can find it outlined in the book of Nehemiah. God showed Nehemiah how to accomplish his task of rebuilding the walls of Jerusalem and he will do the same for you as you study the book of Nehemiah and ask God to apply its wisdom to your life as you go about rebuilding your own walls.

Gaining wisdom by becoming familiar with the challenges Nehemiah faced and the progress that he made will help keep you from being blindsided by anything that's thrown at you to hinder your progress. Your ability to recognize the well-worn tactics of the enemy will help you stay on track, ready to implement God's game plan and sidestep the enemy's wiles.

Although names, places, and situations will obviously be different, the tactics of the enemy will manifest in pretty much the same way in your situation as they did in Nehemiah's as you take steps toward repairing your life. This may happen many times throughout your rebuilding process. The circumstances may vary and the order in which the tactics come your way may differ; but most of the time, you can be prepared for them because you'll know the general format used by the enemy to stop any work or worker of God.

You Are Being Called

God called Nehemiah to rebuild the wall around the city of Jerusalem, which had been destroyed many years before God placed this assignment on his heart. Because of the disrepair of the city walls, the people of God were in disgrace. What used to protect the inhabitants was no longer securely in place, leaving them helpless against the onslaught of their enemies. That broke his heart and made him move in the direction God had for him.

Nehemiah 1:4 NIV When I heard these things, I sat down and wept. For some days I mourned and fasted and prayed before the God of heaven.

From the very first pages of this book, you have been told of the damage that's been done to the men who are attempting to follow Jesus. From the purest perspective, our representation of Jesus to a world that is out of answers could be described as fairly disgraceful. This representation is of paramount importance to God and it should be a priority for us. The disgrace of God's people in Nehemiah's time drove him to repentance and heartbreak. His desire to honor God drove him to his calling and direction. His petitions equipped him with a promise and a mission straight from the heart of God. He could be used mightily because he cared about the same things that were on God's heart. Because of that heart position, he could be trusted to be an instrument of change in the hands of God.

Having the heart of God is where you want to head. Without the heart of Jesus, all of your work will be little more than religious activity that stirs up a bunch of religious dust but has little eternal impact.

Nehemiah 2:4-5 NIV The king said to me, "What is it you want?" Then I prayed to the God of heaven,

5) and I answered the king, "If it pleases the king and if your servant has found favor in his sight, let him send me to the city in Judah where my fathers are buried so that I can rebuild it."

Nehemiah 2:7-8 NIV I also said to him, "If it pleases the king, may I have letters to the governors of Trans-Euphrates, so that they will provide me safe-conduct until I arrive in Judah?

8) And may I have a letter to Asaph, keeper of the king's forest, so he will give me timber to make beams for the gates of the citadel by the temple and for the city wall and for the residence I will occupy?"

You Are Being Empowered

Once called and commissioned, Nehemiah understood that he needed tools and provisions to accomplish his mission. To live as proper heirs, we have been given fruits and gifts by God.

Our most important tools are the fruits of the Spirit: love, joy, peace, patience, kindness, goodness, faithfulness, gentleness, and self-control (Gal. 5:22.) This is what will allow the character of Jesus to be seen in each of us. These fruits are developed over time as we continually say "yes" to God and allow Him to change us. If we try to remain in control of our lives, living selfishly rather than for the good of God and others, we cannot expect to see these fruits evident in us to any great degree.

Another important set of tools is the gifts of the Spirit. The first thing that needs to be mentioned is that the gifts work most effectively in conjunction with the fruits of the Spirit, especially love (see I Cor. 13.) Let's examine I Cor. 12:7-11 to see what the gifts of the Spirit are.

I Cor. 12:7-11 NIV Now to each one the manifestation of the Spirit is given for the common good.

8) To one there is given through the Spirit the message of wisdom, to another the message of knowledge by means of the same Spirit,

9) to another faith by the same Spirit, to another gifts of healing by that one Spirit,

10) to another miraculous powers, to another prophecy, to another distinguishing between spirits, to another speaking in different kinds of tongues, and to still another the interpretation of tongues.

11) All these are the work of one and the same Spirit, and he gives them to each one, just as he determines.

All these gifts are intended to equip the heirs of God for service and are apportioned to us as the Holy Spirit chooses. I encourage you to seek the Lord for those gifts He would like you to utilize for His glory and also seek out others who function reliably in the gifts of God to help you as you seek a life of significance in God.

You Need to Crave Every Tool the Lord Has Provided – for the Good of Others

II Cor. 10:3-5 AMP ...For though we walk (live) in the flesh, we are not carrying on our warfare according to the flesh and using mere human weapons.

4) For the weapons of our warfare are not physical [weapons of flesh and blood], but they are mighty before God for the overthrow and destruction of strongholds.

5)[Inasmuch as we] refute arguments and theories and reasonings and every proud and lofty thing that sets itself up against the [true] knowledge of God; and we lead every thought and purpose away captive into the obedience of Christ (the Messiah, the Anointed One), ...

I would like to suggest that all the gifts mentioned in I Cor. 12:7-11 have for too long been classified as "for those other guys." In many church circles, we have been taught to recognize those who function in full-time ministry as the gifted ones. I believe we have short circuited the plan of God and His intended use for these gifts. Although these gifts are given in fullness to some for consecrated works of service, they are also available to us as weapons of warfare when it comes to the war on our marriages, our families, and our church communities, whether God allows those gifts to function in us or brings people our way when we have need of a word of knowledge or wisdom, healing, discernment, etc.

The Gifts of God – Weapons and Provisions for Your Mission

Romans 1:11 NIV I long to see you so that I may impart to you some spiritual gift to make you strong-

Very much like the tools of a tradesman, which help him to accomplish a given task, the gifts of the Spirit allow the significant life seeker to enter into the spiritual realm and draw from it wisdom and power as led by the Holy Spirit. A major controversy in church circles today is whether or not the gifts of the Spirit mentioned in the Word are even for today; and if so, are they for every Christian? Much time is spent arguing and debating over gifts like speaking in tongues, words of knowledge, prophetic utterances; and probably the hottest topic of all, the Baptism in the Holy Spirit. However, remaining permanently in the debate stage is not going to get the job done.

[The spiritually impotent debate whether or not the spiritual gifts are for them. The overcoming, mature heart petitions God for these tools to reach others.]

Instead of being bogged down by endless controversies and discussions, I believe that the man who is heading for a significant, overcoming life sees the need of those who are impotent or perishing with God's eyes; and because of that, he seeks to find the heart of God for every tool he needs to reach others and discerns which ones he is apportioned for use in his personal service. He petitions for whatever gifts he needs, so he can operate at full capacity to accomplish God's goals for his life in reaching others in conjunction with the fruits of the Spirit that are being developed in him. He sees the gifts God has for him as powerful tools to help pass on the wonder of God and equip him for service – all for the glory of God and for the good of others and their needs.

I see this combination – the fruits and gifts of the Spirit – as vital for being able to see things from God's perspective and flow in the life of Christ. Many have become shipwrecked and self-focused in seeking the gifts while neglecting the less "glamorous," lower profile, more difficult endeavor of allowing God to work the fruits of the Spirit into their lives. It's no wonder we have such controversy even today, as it can't be denied that much harm and abuse as well as good have come about as the body of Christ has attempted to function in what the Lord has given to build up His kingdom. Unfortunately, the gifts of the Spirit have at times become a weapon of destruction, something God never intended. How it must grieve the heart of our Father to see His children misrepresenting Who He is and what He's provided for good purpose.

200

What if each and every one of us longed for, pursued, and desired with a pure heart whatever gifts the Lord may have for us to live an abundant life in Christ? We could petition our Father in heaven for tools of service and then use those tools to fulfill our personal commission for the growth and betterment of our fellow heirs, thus creating a significant legacy for our Father God. Then, not only would we become equipped, flowing in what God has for us, and sent forth; but as we would submit to the work of the Holy Spirit in us, the Lord could use us to help equip others and send them forth.

Touching on the Baptism in the Holy Spirit – Ouch!

Putting aside which side of the fence you're on when it comes to the Baptism in the Holy Spirit, please allow me to share my heart with you at this point. I would then encourage you to stop and spend time with the Lord and the Word to see what He may have to say regarding what's on my heart to share.

Having said that, I believe the Baptism in the Holy Spirit is a timeless power that's available to all believers, so they can live a victorious life in Christ, and avoid being defeated and worn down by life and its circumstances. Granted, it is one of the most misused gifts ever given to believers by those who consider themselves more important because they speak in tongues. That, however, should never be the criteria for discarding this important provision. I'm convinced God has given His new spiritual creation a spiritual language to communicate spirit to Spirit with Him.

You may disagree with me, but I truly believe the Baptism in the Holy Spirit is a mighty important tool for living a sanctified, significant life in Christ. Satan hates the idea that a believer can be ministered to and empowered in his or her inner being, and given the ability to receive the enormous wealth of the third Person of the Trinity, who will always point you to the life and the spiritual wealth of Jesus.

Rom. 8:26-27 NIV   In the same way, the Spirit helps us in our weakness. We do not know what we ought to pray for, but the Spirit himself intercedes for us with groans that words cannot express.
27) And he who searches our hearts knows the mind of the Spirit, because the Spirit intercedes for the saints in accordance with God's will.

The Holy Spirit will always be there to deliver you from lifeless prayers, dismal sessions of dryness in your prayer closet, and a fruitless spiritual life. If you are serious about the deep things of God, I ask at this point that you at least temporarily suspend any prejudice that would hinder you from seeking the Lord concerning the Baptism in the Holy Spirit and go to God Himself and His Word. Present the Lord with your doubts. Immerse yourself in the Word of God. Seek out honest, humble men of integrity who function in the fullness of the Holy Spirit. Pray for truth. Then wait on the Lord to show you how to proceed. (By the way, the speaking in tongues associated with the Baptism in the Holy Spirit is not the same thing as the use of tongues as one of the gifts of the Spirit. The gift of tongues is used to edify the body of Christ. Speaking in your own prayer language is meant to edify you and help you to pray in the perfect will of God.)

[Armed with a heart that holds God's desires, His Word, and the gifts and tools He's made available, it's time to implement your lifetime strategy of reversing spiritual impotence, while building a significant heritage for God.]

Back to the Hindrances That Will Come Your Way

Nehemiah 2:10 NIV When Sanballat the Horonite and Tobiah the Ammonite official heard about this, they were very much disturbed that someone had come to promote the welfare of the Israelites.

As you study the book of Nehemiah in depth, you will find six basic strategies used by the enemy to hinder your progress and stop you from succeeding. He will attempt to:

1) Rob you of your mission

Nehemiah 2:19 NIV But when Sanballat the Horonite, Tobiah the Ammonite official and Geshem the Arab heard about it, they mocked and ridiculed us. "What is this you are doing?" they asked. "Are you rebelling against the king?"

2) Ridicule you and your zeal

Nehemiah 4:1-3 NIV When Sanballat heard that we were rebuilding the wall, he became angry and was greatly incensed. He ridiculed the Jews,
2) and in the presence of his associates and the army of Samaria, he said, "What are those feeble Jews doing? Will they restore their wall? Will they offer sacrifices? Will they finish in a day? Can they bring the stones back to life from those heaps of rubble—burned as they are?"
3) Tobiah the Ammonite, who was at his side, said, "What they are building—if even a fox climbed up on it, he would break down their wall of stones!"

202

3) Discourage you to the point of despair

Nehemiah 4:7-12 NIV   But when Sanballat, Tobiah, the Arabs, the Ammonites and the men of Ashdod heard that the repairs to Jerusalem's walls had gone ahead and that the gaps were being closed, they were very angry.

8) They all plotted together to come and fight against Jerusalem and stir up trouble against it.

9) But we prayed to our God and posted a guard day and night to meet this threat.

10) Meanwhile, the people in Judah said, "The strength of the laborers is giving out, and there is so much rubble that we cannot rebuild the wall."

11) Also our enemies said, "Before they know it or see us, we will be right there among them and will kill them and put an end to the work."

12) Then the Jews who lived near them came and told us ten times over, "Wherever you turn, they will attack us."

4) Deceive you in any way he can to cause you to quit your mission or at least have you stop short of complete victory

Nehemiah 6:1-3 NIV   When word came to Sanballat, Tobiah, Geshem the Arab and the rest of our enemies that I had rebuilt the wall and not a gap was left in it—though up to that time I had not set the doors in the gates-

2) Sanballat and Geshem sent me this message: "Come, let us meet together in one of the villages on the plain of Ono." But they were scheming to harm me;

3) so I sent messengers to them with this reply: "I am carrying on a great project and cannot go down. Why should the work stop while I leave it and go down to you?"

5) Threaten you by pointing out the harm you could cause by becoming "too spiritual" or some other such lie

Nehemiah 6:5-8 NIV   Then, the fifth time, Sanballat sent his aide to me with the same message, and in his hand was an unsealed letter

6) in which was written: "It is reported among the nations—and Geshem says it is true—that you and the Jews are plotting to revolt, and therefore you are building the wall. Moreover, according to these reports you are about to become their king

7) and have even appointed prophets to make this proclamation about you in Jerusalem: 'There is a king in Judah!' Now this report will get back to the king; so come, let us confer together."

203

8) I sent him this reply: "Nothing like what you are saying is happening; you are just making it up out of your head."

6) Entrap you in some way to bring compromise to your mission

Nehemiah 6:10-13 NIV One day I went to the house of Shemaiah son of Delaiah, the son of Mehetabel, who was shut in at his home. He said, "Let us meet in the house of God, inside the temple, and let us close the temple doors, because men are coming to kill you—by night they are coming to kill you."
11) But I said, "Should a man like me run away? Or should one like me go into the temple to save his life? I will not go!"
12) I realized that God had not sent him, but that he had prophesied against me because Tobiah and Sanballat had hired him.
13) He had been hired to intimidate me so that I would commit a sin by doing this, and then they would give me a bad name to discredit me.

It would be wise to expect the enemy's tactics to surface over and over as you progress toward the repair of your relationship with God and the rescuing of your marriage and family. These tactics will come in many different forms and their modifications, varying degrees of intensity, and from various sources - some of them very clear, some very subtle.

Read and study the chapters of Nehemiah at least to the point where the wall is completed at the end of chapter 6. Read them every time you find some sort of roadblock in your journey. More than likely, that roadblock will take on one or more of the above-mentioned tactics. Observe Nehemiah's responses to the tactics. Once you can see the ploy of the enemy, you will be able to seek the Lord for His response and His power to overcome.

You need to remember that the enemy of your soul despises giving up any stronghold he has established against you. When you make the all-important decision to no longer offend God with your life and seek all of God's spiritual wealth for you and your family, you can plan on challenges coming your way from every direction. Many will come from those members of the church who choose to remain in their impotence. Many of those who purport to be your best friends will be the ones who become the most steadfast in their zeal to help you remain as you are. You need to understand this, anticipate the kinds of opposition that will come your way; and have a game plan ready to counteract any deterrents by continuing on with wisdom and zeal. Let me say once more that you need to remember your battle is a spiritual one, not a war against whoever is used to attempt to hinder your submission to Jesus and His ways.

Never Give Away Your Seed

Nehemiah 2:11,12,16,17 NIV   I went to Jerusalem, and after staying there three days.

12) I set out during the night with a few men. I had not told anyone what my God had put in my heart to do for Jerusalem. ...

...16) The officials did not know where I had gone or what I was doing, because as yet I had said nothing to the Jews or the priests or nobles or officials or any others who would be doing the work.

17) Then (my emphasis) I said to them...

Have you ever enthusiastically gone to someone to explain a Rhema Word, a word the Holy Spirit ignited in your spirit as you read the Bible, one that changed your life, only to have them respond with something like, "That's nice"? If his response, or lack thereof, didn't completely deflate your joy or rob you of your Word from the Lord, have you ever continued to try to explain the impact of what you heard, only to see his eyes wander off someplace as you stood in big-eyed enthusiasm before him? If that's happened to you, it would be good to thoroughly learn the following lesson from the book of Nehemiah.

There is danger in giving away the seed of what you've been given before the Lord brings it to maturity. In parable form, it could be expressed as the seed a farmer buys in order to plant his crop and reap a harvest. When the seed is planted in the ground and nurtured to maturity, it produces a bountiful supply that can feed many people, giving them nourishment for years to come. If that same farmer sees the needs of the people around him and decides to offer his unplanted seed to satisfy their immediate need for food, it could temporarily quiet a few hunger pangs; but it would have an infinitesimal impact in comparison with what it could have accomplished as a mature crop.

The point of the story is that it's important to wait for the Lord to bring the word He gives you to maturity in your heart before you try to share it with others. This is something that's not often considered and has no doubt derailed the work of the Lord in many instances as those called by God shared their word or vision prematurely, only to be met with words of discouragement and lack of enthusiasm from those who had not spent any time with the Lord concerning His plan.

In the following chapters, you will be working hand in hand and heart to heart with the Lord on the way to wholeness for both you and your family. Your interaction with the Lord and subsequent submission to His ways will give you clear direction and positive steps to initiate. It is so important that you never act on nor give away your seed of wisdom before it has matured. If you do, you will wonder why your steps - even though you know they are ordered by the Lord - produce little benefit and maybe even cause harm to those around you.

Nehemiah understood this concept. Even though he grasped his calling, had the provision he needed to complete the task and knew he was in the perfect will of God, he used wisdom to avoid being robbed of his mission before he even got started. Even though the seed of his mission was firmly rooted in his heart, he told no one what he was about to do until the proper season when all was in place and he was ready to act.

Can you imagine the negative impact your words would produce if you finished this book with a command from the Lord to change your life, announced you now understood your spiritual impotence, told your wife she would have to submit to the changes you would be making; and then had a conference with your children, explaining that you were going to rescue them from their sin and help them radically alter their lifestyles? Then, continuing in your folly, you went around to all your friends, spouting your intentions to become a real man of God from that day forward?

Obviously, those actions would produce little or no fruit, even though you tried to share what the Holy Spirit revealed to you. The less than enthusiastic response of your family and friends would no doubt rob you, at least to some degree, of the hope you'd been given. It would give the enemy opportunity to try to nullify God's plan for your life and destroy your witness and reputation with your wife, your family, and your friends, possibly for the rest of your life – all because the timing was premature.

Colossians 3:12 NIV Therefore, as God's chosen people, holy and dearly loved, clothe yourselves with compassion, kindness, humility, gentleness and patience.

On the other hand, if you complete the following chapters of this book, set it down and determine to wait on the Lord to give you new seed for your every need and every step; and allow Him to bring it step by step to maturity before you move step by step in love, your life will have untold eternal impact on those around you. It will be significant to God and significant to others. You will learn to wait on the Lord for His heart. You will be taught to approach others with the integrity, love, and character of Jesus, Who has full residence in your heart. You will walk fully in the power of the Holy Spirit to change your life and your world for God's honor and glory. You will be able to stand and watch as the Lord redeems your life and the lives of those around you and develops an honorable, lasting legacy through you and those who also choose to follow in His footsteps because of your example.

Wait for specific direction from God!

Obedience to the Lord in all things is of far greater importance than a myriad of good deeds done on your own initiative. He is far more concerned with the condition of your heart than in what you can do. Paul had been told through a prophet that his life would become difficult if he went to Jerusalem. He knew he would be bound and taken into captivity because of his appearance there. None of that mattered to him.

What was of primary importance to Paul, however, was his obedience to the Lord and what He had called him to do. Nothing could rob him of his purpose for living. He knew that his mission, commissioned and anointed by God, would allow His Lord's will to be accomplished. That was all that mattered to him.

As you move forward, there will be many good things you could do to change your life and the lives of those around you. There will be many choices you will have to make and many people with whom you'll be involved. However, only those things that are done in prayerful obedience and birthed through waiting on God and His timing will be truly fruitful and eternal. Anything else may possibly be a good thing, but it will fall far short of what God intends if you initiate your own marching orders and then ask God to bless your efforts. As Nehemiah did, as Paul did, move only when you are told to move and go only where you are told to go. Then have confidence that you're moving hand-in-hand with the Lord no matter how hard the challenge might be.

Wait for the presence of God!

Exodus 33:13-16 NIV "If you are pleased with me, teach me your ways so I may know you and continue to find favor with you. Remember that this nation is your people."

14) The Lord replied, "My Presence will go with you, and I will give you rest."

15)Then Moses said to him, "If your Presence does not go with us, do not send us up from here.

16) How will anyone know that you are pleased with me and with your people unless you go with us? What else will distinguish me and your people from all the other people on the face of the earth?"

The love of Christ is always the primary attribute in the presence of God. As children of God, through Christ, we are to act like Christ would in every situation. As you are called to make decisions to effect change in

207

your world and rescue your children, you will need to move in decisiveness and candid truth toward those with whom God has called you to deal. As stated before, they are never your enemy. They may see things differently than you do, but they are greatly loved by God. You are to love them as Jesus loves them.

[The spiritually impotent man spends his time protecting his personal doctrine and arguing its soundness, rather than seeking God for everything available to him for the glory of God and the good of others.]

God's presence and anointing will make the difference between fruitless, religious activity and changes that affect your world and the world of those in your circle of influence for eternity. For every step you take, make sure you have waited for the heart of God to be planted in you toward those with whom you will be dealing. Without it, your words and your intent will have little compassion; and, therefore, little spiritual effect. You may be moving in obedience, but your motives will not have the love and purity that Jesus exhibits as their basis. When this is the case, you may be right in what you are doing; but no one will see Jesus in you and be drawn to Him by actions carried out with impure motivation and the absence of His love.

Wait for the power of God!

Matt.16:19 AMP I will give you the keys of the kingdom of heaven; and whatever you bind (declare to be improper and unlawful) on earth must be what is already bound in heaven; and whatever you loose (declare lawful) on earth must be what is already loosed in heaven.

Jesus said and did everything He did with authority, because He knew that all of the desires of His Father were behind His every move. He only did what He had been told to do. He was always where He was supposed to be, doing what he was supposed to be doing, when He was supposed to be doing it. Therefore, He was confident that all of the power of the heavenlies was with Him.

If you notice in Matthew 16:19, Amplified version, there comes a time when whatever needs to be done is accomplished in the heavens. Only then are we to follow through with our part as it is accomplished on the earth. Study that verse until the Lord reveals the incredible freedom and power it contains for you in any work in which you are called to be a part.

[Praying for others changes you.]

208

Many times I have prayed for something or someone, sometimes binding influences that He told me were involved. The Lord would then have me wait on Him in prayer, sometimes for days, weeks, months, or even longer. My part was to hold my petition before Him as the work was being accomplished in the spiritual realm. Often, without fanfare of any kind, I would get a word in prayer, or from His Word, or even from someone else who heard from God. Somehow, I would be told that what I had been praying for was completed. As I would go to the Lord in thanksgiving, He would tell me to now loose what had been accomplished in heaven here on earth. Amazingly, what was needed would occur as easily as a hot knife goes through butter. When the power of God is manifest, nothing can stand against it. That power is yours through Jesus as you work closely with God in any given situation, having Him guide you and direct your every step. We are privileged to be included in what God is doing here on earth.

It's Time for You to Begin Your Journey

Now, you go! Armed with the command you've been given, motivated by the love of Jesus and His love for others, empowered by the Holy Spirit, be a man of God who is on his way to living a significant, world overcoming, life. Act as Jesus would toward others. Love as He loves, live as He lives, honor your Father in everything you do, just as He does.

Hebrews 12:1-3 "Therefore, since we are surrounded by such a great cloud of witnesses, let us throw off everything that hinders and the sin that so easily entangles. And let us run with perseverance the race marked out for us,

2) fixing our eyes on Jesus, the pioneer and perfecter of faith. For the joy set before him he endured the cross, scorning its shame, and sat down at the right hand of the throne of God.

3) Consider him who endured such opposition from sinners, so that you will not grow weary and lose heart."

Hebrews 11:6 NIV And without faith it is impossible to please God, because anyone who comes to him must believe that he exists and that he rewards those who earnestly seek him.

Chapter 18
MASH icu Study Questions

1) Do you see how Nehemiah's plan will apply to your spiritual life as you take the next steps toward wholeness?   Y/N

2) Do you understand that you will need to remember these lessons throughout your life, referring to them as needed in your journey?   Y/N

3) Do you understand your battle is not against people, but against spiritual forces of evil in the heavenlies and your own flesh, and that God will accomplish the work that needs to be done in you?   Y/N
(See Eph. 6:1 and Phil. 1:6)

4) Are you ready to learn to love others as Jesus loves them throughout your healing, being sensitive to your Father first and then to others?   Y/N

Father,

Without Your wisdom, I will accomplish nothing for You. Without the love of Jesus flowing through me, I will continue to cause You harm and possibly eternally harm those around me. Teach me to remain still until Your presence is with me. Show me the pitfalls that have been laid out for me by the enemy. Teach me to do only what is important to You as I interact with my wife, my family, my church body, and my community. I desperately need You, Lord. Thank You for being with me as I come to You.

Chapter 19

Reclaiming Your Office of Husband

The place of God's power, mercy, and presence

I sat in the court room, unable to talk to my first wife unless I communicated through her lawyer. My recent commitment to the Lord allowed me to see what I could never see during the twelve years of our marriage. Through her mask of anger, I saw pain so deep, violations so harmful, and sorrow so intense that she would probably deal with them in some form for the rest of her life - and I was responsible for them.

She and I were friends through high school, and we started dating seriously the first years of college. She was a bright, very beautiful woman and I was the envy of most of my friends for my ability to "land" someone so beautiful and devoted to me, something I myself really didn't comprehend. She was a naturally loving person, someone who very clearly understood and lived out words like love, commitment, devotion, compassion and marriage for life. I understood work, cars, beer, parties, sports, business success, lust (not love,) and stupidity, and devoted myself to them with vigor.

To make a long and very painful story short, my first wife did nothing but devote herself to the marriage commitment she had made and I did nothing but violate it with my selfishness and stupidity over and over again until she could take no more. I was clueless as to what marriage really entailed and proved it with every breath I took and every emotional harm I sent her way.

One of the most amazing things about that whole timeframe is this: I didn't even know how far off I was. I was just doing the best I could. All I knew was how to follow my own selfish desires and wants; and I was oblivious to the fact that my wife, who had opened her heart completely to me, was being pierced over and over again until she was emotionally bloody.

I know that I'm forgiven by God. I have repented often, and I believe she has even forgiven me because I have asked her forgiveness over the years; but I certainly wish there could have been more in me at the time that understood how life and marriage are really supposed to function. It saddens me deeply that she, an innocent victim who only wanted to love and be loved, had to pay the price for my ignorance.

[The Holy Spirit needs to break your heart over your sin, because it breaks the heart of Father God.]

In His mercy, God has since given me another chance to understand what marriage is all about in His eyes. He has entrusted me with one of His wonderful children. Merry and I have been married for almost twenty-eight years. She is an astoundingly bright, beautiful woman of God, an incredible companion and helpmate; and a gift I really don't deserve and certainly have not earned. She is also someone for whom I am accountable when standing before God.

The following verses have often been used to place women in bondage through a confused husband, a disregard for the intent of the verses during the time they were written, or by counselors who have dismissed the heart of God and only see the law.

Ephesians 5:22-24 (AMPC) Wives, be subject (be submissive and adapt yourselves) to your own husbands as [a service] to the Lord. [23] For the husband is head of the wife as Christ is the Head of the church, Himself the Savior of [His] body. [24] As the church is subject to Christ, so let wives also be subject in everything to their husbands.

Colossians 3:18 (AMPC) Wives, be subject to your husbands [subordinate and adapt yourselves to them], as is right and fitting and your proper duty in the Lord.

1 Peter 3:1,7 (AMPC) In like manner, you married women, be submissive to your own husbands [subordinate yourselves as being secondary to and dependent on them, and adapt yourselves to them], so that even if any do not obey the Word [of God], they may be won over not by discussion but by the [godly] lives of their wives, ...

[7] In the same way you married men should live considerately with [your wives], with an intelligent recognition [of the marriage relation], honoring the woman as [physically] the weaker, but [realizing that you] are

214

joint heirs of the grace (God's unmerited favor) of life, in order that your prayers may not be hindered and cut off. [Otherwise you cannot pray effectively.]

Matthew 19:5 AMP "And said, For this reason a man shall leave his father and mother and shall be united firmly (joined inseparably) to his wife, and the two shall become one flesh?"

Acts 10:34 AMP "And Peter opened his mouth and said: Most certainly and thoroughly I now perceive and understand that God shows no partiality and is no respecter of persons...

<u>It all has to do with the fulfillment of the offices given both husband and wife by God.</u>

1 Peter 3:7 (AMPC) "In the same way you married men should live considerately with [your wives], with an intelligent recognition [of the marriage relation], honoring the woman as [physically] the weaker, but [realizing that you] are joint heirs of the grace (God's unmerited favor) of life, in order that your prayers may not be hindered and cut off. [Otherwise you cannot pray effectively.]

If God is no respecter of persons and considers everyone joint heirs and equal in value, then the minimizing of women in any way does not fit Who He is and what He intends in His Word. However, if we apply the above verses to the offices He created for both men and women to provide structure to His plan for the family, we find they rhyme with the beauty, love, and proper order that show marriage to be the perfect representation of the relationship between Christ and His church, as stated in His Word.

Picture the man as a structural beam or covering header that holds up a roof and the woman as a supporting pillar of that beam or header. The two, in essence, become one; and they need each other. The header (covering) cannot stand and function properly without a strong support pillar; it will collapse. Likewise, the pillar cannot fulfill its purpose without the beam overhead in place. The husband is intended to be the spiritual covering the wife needs to protect her from the torments of this world. The wife lifts her husband up and supports him, so he can fulfill his God-given office. Once a marriage covenant takes place, the heart of God is grieved when separation occurs between husband and wife. The relationship can't function as God desires in that condition.

In the previous scriptures, the woman is to be subject to the *office* of the man, supporting it and submitting to its role. The word *weaker* is to be interpreted as *secondary in the order established by God*, not less important. Harmony occurs when both men and women subject themselves in Christ-like love to the offices (roles) each has been given, and become one in purpose as they provide a covering for their children.

Where there is a full understanding of the offices God has established, dominance or the minimizing of the woman by the man is foolishness, and horribly destructive to the family structure if allowed to continue. Conversely, if the woman attempts to take on the role established for the man, disorder and confusion ensue for everyone in the family, whether it is recognized or not.

Either way, when God's ordained structure is disrupted, the family fortress weakens and becomes vulnerable to the onslaught of the enemy. He is relentless, insidious, and bent on destroying the family, so that it doesn't overcome the world as Jesus did. A weakened or nullified family structure gives little hope of providing children with the ability to pursue a significant spiritual life in Christ.

An Example of How God's Family Structure Affects Decision Making.

A husband and wife are to approach decision making - those decisions that affect the whole family or are crucial to family harmony - with the attitude of what is best for God, each other, and the children. The decision is then fertile soil in which the parents and children can prosper and become everything God designed them to be. Obviously, some decisions are for parents alone; but, in order to bring worth to the lives of children and give them an understanding of their importance, there are times when family challenges should be presented to children. If the children are old enough and reasonable in their walk in Christ, they should be provided an opportunity to present their opinions for consideration by their parents.

Whether simple decisions between husband and wife or decisions where children are involved, a husband and wife come together for the best interests of each other and for the children. Then they pray, consider all the options, and make a determination in line with the heart of God.

Should they have an impasse and are unable to agree, even after much prayer and submission to one another, the husband should go to prayer and make the decision - *one that is best for his wife and his children.* While making this decision, his posture must be the same kind of sacrifice that Jesus made. He is to lay down his rights, opinions, and personal gain to be able to hear clearly. Knowing this, the wife devotes herself to prayer for her husband to hear clearly and then submits to the decision that is made. Any decisions that involve the children are then presented to them by both parents, who are in agreement.

Your New Life

It is vitally important to remember that from this moment on, as you are in the process of rebuilding your marriage and restoring your family, you may be fighting conventional thought, bucking religious traditions; and breaking loose from whatever spiritual bondages hinder you or your family from living world overcoming lives before the Lord. You may need to minimize your relationship with those who cannot see what the Lord has shown you. You may even need to sever some relationships that hinder you or your family from following God in the manner in which He directs. Remember that you are destroying spiritual bondages.

As you focus on restoring your marriage and rescuing your children, you may have to make some definitive choices that may not be understood by those around you. You may need to be very direct at times. One more time, it is critically important that you immerse yourself in prayer, seek wise counsel, and move only after you and your wife are agreed. She is your most important ally once your marriage is restored.

Remember, in all of the following chapters you are embarking on an eternal work that's inspired and directed by God. Remember also that the steps you are taking are very important to Him. Remind yourself every moment of every day to move only as you are directed in prayer and only in God's timing and the love of Christ.

Love is the key to every eternal action. Everything God does for us is motivated by love. Everything we do must have love as its motivation.

I Cor.12:31b NIV ...And now I will show you the most excellent way.

I Cor.13:1-13 NIV If I speak in the tongues of men and of angels, but have not love, I am only a resounding gong or a clanging cymbal.

2) If I have the gift of prophecy and can fathom all mysteries and all knowledge, and if I have a faith that can move mountains, but have not love, I am nothing.

3) If I give all I possess to the poor and surrender my body to the flames, but have not love, I gain nothing.

4) Love is patient, love is kind. It does not envy, it does not boast, it is not proud.

5) It is not rude, it is not self-seeking, it is not easily angered, it keeps no record of wrongs.

6) Love does not delight in evil but rejoices with the truth.

7) It always protects, always trusts, always hopes, always perseveres.

8) Love never fails. But where there are prophecies, they will cease; where there are tongues, they will be stilled; where there is knowledge, it will pass away.

9) For we know in part and we prophesy in part,

10) but when perfection comes, the imperfect disappears.

11) When I was a child, I talked like a child, I thought like a child, I reasoned like a child. When I became a man, I put childish ways behind me.

12) Now we see but a poor reflection as in a mirror; then we shall see face to face. Now I know in part; then I shall know fully, even as I am fully known.

13) And now these three remain: faith, hope and love. But the greatest of these is love."

A Significant Marriage

This chapter deals with the Christian marriage, the second most important priority on God's heart regarding relationships. Obviously, the first priority is the restoration of your first love relationship with Him. After you have reclaimed your cross-earned right to love Jesus with your whole heart and your covenant place before God, the Lord desires to restore your office of husband, if you are to present Him with an overcoming life. In His present end-time economy, the Christ-centered husband will be at the forefront in his office as God brings about the healing in His men.

The office of husband is one of the key ways in which God wants to clearly represent who Jesus is and how He would function in this day and age. He will use this office to implement His very heartbeat to a world that is falling deeper and deeper into the darkness of the final playing out of the sin of all mankind. The world needs to see a Christ-centered husband if they are to gain a picture of Jesus Christ. The church needs the very same thing for the very same reason.

There is no more powerful position in God's economy than the office of husband as God intended it when it comes to portraying who Jesus is. The man given the stewardship of this office is there to guide and direct the family unit, which is the springboard for every other position known to man. A man who functions in the office of husband is answerable to God for the spiritual impact that his marriage and, subsequently, his family have on furthering the kingdom of God within their circle of influence. You have been given the power of the Holy Spirit to overcome every situation that's out of order. It's time to embrace that power to overcome any hold the world has on your marriage and family.

Let it be stated here loud and clear that it is the office of husband that ranks higher in God's eyes, not the husband himself. He is no better than anyone else as far as God is concerned, because the Word makes it

218

very clear in the book of Acts that He shows no partiality to anyone. Just as God has different rankings of angels established in the heavenlies, it is the same here on earth. The office of husband carries far greater accountability than any other office ordained by God. My wife, Merry, has said on more than one occasion that she feels she got the better end of the deal once she understood what God expected of a husband and wife in marriage.

Every follower of Christ is His ambassador, but the husband has the greatest responsibility and accountability. In light of that, is it any wonder that Satan would spend great effort in attempting to nullify a man's position in the home, the church, and society? Spiritual impotence is indeed a tragedy of monumental proportions when you view God's overall plan and consider the fact that a man who holds the office of husband will be held accountable for the success or failure of the marriage. Let's all turn to God, so He can turn it around!

Do You Remember?

While the offices of husband and father are the highest offices ordained by God, marriage and, subsequently, the family are the highest institutions given to mankind by Him! He esteems them high above all the institutions that oversee earthly nations, governments, or kingdoms. Marriage is the one institution that is called the earthly representation of the relationship between Jesus and His church. That is no insignificant thing to God or to us for that matter, because our relationship with Jesus Christ is the turning point that reestablishes our relationship with Father God, which was initially lost by Adam and Eve in the Garden of Eden.

Eph. 5:31-32 AMP For this reason (my emphasis) a man shall leave his father and his mother and shall be joined to his wife, and the two shall become one flesh.
32) This mystery is very great, but I speak concerning [the relation of] Christ and the church.

The cross of Jesus Christ is the one event on which the past, present, and future hinge. Even the year in which we live is calculated according to what many believe is the year of His birth. As you will come to realize in the pages ahead, marriage was designed to be the premier exhibition of the power of the cross throughout the ages. Yes, that's a bold statement, but keep reading and you will begin to see the truth of it. It is the springboard for the family and every position of leadership in government and society. If a marriage is truly functioning properly, it will be the example of God's unconditional love for mankind and a mirror of who Jesus is.

[You love her first, even if she can't love you back.]

In the office of husband, a man has not only some pretty awesome, God-given credentials, but some pretty heavy responsibilities as well! The world is supposed to see the relationship that God has established with His people when they observe the relationship a man has with his wife and also his children in a Christian marriage.

(Do you fully understand that last statement? Dwell on these last paragraphs until Father God reveals to you how little value you may have placed on the institution He considers to be most important. Your concept of marriage vs. His is an indicator of the depth of your spiritual impotence.)

Is it any wonder that the enemy has focused on minimizing the importance of marriage and continually attempts to redefine it, so it doesn't even resemble the plan God has for it? The plot of the enemy of God is to destroy the institution of marriage and the family, so that it's no longer a Christ-centered, Christ-presenting unit. He is systematically doing all within his powers of deception to make it spiritually impotent, thus rendering it ineffective in the plan of God to reproduce the character of Jesus in His children so that others will see and embrace Him. He is succeeding in his plan by creating a spiritual impotence in men, the lynchpin in this unit, with their ignorant perspective on marriage and their inability to function in it. Even a surface look at society or one night in front of the TV makes his plan abundantly clear.

God, on the other hand, is planting a desire in the hearts of His men to reclaim their offices of husband and father through the power of the Holy Spirit, so that Jesus is properly represented in these closing hours of His timetable. His call is undeniable to those of you who have ears to hear it. Open your heart and hear the call God has for every area of your life. Embrace that call and see how the Lord responds with His power to rebuild what has been destroyed.

In the following chapters, we'll dissect the properties of a Christ-centered marriage and examine our responsibilities as men of God within our marriages and families, so that each of us can continue to turn completely to God as we discover what is involved in our offices of husband and father.

Reclaiming the Spiritual Office of Husband

Eph. 5:21-32 AMP Be subject to one another out of reverence for Christ (the Messiah, the Anointed One).

22) Wives, be subject (be submissive and adapt yourselves) to your own husbands as [a service] to the Lord.

220

23) For the husband is head of the wife as Christ is the Head of the church, Himself the Savior of [His] body.

24) As the church is subject to Christ, so let the wives also be subject in everything to their husbands.

25) Husbands, love your wives, as Christ loved the church and gave Himself up for her.

> *26) So that He might sanctify her, having cleansed her by the washing of water with the Word.*
>
> *27) That He might present the church to Himself in glorious splendor, without spot or wrinkle or any such things [that she might be holy and faultless].*
>
> *28) Even so husbands should love their wives as [being in a sense] their own bodies. He who loves his own wife loves himself.*
>
> *29) For no man ever hated his own flesh, but nourishes and carefully protects and cherishes it, as Christ does the church,*
>
> *30) Because we are members (parts) of His body.*
>
> *31) <u>For this reason</u> (my emphasis) a man shall leave his father and his mother and shall be joined to his wife, and the two shall become one flesh.*
>
> *32) This mystery is very great, but I speak concerning [the relation of] Christ and the church.*

If we take the above verse by verse, we can see the incredible plan of God, how far we as men have fallen from God's plan for us; and how much we have violated the offices of husband and father. Instead of being the benchmark example of love and servanthood God desires us to be, we are at best no different than the world and at worst a glaring example of impotence because of our inability to even desire to have the character of Christ reproduced in us, let alone be used so that His character can be reproduced in others. But you can change that!

<u>Verse 21 Be subject to one another out of reverence for Christ (the Messiah, the Anointed One).</u>

Be subject to one another. WOW! When was the last time that crossed your mind? Have you ever in your life thought about it? Have you ever craved being subject to your wife in your heart for the simple reason of revering Christ? Being "subject to" your wife means that you consider her more important than you consider yourself.

The proper posture of both husband and wife is like that of being bondservants to each other. A bondservant is one who has been given his freedom, yet he chooses to remain as a servant.

In the marriage covenant ordained by God, any lifting up of self or any posture of dominance over the spouse does not revere Christ. It does not glorify Him. Men, if you lift up yourself when you have covenanted to serve your wife as God expects of you, you bring the character of Christ into a carnal perspective as far as the world is concerned. They see Jesus, not as a godly King who gave up everything in His life for them, but as a worldly, self-serving man, the same as you.

Verses 22-24   Wives, be subject (be submissive and adapt yourselves) to your own husbands as [a service] to the Lord.
23) For the husband is head of the wife as Christ is the Head of the church, Himself the Savior of [His] body.
24) As the church is subject to Christ, so let the wives also be subject in everything to their husbands.

It is a part of God's plan in marriage that the wife has the safety of a protective covering, which should be provided by her husband as stated above. When her husband is spiritually impotent, the wife loses her sense of spiritual protection that he is supposed to provide. Her natural reaction is to take control in some form, so that she and her children, if there are any, will experience protection and well-being from her standpoint. Seeking safety for herself and her offspring, she manipulates her world to fill the void left by the spiritually absent husband. Often this violation of her office as wife is less noticeable, because the honorable woman will normally seek the Lord diligently in the midst of her husband's spiritual absence, relying on Him as her covering. It is said that when a husband becomes weak, especially spiritually, the woman takes on the role intended for the man.

Although out of line with God's original intent for marriage, it is an alternative He can use to help implement His plan for mankind. Her desperate need and her spiritual integrity initiate a desire for a closeness to Jesus. This association - even though it bypasses the spiritually atrophied husband out of necessity – has been used by God to further His kingdom through her offspring and others who see Jesus in her.

As good as this may be in some respects, it has occurred far too many times, even in Christian homes, until this travesty of God's plan has become the norm. Women are now expected to be the "spiritual one" in the family, while the man goes about doing "manly" things, because "that's just the way it is." Well, that is not the way God intended it to be. The manliest part a man can play is in the fulfillment of his office of husband and father under the complete and absolute Lordship of Jesus in service to his wife.

As it stands, there has been generation after generation of men who never responded to the Holy Spirit's call to truly flourish in the office of husband and the office of father. A spiritually impotent man cannot pass along what he does not own himself and a mother cannot convey to her children what a father needs to convey, especially by example, because she obviously is not a man. In all likelihood, she cannot even tell her boys how

222

to be a spiritual man, because she has never experienced it in her husband, father, or grandfather. Sadly, she also has little to pass on to her daughters when it comes to explaining either a man's or woman's role in God's plan for marriage because she has never experienced it herself.

As if that isn't enough, problems also occur in the wife's relationship with Jesus when the husband is in violation of his office. She must come to Jesus so He can fill the office her husband can't, submitting to Him as her covering, just as a single mom must do. Although this looks like a step up, she is robbed of being able to fulfill her God-ordained offices of wife and mother under spiritual submission to a Christ-centered man, the way God designed things to flow.

Does your life provide fertile ground
so your wife can prosper in Christ?

The world is rampant with controlling women and matriarchal families as a direct result of the spiritual impotence of men. So many marriages within the church suffer this disastrous plight because we, gentlemen, have violated our offices of husband. Because of our spiritual impotence and lack of desire to fulfill the plan of God through our marriage as our priority in life, we cause women to unknowingly violate their service to the Lord. Although they are ultimately responsible for their own sin, our incapability of acting toward them as Jesus would is the catalyst for them to stumble spiritually, as they find ways to fill the unquenchable need within them that can only be filled by a spiritually sound husband. Every one of us will be held accountable to God for that offense.

Verses 25-30 Husbands, love your wives, as Christ loved the church and gave Himself up for her.
26) So that He might sanctify her, having cleansed her by the washing of water with the Word.
27) That He might present the church to Himself in glorious splendor, without spot or wrinkle or any such things [that she might be holy and faultless].
28) Even so husbands should love their wives as [being in a sense] their own bodies. He who loves his own wife loves himself.
29) For no man ever hated his own flesh, but nourishes and carefully protects and cherishes it, as Christ does the church,
30) Because we are members (parts) of His body.

These verses command husbands to love their wives as Christ loved the church. He went to the cross for the church. He was obedient unto death for the church. His whole purpose for leaving heaven was to place himself in a position to save those who would accept Him.

223

The office He held as Servant and Sacrifice is the same posture we are to take as a man in our office of husband. Our lives are to be a sacrifice for the mate God has given us. When we get our spiritual lives in line, our wives will be able to see how their lives are to line up with the Word of God. This is a spiritual cause and effect, unperceivable unless we address it and submit to it in the spiritual realm.

There is no room in the Christian marriage for a man to demand that his fleshly wants be fulfilled either by his wife or the world around him. There is no provision by God whereby a man is to attempt to maintain his comfort zone, while denying the requirements of the office he has been given - to be an example of Jesus and treat his wife as Jesus would.

The office of husband is one of total and complete service, designed specifically so he can provide fertile ground for his wife to become all she can possibly be in Christ by the power of the Holy Spirit. All of the "she really turns me on, she is really good for me, she fulfills me, she whatever" has no bearing on the reason any of us are to be married. If any of those carnal ideas form the basis for our marriages, we are eventually doomed to an average marriage at best, one that's only a shadow of what God has available to us. It's our choice.

Yes, men, you and I have the key to a successful marriage, one that is significant in the eyes of the Lord - where it counts. Our Christ-like actions or lack of them determine whether we have a good and honorable marriage that glorifies God or one that has been nullified by the plans of the enemy. Our Christian walk, placed under the complete and absolute Lordship of Jesus Christ, is the single most important factor in furthering the kingdom of God in our circle of influence and through our marriage.

I told you earlier that the Lord brought Merry and me together as husband and wife. It took about six years for Him to prepare my heart enough to even begin to understand the husband's role in marriage. Because Merry is a magnificent woman of God, I found that she did not attempt to satisfy my male ego, but strove to nurture our spiritual relationship. The Lord commanded me to hold her in the highest esteem, even higher than I held myself. Not only had I never heard that before, I was incapable of doing it even on a good day. I initially had no concept of her value in God's eyes.

At first, we dated on and off and then the Lord separated us so He could work with each of us on an individual basis. I needed to shed the fears of my past and Merry needed to learn to depend on the Lord rather than on me.

Over time, it became clear I was to ask Merry to be my wife. It all started when the Lord woke me one night and told me Merry was the person He had chosen for me. At that time, I was so dead in my heart toward her regarding the normal passions and emotions I usually had toward the

224

women in my life, that I had to ask Him, "Mary who?" We had been separated long enough that I saw her as little more than a close and trusted friend; and because of my spiritual impotence, I couldn't see how those qualifications were anything on which to base a marriage.

During our time of separation, Merry held in her heart the firm belief that the Lord intended us to be married. She even prayed for its removal at one point because she didn't want to continue to hold a place in her heart for something that could be of her own making. As time went on, she became very involved in worship within churches and lost track of what was going on in my life. She tells me that when the Lord began to bring us back together, she asked Him why He was doing it at a point when her life was so focused in another area.

After much fervent prayer and much counsel, I finally decided to be obedient to what I was convinced God had called me to do. I asked her to marry me. Being the romantic guy that I am and having only obedience in my heart as the stimulus for my marriage proposal, it went something like this. "Uh, Merry, I believe the Lord has told me that you're to be my wife. Will you marry me if you believe that it's God's will?" Pretty slick, huh?

Her response to my unusual proposal was, "If it is God's will, I will marry you." So, we both married in obedience to what we believed God wanted for our lives.

The Lord spent the next two or three years putting to death in me any fleshly thoughts, concepts, expectations, and preconceived notions I had as to what a marriage should be. Often I would find myself reeling in agony as the Lord was killing my selfish flesh and teaching me how much He cherished Merry, how He demanded that I do the same, even if it cost me every ounce of my comfort zone. There is no question in my mind that Merry had an anointing in those years to hold me before the Lord until I could hear His voice and begin to function properly in the office of husband and, at times, was mercifully unaware of the inner turmoil I experienced. Her quiet patience and unfailing love allowed me to grow in Christ, despite my flailing about like a fish out of water as I struggled against the will of God for me.

God was and is teaching me to die daily to any fleshly assumptions I may have in regard to what a husband should be and to live only in those things He considers important to a marriage. He was teaching me to serve as Jesus would serve, to love as He would love.

Just a Moment

What has been said so far would be sufficient to warrant going on to the next point, but I would like to make a comment to all you men who are struggling with your marriage. As I eventually received a supernatural knowledge of how important Merry was to God and was also given the

225

desire to be obedient to Him during those years when He was refining my priorities in marriage, He also made His power available so that I would not allow my flesh to sabotage our marriage as it had in past relationships, even though there were many times of dismal failure on my part.

When the clouds of my own selfishness were lifted and I began to see Merry as God saw her, a new kind of love entered my heart for her. It was His kind of immovable, unshakable, and I guess, holy love. Although I still fail Merry, I love her in a way that I never thought I was capable of loving someone else.

The love that has been placed in my heart supernaturally has no restrictions on it. There are no demands on Merry to be anything other than what God wants her to be. I am now fulfilled when she is fulfilled, something I never in a million years thought possible. For the very first time in my life, I am at complete peace, knowing that I'm in the very center of God's will for my life as I cherish and cover her life with the love of Jesus, which He gives me the strength to do. The love that God has placed in my heart for her is far beyond anything I could imagine or desire. Until He stepped in, I never even knew it was available to me.

You may think that your marriage has become so dulled that it's impossible for it to be rekindled into the vibrant, Christ-like representation God intends it to be. Well, you will have no opportunity to find out how powerful God is until you make the decision to place your marriage and your spiritual impotence under the Lordship of Jesus and commit to allowing God to reinstate your office of husband. Just decide to do it!

In doing so, you enter into the direct plan God has for His men to become the leaders He needs for the coming days. Moving with Him and flowing in His desires for men during these times means that you will be moving in the unbeatable power of the Holy Spirit. What awaits you, if you choose to move with God - especially by allowing Him to restore your office of a Christ-like husband - is far, far beyond your wildest imaginations and scope of thinking. The Lord will have to expand your heart to contain the love He desires you to feel for Jesus and your wife. Go for it! God is waiting to hear you say that you're sick and tired of being sick and tired and lifeless.

Verse 31 <u>*For this reason*</u> *(my emphasis) a man shall leave his father and his mother and shall be joined to his wife, and the two shall become one flesh.*

God's kind of marriage is something to be admired. He is waiting for His men to be wise enough to choose His ways over theirs concerning their marriage. He desires to impart His "well done" to those who decide to follow His plan.

226

As far as God is concerned, there is only one reason a man is given permission to take a woman as his wife. That reason is so he can be the example of Jesus to her and lay his life down for her as Christ laid down His life for the church, all so that she has fertile ground to become all she can be in Christ.

Men, the Word of God does not lie and is never taken lightly by Him. This is the criteria by which you and I will be judged when we stand face to face before God. The life and character of Jesus will be the plumb line with which our relationship with our wives will be judged. The heart service He had for the church will be the benchmark when God examines our hearts toward our wives.

We may not fully understand it until we get in line spiritually, but if our marriage is mediocre and impotent, and does not reflect the relationship Jesus has with His church, it is because we are violating the office to which God has called us. It's one of the primary reasons that our lives are deemed insignificant before the Lord. It will be next to impossible for us to get in line with the plan God has for our marriages until He gets our hearts in line spiritually. It's our task to seek Him for taste buds for the real things of God, so that our marriages and our families can be the example they're intended to be from God's perspective.

Which brings us to *verse 32 This mystery is very great, but I speak concerning [the relation of] Christ and the church.*

The world is dying in its sin and, without knowing it, looking for an example of the relationship Christ had with His church, so they can have the opportunity to understand the concept of His heart service and His love for them. The Christian marriage, our spiritual servant's attitude toward our wives is to be that example.

The marriage covenant and our participation in it is much, much more than "She's cute, I think I'll marry her." It is held in very high esteem by God, because it is supposed to be the representation of the life of Jesus to others. God deems that of great significance. To have our marriages classified as significant in His eyes, they must be in line with His Word and we must be in line with His Word toward our wives. How do you fare?

One More Very Important Point!

If you are spiritually impotent and in violation of your office of husband, the natural instinct for a woman is to seek to control her environment. Your failure to spiritually cover her automatically stimulates her to seek safety. Some women bury themselves in maintaining the household, taking care of the children, or finding their own career as a priority over their relationship with their husbands. Long ago, they gave up

227

on their husbands' ability to be completely guided and directed by God, so they take things into their own hands to experience a sense of safety. Most women dig in deep with the Lord, which is a very good thing and probably one of the reasons you are beginning to hear from Him at this moment. Her heart prayers are being heard.

Some women, however, seek to find the comfort they miss because of your ignorance and spiritual absence in material things. Unknowingly, they have attempted to fill that gnawing absence with "stuff" in the same way you have, neither of you realizing that it stems from your spiritual impotence. Her need for a bigger house, better social standing, more clothes, more jewelry, more, more, more is a cry for you to get back to God so that she can feel complete. In spiritual reality, because the two of you are one in the spirit, she can only be complete when you are in line with the Word of God.

[What price is too high to pay to rescue your marriage?]

A truly spiritual woman will say that her real safety is in the fact that she is confident you are seeking God for the answers to everything in your life and in your marriage. When she knows you have the Lord as your only source for anything in your life, she can rest and be at peace because she knows that He is reliable. Her confidence is in His ability to make you the man you need to be.

Here's Your Challenge, Men

Because you may have violated your wife's trust at almost every turn throughout the many years of your spiritual impotence, she may not be able to trust you completely until you show that you're trustworthy in following God. If you really turn everything over to the Lordship of Jesus Christ, your tastes, desires, and values will change. You will begin to desire the ways of God for your life. In most cases, if you are married to a woman who follows Jesus also, this will be a welcome relief for her. She will most likely embrace your new life and all that comes with it.

However, your wife may have been wounded by your spiritual absence for so long that your new lifestyle may not be readily embraced by her. She may still need things and stuff to make her feel secure, until she is convinced of the work God is doing in your heart. The idea of making any significant, God-directed changes may not be extremely exciting for her right away. She may not be ready to know the guy you're becoming at first.

If the last scenario is closer to your situation than the first, now is the time for you to keep your mouth quiet and your prayers ongoing. To expect your wife to be quickly moved from her position of needing to

228

control her environment to one of complete submission to the ways of God is unreasonable unless the Lord does one incredible work in her heart. More than likely, it will be a process. There may need to be small adjustments and minor changes made, which will allow her to begin to trust you and eventually fully embrace the relationship the Lord is forging between the two of you. You have violated her trust over the years with your ignorance of God's ways. Now you need to be Christ-like to her so she can heal from the wounds and needs she may have taken on because you did not understand and function properly in your office of husband.

Be patient, men. Be like Jesus would be to your wife. When she sees that you fully trust Him, she will start being able to trust you. Remember, flowers and a night out every six weeks won't do it. We're talking lifestyle here!

There Must Come a Time to Stop the Bleeding!

During the course of a significantly dysfunctional marriage, many violations of trust occur, and they little by little erode the safety of the marriage. The spiritual seal of the marriage has been broken, which allows inroads for continual harm if these violations persist. Let's rediscover the brilliant plan of God to preserve the safety of your marriage, so that you can rebuild it into a powerful unit that affects the world the way God originally intended.

One of the most important yet often ignored aspects of a marriage is the violations of trust by either the husband or wife. Sometimes they occur with the help of devoted, unknowing friends who are more than willing to walk with you through all the wounds you and your spouse have received from one another. Sometimes these violations are even brought into play through professional counseling. Another avenue in the body of Christ that can lead to trust issues between husband and wife is the prayer request that concerns your marriage. Whatever form it takes, these are all an open window into the privacy of your marriage, and a hindrance to any healing that's vital in making your marriage a powerful force in the hands of God.

A healthy marriage is a place of safety where two less than perfect people are privileged by God to see the inadequacies and failures of the other, all so they can hold each other before the Lord so healing can take place. The covenant marriage is sealed from any outside influence, so each party has a safe place to fail without the fear of the scrutiny of others and the detriment of gossip. If there is a need for counseling to clear some things up so that you can continue, you must set parameters that protect the privacy of both parties. Walking prayerfully within those parameters reseals your marriage and places God back in charge of your relationship. The bottom line is this. How can you and your spouse truly trust and be vulnerable with one another if you continually wonder what everyone else knows about you, whatever form that takes?

Here's Your Challenge, Ladies (Merry Here)

If you want your marriage to be under the covering of a man who fervently seeks God, you need to provide a green light and enough room for him to become one. Is there something you can do to relieve him of certain things that need not demand so much of his time, so that he can spend more time with the Lord? Are your expectations beyond what is necessary or reasonable regarding what he needs to materially provide for you and your family? Ask the Lord for an accurate assessment from His perspective. Remember, your encouragement and support are crucial if your husband is to experience the freedom to seek God wholeheartedly. I can assure you that the sense of security you seek as a married woman lies in the assurance that you have a husband who follows hard after God.

Maybe you are in the opposite situation, and your husband doesn't seem interested in going deeper with the Lord. Trying to constantly herd him in that direction will probably have the opposite effect. Your most effective tool to help him move in the Lord's direction is prayer – for God's benefit and your husband's good. At this point, it's not about your life getting better; it's about God being glorified in your marriage. As you continue to pray and allow the Holy Spirit to move on your husband's behalf, God will be glorified, and you and your children will benefit. It's a win-win-win situation!

If you are a woman contemplating marriage, begin now to look to Father God to fulfill your needs and desires, so the burden is not on your prospective husband. It's not his job to carry that burden. It is his job to submit to the Lord and seek to serve you as He desires. Determine in your heart to allow him the freedom to follow hard after God and encourage him to do so. He shouldn't ever have to feel guilty for prioritizing the Lord over other things that come along in daily life. Rest assured; daily life will fall into place as you both seek the Lord together. Be the support pillar for his covering.

If your marriage is in trouble for whatever reason, first seek the Lord to reveal if you are functioning properly as a wife. If changes are needed, enthusiastically repent and surrender fully to the Lord so you can become who He desires. Ask God to heal both you and your husband of the wounds you may have caused each other. Remember this: you are both doing the best you know how at this point, so leave room for God to move and for both of you to grow.

Open the door for God's power to make the seemingly impossible possible. You have more power available than you may realize at this time. God is very willing to prove Himself strong on your behalf as you surrender

230

to Him. If your husband should find the path to repentance and the Lord begins healing him, allow your husband the freedom to pursue the changes he is being shown to make. Love him through it. Be patient. It will be worth it!

God, You're So Good!

Finally, are you prepared to be overwhelmed when the Lord restores your marriage to the standards He has chosen for a marriage that's bathed in the presence of God? If your heart has presented it to the Lord so He can make it honorable in His eyes, you must prepare yourself to see it transformed - maybe overnight or maybe over a long period of time, but transformed none the less. Are you preparing your heart to be overwhelmed by His goodness, experiencing more than you could ever ask or think on that day? You should be!

[Ask the Lord to show you any way that you are not walking in Jesus' kind of love.]

Chapter 19
MASH icu Study Questions

1) Did you marry your wife to please yourself? Y/N

2) Do you provide a fertile garden in which your wife can grow spiritually? Y/N

3) Do you care at all if your marriage pleases God and represents Jesus to the world? Y/N

4) Are you willing to pay any price requested of you to have God restore your Christ-like office of husband, knowing that it is an office of absolute service and makes no provision for your own comfort zone? Y/N

Father,

Please place Your love for my wife in my heart. Teach me to love her as You love her. Teach me to serve her and cherish her more than life itself. I desire to be like Jesus to her. Complete Your work in me, Lord, that I might glorify You in our marriage. Thank You, Lord!

Chapter 20

Reclaiming Your Office of Father

It is your right, your privilege,
and the road to an honorable legacy.

Luke 17:2 AMP It would be more profitable for him if a millstone were hung around his neck and he were hurled into the sea than that he should cause to sin or be a snare to one of these little ones [lowly in rank or influence].

"You stupid jerk, can't you do anything right?" Don fumed at Carrie, livid with anger as he threw a plate of spaghetti at her so hard that it caromed off her forehead and hit a nearby wall. Carrie felt the welt that was starting to form and retaliated with her own plate that dealt Don a glancing blow to his right shoulder.

"I must have been an idiot to ever marry you," she screamed, following him to the door, while she spewed loud curses at him as she had done so many times before.

Don, almost beside himself, would one more time go to his parents' house or sleep in his car, cursing his wife of five years off and on through a night of fitful sleep.

"At least I don't have to spend the night in jail this time," he thought. He hadn't been the only one to strike a blow, so he knew Carrie wouldn't call the cops on him.

"Don't be afraid, Jessica," Pamela comforted her quivering little sister as they huddled together under the kitchen table. "Mommy locked herself in her room and Daddy's not here, so they won't hurt you."

Your children are not your own as you suppose.
They are Mine.
I have only lent them to you,
so that you can give them back to Me
prepared to live a significant life in Jesus.
Be very careful how you nurture their hearts.
Be very careful how you direct their lives.
You are accountable to Me for their lives.
Guard them, protect them,
guide them to eternal safety.
I will call you to account for the legacy
you have instilled in them.

How dare we expose our children, "God's little hearts," to our stupidity and sin. In God's economy, children are really His; but He gives them to us so as good stewards we can lovingly nurture them with one purpose in mind – that at some point they will choose to serve Jesus with their whole hearts. We are to nurture them so they can hold His hand willingly. That is the real purpose for a husband and wife to bring children into the world. As we are heirs with Jesus, they are our heirs. They are our legacy.

Satan has always attempted to kill the heirs of God, no matter what timeframe they live in. Since the Garden of Eden, he has been devising plans against God's people to disrupt their ability to maintain generations of families devoted to serving God. God purposefully had to keep the blood-line clean to bring us Jesus.

Once God was with us in the flesh through Jesus, Satan mounted a campaign to destroy the Heir of God by enticing a proud king to order that every male child two and under be eliminated, in hopes that God's plan to establish a spiritual King would be thwarted. When that failed, he devised another plan which resulted in the death of God's Son at the cross, not realizing until it was too late that this furthered God's plan rather than prevented it.

Since any of us who have confessed Jesus as Lord are heirs of God and joint heirs with Jesus, the enemy is now after those who have a desire to serve God with all their hearts. They are dangerous to his kingdom. Men, Satan is after your heirs, especially if you have attempted to teach them to live as Jesus lived while walking on this earth. He will either try to make you impotent to teach them, or he will do whatever it takes to derail their lives in Christ. If that doesn't make you determined to dig in with God and allow the Holy Spirit to powerfully move on behalf of you and your children, you need to realign your thinking and your priorities.

Because of the deterioration of the family and the depth to which it has fallen, it is paramount we observe the family unit from God's perspective and not attempt to address all the family combinations that have developed through carnal influences and sin over the years. You, as the reader, must seek the Lord and discover how He will direct you to adapt this chapter to minister to your circumstances and help you recoup what has been lost as you repent and the work of the Holy Spirit brings you in line with the Word of God. Single dads, single moms, and second families that result after divorce are only several of the challenges that need to be faced with wisdom, understanding that grace and mercy from the throne room of the Lord must flow in your direction as you seek how to restore what is out of order.

With the presentation of the ideal family unit as the example, you as a man of God will need to recoup what you can from your personal circumstances and adjust your life to pick up as many broken pieces and people as you can through the power of God, the great Restorer. If you are privileged enough to have an original family that is attempting to serve God, you have a wonderful chance to build a significant heritage from the start, without having to factor in all of the influences of your past mistakes as you surrender to His will from this time forward.

[When a terrible shaking of things becomes evident, when personal and economic stress becomes more prevalent, God is empowering His men to reclaim their proper offices of husband and father as the key to managing their lives through these difficult times. He is raising up stellar examples of the power of the cross of Jesus Christ for the world to see. He is calling forth valiant, courageous men who will stand with Him against the onslaught towards their children and the destruction of the nuclear family. He is clearly defining what it means to live a significant life empowered by the Holy Spirit, building an honorable legacy to present to Him. Chaos in any form cannot touch the man who has been restored to spiritual health.]

The Family

Most people have little understanding of why God set human reproduction in motion, and worse yet, often consider it a by-product, an afterthought of fulfilling one's selfish desires. Parents who are not completely aware of the spiritual nature God has made available to them - whether in the world or the church – have no idea the harm their rebellion causes in the lives of their children in both the physical and spiritual realms. If it is not discovered in this lifetime, it will be a very rude awakening for some parents when they stand before the Lord. God has a plumb line to which He adheres. Anything other than vibrant, Christ-like character developed in our children is unacceptable to God.

237

Through the spiritual impotence of society as a whole and each man individually, this eternal concept has been basically nullified. Generation after generation have failed to reproduce the pattern God designed for us.

The order that God has established for mankind is centered around and implemented through the offices of husband and father. As husbands and fathers, we preside over the unit of government called the family. God, however, has not called us to be disciplinarians or life monitors, who point out all the things our children do wrong in order to teach them what is right in society's eyes. We are to be encouragers and nurturers, pointing them to Jesus and His ways.

Under full submission to the Lordship of Jesus, we are commissioned to guide, direct, pray for, and serve our wives and children as they navigate through the challenges and pitfalls of life. We are to provide fertile soil for them to embrace the fullness of the love of Jesus they observe in us. We are to guide them to spiritual wholeness, so they can represent the power of the cross as a loving, spiritually powerful unit to those around them.

As servant leaders, we are called to invest in our children as the priority right after our relationship with our Lord and our wife. Our purpose is to make it very clear to them throughout their lives that they have eternal worth, and that God Himself designed a very specific plan for their lives. He had good reason for giving them breath.

We are to instill in them a sense of incredible value, not determined by what they accomplish or how well they fall in line with the standards of society; but an intrinsic value established by God. They are simply valuable and should be told often and shown so by our actions. They are valued members of the family and the family of God. (Please don't confuse this with the secular term "self esteem." That's not what I'm talking about.)

They must know in their hearts that their family has a common, eternal purpose of which they are a part, and that their own individual lives have purpose. The bottom line in leading them to a life of integrity is to instill in them that they have the honor of representing Jesus and their family. Children have a sense of belonging when they fully understand their world centers around the safety of an honorable family, and that they have a much bigger destiny than social pressures and peer groups. The plan of God for their lives is far greater than their immediate little worlds.

Above all, it is paramount that children understand they are deeply loved by God and their parents. This kind of love is not only portrayed with words, but with every action every moment of every day from the time they are born.

You and I, men who say that we follow Jesus and have been given an incredible opportunity to have a significant legacy, also have a

238

monumental problem if we have chosen to submit ourselves to the spiritual impotence process of the enemy. If we have violated our offices of husband and father, we are impotent to see the life of Jesus reproduced in our family unit, because of our inability to represent Him, particularly to our children. We will answer for the stewardship of their little hearts, hearts owned by God, no matter what chronological age they may be.

Obviously we will not be held accountable for the individual choices they make, but we will be held accountable for providing the proper atmosphere so they become able to make proper choices while their spiritual growth is being nurtured in our care. That responsibility, in some instances, may cover their complete lifetimes.

We, as men, will be held accountable for the prayer we have presented on their behalf, the counsel they have been given, the choices we have made for their welfare; and the path to which they have been exposed by our exhibition, or lack thereof, of the life of Jesus we lived in their midst. We will be held accountable for the quality of investment we have made in them. There will be no provision made for our excuses, like how hard it would've been to sacrifice, or how we had our own dreams to fulfill. We must do all we possibly can to allow Christ to be seen in us by our children; so they, in turn, can be open to our example and allow the Holy Spirit to make the same changes in them.

Think back, when did you start to allow Satan to rob you of your children?

Let's state something that bears repeating. Spiritual impotence ensures that the one made impotent will lack the intense, obedient, spiritual desires Jesus had. This person no longer has the God-given desires to do the Father's will in all circumstances. This includes playing his part so that Jesus' life can be free to flow in those around him so that none should perish, even if it means extreme personal loss or even death. Most of the time, he doesn't even know how far he has fallen.

The stewardship of children is no exception. An ineffective father, who holds only a large home, big cars, the newest technological gadgets, his children's college degrees, or even their financial security in his hands when his life is judged, will not please God. All of these carnal treasures are insignificant to the heart of Father God if that earthly father hasn't done all he could through his actions, words, prayers, and sacrifice to facilitate the fullness of the life of Christ being reproduced by the Holy Spirit in his children, thus saving them from traveling the road to spiritual impotence.

As far as God is concerned, there is no cost too high to pay for the spiritually potent man who is helping to create a full, vibrant life and a significant legacy in his children. A father's calling is to teach his son to be a godly man and his daughter to be a godly woman, who both know and understand the character of God through his actions. God asks the same

239

price from men that Jesus paid - everything. The perfect fulfillment of the plan of God rests squarely on the shoulders of His men, who are to help reproduce taste buds for Jesus in their children, and hopefully this will continue generation after generation until the coming of Jesus.

Men are commanded to intensely follow the perfect man, Jesus, throughout their lives. That means you! To do less opens the door in every generation to spiritual impotence as Satan attempts to thwart the plan of God by hindering the work men are called to do within the family.

Let's look back at what we've learned regarding the significance God places on the family. Remember, the family unit brings forth kings, presidents, governors, pastors, business and community pillars, teachers, and every other form of leader that is needed to govern His world and fulfill His plan for mankind. If the husband is not following hard after God, the spiritual growth of his children suffers. If a child's spiritual growth is stunted, that child, destined to be a king or a president, will more than likely fulfill his calling by functioning according to worldly standards. If you live to appease your flesh, so will the children unless God intervenes. Instead of learning to be spiritual leaders and Christ-like influences to the world while they grow in the family, they will follow only what they have seen in you, the parent.

Those little children, of whom you've been given stewardship, have a very specific calling on their lives to further the plan of God. They are to become heirs of God and seek to have others become heirs also. You are the one God has chosen to guide those children in their specific direction, first by paving the way for the desire to love and serve Jesus to bubble up in them because they saw Him in you; and then by becoming a study of them to guide them into the calling in which others will see Jesus in them.

Proverbs 22:6 AMP Train up a child in the way he should go [and in keeping with his individual gift or bent], and when he is old he will not depart from it.

The Ideal Profile of a Child Who Functions in a Christian Household
(Remember, this is God's ideal scenario.)

A child who flourishes in an ideal Christian household is an honor to God and is well on the way to creating a legacy of a significant life. Having been studied by the father and mother from birth to determine his (generic use) bent in every aspect of life and then nurtured along those lines, the child flows with relative ease in response to challenges sent his way, heading successfully from one stage of life to the next on the path to his personal, God-appointed calling.

240

Free from the perils of typical worldly peer groups due to life decisions the family has made concerning school and friendships, the Christian child can peacefully navigate his way to godly wisdom and positive social skills. If possible, he is educated at home with a combination of curriculum and life experiences that are tailor-made to bring out the best in him and prepare him to truly function as a contributing member in society. If home schooling is not possible, the family unit is to be the positive influence for the child over and above what is taught outside of the home.

Because of the continual interaction and supportive atmosphere within the family, the Christian child comes to understand his role before God and within his social structure, and the quality of interaction at home carries through into relationships outside the home. He initiates and participates in his circle of influence with integrity and Christ-like character, which continues to grow and develop with age. He is courteous and respectful, and cares for the needs of others as Christ would, completely at peace with his supportive family and in his heart.

Anything you read and study in this book is not a fairy tale, but a process – one that will require much time, devotion, and patience. However, it is well worth it. I assure you this from personal experience. You also don't have to do it perfectly to reap the benefits. We are far from perfect.

What's This Generation Gap Thing?

Did you know that in God's eyes there is no such thing as a generation gap? That whole concept is nothing more than spiritually ignorant, psycho-babble hogwash. Spiritually alive parents who have chosen to invest in their children, considering them more important than themselves and spiritually alive children, who have chosen to invest in the family by the power of the Holy Spirit, have no time to buy into that ridiculousness. The generation gap concept was created by spiritually impotent people, who attempted to incorporate their impotence into guiding and directing their offspring. It is nothing more than a way to excuse their inability to lead their children as they continue to walk in their own ways and thinking. What they really need to do is submit to God through Jesus Christ so the life of Christ can flow in them through the power of the Holy Spirit. It is God's wisdom, strength, love, etc. that we need – not ours. Ours will not truly get the job done. Of course, each generation has its own tastes and preferences; but communication, understanding, mutual love and respect, discernment, and prayer overcome any differences and allow generations to flow together with peace and harmony.

Raising godly children requires a lifetime of investing in them, most of the time in ways that violate our personal comfort zones. It is going to take a lot of surrender of our own ways to the Lord, a lot of prayer, a lot

241

of selfless choices, placing their well being above our comfort; and a lot of heart work. Yes, heart work. However, the eventual satisfaction and rewards of seeing a child being formed by God and the character of Jesus going forth through our children more than compensates for whatever price we may have to pay.

Godly children, who eventually become godly adults, are the goal and heart desire of Father God for both marriage and family. His standards are higher than the world's standards and most of the standards in the typical church of today. He is after the heart of our children, not their compliance. His methods raise the bar in comparison with "normal" child rearing.

[While education is vitally important and must be part of any child's growth process, which child lives a more significant life – one who has all of the degrees in the world, a successful business, and a mediocre life in Christ; or one who has the priorities of God as his priority, dedicating himself to bringing others to significance while having few of the successes of the world?]

Investing in our children God's way creates generations of strong, healthy children, who are full of integrity and inner wealth and capable of not only overcoming any of the challenges that come their way, but actually prospering because of them. Raising children God's way brings proper credit to the life, death, and resurrection of Jesus Christ and a testimony of His eternal work.

Knowing this, each of us has a choice to make at some point in our lives. This moment may be that time for you. You can approach child rearing with an attitude that your children are the ones who need to conform to His ways on their own, or you can settle it in your heart, once and for all time, that who you are and who you become in Christ is a major factor in determining who they will become.

You Cannot Be a Significant Father in Your Own Strength

Every source, human or otherwise, that teaches your child is vying for a place in your child's heart and becomes direct competition to your way; which, hopefully, is God's way of approaching life. Television, peers, video games, school systems, movies, music, books, computer interaction, cell phones, whatever social media is currently in use, even choice of career - in essence, everything your child faces in life - have their own agendas, most of them ungodly. Their constant barrage of choices is so prevalent that there is very little chance of your influence being the continual primary presence in their lives without supernatural help.

242

All you need to do is look around at most children from the ages of twelve to twenty-one. Look at the statistics of wayward children. Observe what influences their life choices. In most cases, they have long ago minimized their parents' values and opinions and replaced them with the values and choices given them by their peers and outside influences. That is Satan's plan.

Look at your own children. How much do they love Jesus and, in turn, really love others? What portion of their future plans includes complete service to Him? Who or what is the greatest influence on their lives? Are you? Other than Jesus, it should be you. How has your spiritual impotence assisted the enemy in gaining access to their thinking and their future – both now and in eternity? You need to fully understand that without the wisdom and power of God and a full-hearted commitment to His ways yourself, you have little chance of being the primary influence in the way your child approaches life even though that's the office you hold in Christ.

God never considers children an accident or an inconvenience. They are never simply an "add on" to a couple's relationship or choice of careers. They are never considered something that would be "nice to have when we are ready." He never, ever considers them a mistake.

In God's eyes, every little heart He creates is vitally important to Him. If He has His way, they are destined to serve Him for eternity after living a life of loving dedication and service to Him on this earth. He has specific plans for each and every little gift of life He gives.

In His eyes, the responsibility of a parent, and especially you as a father, does not end when the child turns eighteen. That is legal foolishness designed by a cold, self-serving world. Only when a child - no matter what age he may be - is in heart service to the Lord through a loving relationship with Him is God's heart satisfied.

A father's responsibility for the spiritual welfare of his children is fulfilled only when they are fully devoted to the Lord and used by God to help Him reproduce that heart in others as their life goal. A spiritually potent father is called to be the guiding force behind his children's life choices by leading them to Jesus through his example. He is to pray for them and live the life of Christ in their midst, so they can become spiritually potent parents who continue the legacy he has established by the power of God as they guide their own children into a significant life in Christ. The role of father never ceases. Hopefully, it will continue in every succeeding generation. That is a significant heritage!

From Our Father's Heart

You need to turn around often to see who is following you.
You also need to check to your right
and to your left to see with whom you are walking.

Often, you need to remember Whom you are really following.
Too often you forget how much you are worth to Me,
not only the value that I place on you personally,
but the value that you are because of what I have made you
and what you have learned.
The only One you are to follow is Jesus;
that you know deep in your heart.
Once that is your only goal,
I can place others to your right and to your left,
people of maturity;
so that your path will be straight and purposeful.
They will not allow you to falter.
You will be safe with them.
Hold them close; value their friendship.
Work for their best interests.
Mark carefully who they are
and allow nothing to separate your hearts.
Study the needs of those whom I have watching you.
They will need to travel some of the roads
that you have already traveled.
Love them deeply. Forgive their immaturity.
Serve them with an honest heart.
Soon they will have others following them
because of the love that you have shown.
If you have no one to your left or your right,
if you have no one following you,
even if the path ahead of you seems clear,
more than likely you are on a path to destruction.
Check your heart. Check your motives.
Check your spirit and the direction it is taking you.
No one on the right path walks completely alone.
It is too dangerous. I would not allow it.
Stop now and see what you might have missed.
Submit to someone who is producing mature, Christ-like followers
and is surrounded by people of integrity.
Repent of your pride.
Become a listener and a follower first, so that one day
you will be mature enough to lead.

*Hebrews 12:1-2 NIV Therefore, since we are surrounded by such
a great cloud of witnesses, let us throw off everything that hinders and the
sin that so easily entangles, and let us run with perseverance the race
marked out for us.*

2) Let us fix our eyes on Jesus, the author and perfecter of our faith, who for the joy set before him endured the cross, scorning its shame, and sat down at the right hand of the throne of God.

Men, if our children are confused by the world's system, hurt emotionally or spiritually, don't understand who Jesus really is, and cannot bask in His love and wonder, it's not their rebellion that's the problem. Don't buy the foolishness of the "generation gap" scenario made up by the carnal minds of the world. We need to face the fact that it's our spiritual impotence alive and at work that has allowed this travesty.

We have been distracted by the trinkets offered to us by the world's system. We have been spiritually dulled. We have no power to exhibit the life of Jesus in their midst. In fact, their confusion and pain may have such little place in our hearts that we find the cost to do what it takes to allow the Lord to create change in their lives too high. If that is the case, we are spiritually made impotent and unable to be awakened enough to function properly in our office of father for the Lord. We have turned over our stewardship of His "little heart" to the world and we actually can't care enough to do whatever it takes to rescue them. It's not that we're doing something wrong in God's eyes; we are doing almost nothing right. What a sad fact that we have no ability to even desire to do what it takes to eliminate their imminent danger. It's time to snap out of it!

In the first chapter of this book, there was a story about Barry and his wife Connie. They did what was necessary to rescue their daughter. Once they decided she was more important than any career, house, job, or social status, the implementation was simple. The reward was incredible. The peace both Barry and Connie experienced after the proper, godly choices were made far outweighed any carnal loss or physical downsizing. They were at peace with God and having established the spiritual potency needed to affect their daughter's life, they were at peace with themselves.

Let's Talk About the Typical, Modern Day Christian Family

I am so very sorry to say that today's typical, modern day Christian family is very much the same as the family that doesn't claim to follow God. The profiles are very similar. In many instances, both parents work to pay for their lifestyle – a lifestyle they've been convinced by outside sources that they absolutely must have - and the children are sent off to school during the day, so they can go to jobs that will help them ensure that they can live the "American dream," or, more recently, simply survive in today's economy.

In a somewhat better scenario, the children are sent to a Christian school which promotes God and His ways rather than a secular school, which has eliminated God altogether. Even this, however, is a deviation

245

from what I believe with all my heart is the way God intended our children to learn – in the home. He gave them to us to raise, to study, to encourage in all facets of life; and to help them discover their purpose in life and stand on a firm, godly foundation. As we help them discover God's desire for their lives, they can eventually specialize in their calling from a place of God-centered, rock solid convictions that came about as we invested our time and energy in their lives.

The Ideal Profile

The ideal profile of a significant, godly family that has overcome the world, is that of a husband and wife who are joined together to glorify the Lord with their marriage and function in the calling they have been given by Him. At the time their first child arrives, both seek the Lord as to the adjustments they will need to make to fulfill the plans the Lord has for the nurturing of that child. Both husband and wife make the necessary adjustments in their lives to allow their focus to remain on the Lord, each other, and now the child. Raising children is not about the convenience of the parent, it's about properly nurturing the child.

The new family now takes on a different dynamic of raising a gift of God as their third priority and ministry, following their personal commitment to God and to each other. In most cases, the husband will need to redefine his business obligations and find a way to properly support his wife in raising the child as the wife modifies her life to fulfill her role as mom. As always, there needs to be room for God to be God. Under special circumstances, possibly even for specific time frames, this typical scenario may need to be modified in untraditional ways. In any case, both parents prayerfully make the decisions that will allow for both of them to nurture their family as God desires. The plan must be tailor-made to suit the needs of the Lord and each individual family. There is no cut and dried formula. The family now takes precedence over either career.

The maintaining of the spiritual offices of husband and father must remain intact. No matter what decisions are made pertaining to the "job description" of both husband and wife in each individual family, there is a bottom line. Each child in the family must be given a clear picture of who God is and enough time must be spent with both parents to impart a clear picture of what a godly man/husband/father, a godly woman/wife/mother and a godly family should be.

Now back to the typical application of parenting. As the husband modifies his life to both provide for the physical needs of the family and be available to participate in the raising of the family to whatever extent is determined, the wife naturally flows into her office of nurturing, loving, and schooling the child in the ways of God and life with full cooperation from her husband. This new family unit is designed to be a united front,

246

implementing the plan of God that none should perish, with each member functioning in his or her individual calling, all desiring to be in God's perfect will. Husband and wife must prioritize the need to invest properly in each child while serving each other.

The husband and wife submit themselves fully to the Lordship of Jesus Christ in this area and gain His wisdom, which allows them to go about the business of teaching their children everything they will need to discover their calling in life. Walking in God's wisdom, they are to study their children to find the bent that most suits them, the way in which they function best. Using that information for teaching, recreation, and discipline, they literally help form the child according to the way God made him, which makes the education process so much easier and gives the child a lifelong, compatible method for learning.

In simpler times here in the United States, it was quite common for children to do their learning in the home. As our nation became industrialized and diversified, fathers worked more and more outside the home. Changes continued to occur in society and outside influences began to erode the close knit bond the family once had. Nowadays, we don't give a thought to the fact that we send our children off to school for their complete, seemingly unquestioned education for approximately thirty-five hours a week or more. As time goes on, there are more and more distractions, more and more destructive influences, more and more ungodly viewpoints and opinions; and we find ourselves spending less and less time with our children. They are more of a target of the enemy than ever before and there is no way to know what it truly influencing our children when they are not with us.

Is it any wonder that the home school movement is gaining momentum? Where else can you establish the kind of family bond it affords? Where else can we be assured that our children will spend the majority of their time with someone who has God's best interests and our children's at heart? Who else will take the time to study our children and specialize in them exclusively? How else can we have a non-stop family adventure where each of us grows in the Lord day after day, side by side?

Although at the writing of this book there is great pressure against it, the home schooling community is still a viable alternative. As long as it is around, it is an incredible opportunity to have wonderful educational and social interactions for both parents and children, a tailor-made curriculum for each one of our children that will bring out the best in them, and the ability to orient everything they learn from a godly perspective. Over the years, it has been found that most home schooled children are competent individuals who possess the ability to communicate and function well in society and in many cases far surpass what the school system can produce.

If there is no other option but to send your children to a public school, you can still influence their reasoning ability, and their personal wealth; but you must become deeply involved with them and their education. It is paramount to make optimum use of your time together when they are not in school and fully understand what is going on when they are there.

Zoning in front of the TV for hours is incredibly detrimental to people of all ages. Get to know computers and the latest cell phones so you're aware of what's available to your children through their use. What's really coming into their minds through those earbuds? Teach them well so they can make proper, godly choices in their viewing and listening habits.

Change your bad habits. Begin new habits that influence your children's environment so they can prosper. If you seek the Lord, no doubt He'd be more than happy to show you solutions that would work well for all the members of your family, especially things that draw you close to Him and each other.

Get to know your children's teachers and what they teach. Also get to know other concerned parents and spend time with them. Begin or join a concerned parents group and become active so there are many voices instead of your single opinion. Do whatever it takes to help with what your children are learning. Never, ever give up your rights to help direct your children's education, if at all possible. God gave you the responsibility and the authority to love them into wholeness. It may be a hard road to travel, but you must travel that road to bring them health as their parent.

There is no question that your investment in them from the time of their birth will go a long way in allowing them to make proper choices throughout their lives. If there comes a time when you have no opportunity to monitor what they are being taught, your prayers for them will help mature the seeds that were planted long ago. You may need to rely completely on God should they be required to be schooled apart from your influence. You can be confident in His protection of them and confident that He will honor your diligence in raising them while you could.

What Do We Do to Help Our Children?

Any attempt to change society or, for that matter, go back to the way things were is foolishness. What is possible, however, is to make an assessment of our personal lives and determine how we can modify them, so they cease to hinder the desires of God's heart mission. When all is said and done, what successes we may achieve by complying with the dictates of society and its drive for accomplishment will fall pale if we have missed the reason the Lord gave us breath. We can live among those who strive for worldly success, but we must follow God and His ways. Always remember that our Father considers His children – and that includes those who have

248

grown into adults - His priority. He wants us, our children, and those we all influence to be with Him for eternity. It's that simple!

[It has been said that some of those children who have been schooled and trained primarily by their parents are not being properly prepared for college. First of all, in most cases, the opposite is true. However, how important is that to God if they are robbed of knowing Him by the world's system?]

Educating a Child to Follow God as He Intended

Most schools, whether public or private (this includes Christian schools,) don't have the ability, time, and/or resources to study and know children the way a mother and father are anointed to know them, especially when those who are teaching our children do not have the same spiritual priorities we do. Because this very important element is missing, the disciplines a child develops become disciplines of compliance to the ways of society, rather than obedience to the ways of God.

Compliance and obedience look the same outwardly, but there is a major difference in the area of heart motive. Compliance is following through with a request or rule because you must, not because you want to do so. Obedience is following through with a request or rule because you know it's the right thing to do and you want to do what's right.

Compliance to the ways of the world always leads to rebellion against the ways of God and we eventually see the deterioration of the society in which compliance thrives. Once a child becomes strong enough, smart enough, or cunning enough to circumvent the pressure applied that forces him to comply in any situation, he stops cooperating. He rebels against whatever is forcing him to do a certain thing, if he doesn't have the desire to do it in his heart.

Romans 6:16-23 NIV Don't you know that when you offer yourselves to someone to obey him as slaves, you are slaves to the one whom you obey- whether you are slaves to sin, which leads to death, or to obedience, which leads to righteousness?

17) But thanks be to God that, though you used to be slaves to sin, you wholeheartedly obeyed the form of teaching to which you were entrusted.

18) You have been set free from sin and have become slaves to righteousness.

19) I put this in human terms because you are weak in your natural selves. Just as you used to offer the parts of your body in slavery to impurity and to ever increasing wickedness, so now offer them in slavery to righteousness leading to holiness.

249

20) When you were slaves to sin, you were free from the control of righteousness.

21) What benefit did you reap at that time from the things you are now ashamed of? These things result in death!

22) But now that you have been set free from sin and have become slaves to God, the benefit you reap leads to holiness, and the result is eternal life.

23) For the wages of sin is death, but the gift of God is eternal life in Christ Jesus our Lord.

The desire for right living is a heritage only those who are living right before God themselves can pass on. Only parents, who are determined to invest in their children the wonder and depth of their own relationship with the Lord, can give the example of right living to their children, which God can use to develop the same desire in them. They can only live rightly because we have set the example and provided fertile soil for our children to thrive in the Lord.

On the other side of the coin, they can only live in rebellion if that is where we have chosen to call home. Remember, rebellion does not mean that a person is openly vicious or antagonistic toward the family or society. Someone in rebellion may be very pleasant, hard working, prospering outwardly, and look very much as if his house is in order; but his heart tells the story. If a person determines "I'm going to do it my way rather than God's way," he's in rebellion.

As far as God is concerned, a person in the state of rebellion is anyone who doesn't have His desire that none should perish as a priority and who also lacks the desire that Jesus had to do His Father's will. Rebellion is the spirit of the world. It breeds impotence when it comes to desiring the things of God. A person who is living right and in obedience to the heart of the Father is the one most beneficial to any society, even though society may not see it that way. If you follow Jesus, you have been given the gifts and wisdom necessary to overcome the world and help your children. Start to walk in them!

Let's Start with Dad

If a father is in rebellion to God, the spirit of rebellion is the dominant spirit within the household. If all areas of his stewardship within the family are not under the Lordship of Jesus Christ, then the father is more than likely making many carnal, worldly decisions and carnal results are permeating the family. This spirit may be dormant or concealed for a time, but it will eventually expose its ugly head. There is no way we should expect our children to flow in true obedience if we don't. If we don't sow proper seed, we will not reap godly results.

250

The spirit of the world is the rebellion that started in the Garden of Eden. Is it any wonder that Christian families who are led by a spiritually impotent father have rebellious, spiritually impotent children? If they haven't rebelled by God's definition of rebellion while they are small, they will as soon as they are able to circumvent the pressure placed on them to comply. It's just a matter of time.

If you don't believe what has been said, simply attend a youth group meeting in most any church, anywhere. Many of the congregation's children, who regularly attend church along with their parents, are like cattle ready to bust down the fences that contain them as soon as they can find a way to do it. Some of them are already on the outside of any form of Christianity, having no desire to come into the fold. Most Christian families send their children to these groups hoping the youth pastor can accomplish in their children what they themselves have failed to do without understanding that he is probably ill-equipped to help them himself.

Somehow, some way, for some reason, the life that's in Jesus hasn't been imbedded in most Christian children. Men, I am convinced this has happened because of our spiritual impotence in providing fertile soil so that their hearts are open to God because they see our hearts open to Him as the example. Our children are smarter than we realize. They take in what we say whether or not it appears that way; and they also watch to see if our actions match our words. It's our actions that speak the loudest and have the most impact. They need a role model and it's us, whether we want the position or not. If a child is ever inclined to live a life of rebellion, we as fathers are held accountable for that life by God.

The child's rebellion is manifesting in great part because of the rebellion in the father that's been passed on. The carnal nature hasn't been eliminated in the child during his formative years, because its destruction through the love and power of Christ has not been the father's priority during those years. The child has been taught the rebellious spirit of compliance by those of us who function in the office of father, yet are spiritually impotent and unable to understand the implications of our own rebellion and unwillingness. More than likely we don't even know that we must do whatever it takes to change, because we are living in compliance to the ways of God ourselves. Remember: going to church and some Bible studies never takes the place of a no-holds-barred investment of love and dedication to God's ways to eliminate rebellion at its core in our own life and in theirs.

Helping Our Children to Overcome Their Rebellion

Rebellion can only be overcome by the blood of Jesus. It can only be eliminated when a person gives himself wholeheartedly to the Lordship of Jesus Christ, inviting the Holy Spirit to rid him of any spirit of the world he still harbors.

The first step in allowing the Holy Spirit to be free to move on behalf of our children is to repent of our own rebellion. If any of us believe that we have no need to repent, we are not only impotent to present the life and character of Jesus to others, we are also deceived and dead wrong as far as God is concerned. Remember, the plumb line is the life of Jesus. That's the life to which our lives will be compared if we call ourselves His followers. There is no repentance necessary if we are always - without exception - as obedient, as loving, and as faithful as He was, never judging Father God or questioning His motives or way of doing things. Anything else is blatant rebellion and consuming pride.

Each of us needs to allow the Holy Spirit to examine every corner of our lives to reveal every ounce of rebellion that exists. Once that's done and we've turned from (repented of) our ways and determined by the power of the Lord to walk in His ways, we can pray confidently for our children, knowing that the rebellion in them can eventually be eliminated because the Lord continually does the same for us. If we have a spiritually potent relationship with Jesus, understand that only He can eliminate rebellion in anyone, and fully understand the power of prayer presented by a father for his offspring, rebellion should not survive in them if we pray diligently and live rightly in their midst. The Holy Spirit will overcome it!

Every person is accountable to God for his own life and his own relationship with Jesus. However, we, as fathers, will stand before the Lord for the diligence we have exerted to be right with God and to exhibit right living in the midst of our families and our circle of influence. If we should stand before the Lord before our child repents of his rebellion, but we have repented of our rebellion against God and His ways and have diligently functioned in our office of father since our repentance by praying for them and living rightly before them, we will be judged on our heart motives.

Investing in Our Children

Jesus made an investment in us. He paid the ultimate price of His life so we could see the kingdom of God and embrace it through Him. Now, every one of us is asked to do the same for our children. We have the incredible honor of investing all the resources we have been given through the life, death, and resurrection of Jesus in them. Please notice, I said privilege, for it is a privilege to guide, direct, and nurture God's future leaders. That is God's perspective of the stewardship of our children.

[We are to prepare our children to love God and overcome the world.
Remember that the most important role you can play is to live the life of
Jesus in their midst so that they give their lives to the Lordship of Christ.

252

They must be born of the spirit or everything they do will be of the flesh, which will produce compliance, not true obedience. Prepare yourself for the time when you or someone else can pray with them to be born again. That will be the beginning of real change and eternal hope.]

God has given us the high honor of studying who our children are. It is our task then to use that information to guide them into a spiritually potent life in Christ, thus fulfilling the plan God has for their lives. This is one of the highest honors God bestows on a man. Having received that honor, what have we done, what are we doing, or what are we going to do to please His heart? You and I will be responsible in eternity for our answer. We are responsible this very day for our actions. There is a joy that is yours if you choose to pay the price. It will honor Jesus.

Life after True Repentance

Once again, if you have chosen to become the father the Lord wants you to be and are submitting yourself to the way He desires you to live, are you preparing to be overwhelmed by the mercy of God as He turns your children's hearts around and instills a desire and delight in them to serve Him? Are you preparing your heart for the day when you, your wife, and your children are moving in concert in the perfect will of God as individuals and together as a family team?

Have you repented of your former life and are you presenting yourself and your children to the Lord? Are you determined to be the father He intends you to be by the power of the Holy Spirit working in you and through you? If you are, then be prepared to be overwhelmed by His goodness! In His perfect timing, as all things fall in place, He will honor His Word and your submission. Prepare your heart to be wonderfully overwhelmed by His goodness!

One Last Thing

Our family has met together at least once a week for as long as we can remember to discuss our unified direction and affirm one another. We meet with the understanding that our time together is to be focused on positive, encouraging conversations, and the struggles of the week are to be left behind. We have determined to use this time to honor God and each other and formally express our love, appreciation, admiration, and commitment to one another.

As often as we can, we each take a turn in affirming the others in the room. (It's really fun when there are non-family members present.) We basically share in one way or another how much they mean to us, what

253

qualities we appreciate in them, and how delighted we are to be a part of their lives. We speak only when we mean it, and take the time to pray for anyone who is having difficulty in affirming someone (sometimes everyone) in the room. We wait as a family until they can.

This commitment has often led to repentance and repair as offenses are laid down, and anger is replaced with a bottom line understanding that everyone is doing the best they can, even if it boils our personal potatoes.

As a father, I have no adequate words to convey how worthwhile these times have been over the years. I am assured in my heart that the Lord has honored our times together and intervened on our behalf, thwarting many attempts by the enemy to create a wedge in our family. I believe that these intimate times together have been instrumental in the steadfast love, understanding, and commitment we have for one another. Go for it, man! You and your family will never be the same.

Chapter 20
MASH icu Study Questions

Please consider the following bottom line questions, which may provide some direction in helping you relate to your children.

1) When was the last time you showed your children that you have unquestioned love for them?

2) When was the last time you encouraged your children for no specific reason other than telling them how well they're doing?

3) When was the last time you told your children they're valuable and they delight your heart simply by who they are?

4) When was the last time you embraced them in your heart as valuable members of your family, and were proud they belonged within its walls of safety?

5) When was the last time you sat down with your children just to get to know them and find out what they value?

6) When was the last time your children had the freedom to talk with you about something without you solving the situation they faced with some form of discipline, or holding what they said against them in some way?

7) When was the last time you assured your children you would always be there for them and love them no matter what they do, with the intent of doing so as your priority?

8) When was the last time you explained to your children how much God loves them?

9) Have you ever met as a family and commissioned each member to go forth in life under his or her specific calling, stating that each member is in full support of the other members?

10) Have you ever anointed your children with oil and commissioned them through the power of God?

11) When was the last time you were vulnerable in front of your children, allowing them to see that you are also under the Lordship of Jesus and trust Him for all your needs?

These questions are only the beginning. Ask the Lord to convict you of those things that are destroying your relationship with your children, and determine in your heart to do something about them.

12) Do you understand that you must repent of your impotent life before God if you want to fulfill your role in leading your children toward a significant life in Christ?   Y/N

13) Do you have a more purposeful direction for your life now that you know the direction you need to take to guide your children?   Y/N

14) Are you willing to pay whatever price is required, so that you can fulfill your office of father to your children?   Y/N

Father,
Please give me Your heart for my children. Allow me to see them as You see them. Show me how I can rescue them and then give me Your courage and strength to do so. Cause me to walk in whatever it takes so they can live a life that is significant in Your eyes. Change me, Lord. Forgive me for my ignorance concerning my responsibility to them. I have violated Your trust in me. I am sorry!

Chapter 21

Reclaiming Your Covenant with Believers

Throughout the Bible, God has been in a relentless pursuit of men through whom He can show Himself strong.

Who Are You Saying Jesus is to Others?

Mark 8:27-30 NLT Jesus and his disciples left Galilee and went up to the villages near Caesarea Philippi. As they were walking along, he asked them, "Who do people say I am?"

28) "Well," they replied, "some say John the Baptist, some say Elijah, and others say you are one of the other prophets."

29) Then Jesus asked them, "But who do you say I am?" Peter replied, "You are the Messiah."

30) But Jesus warned them not to tell anyone about him.

The conversation that took place at that moment changed the lives of the apostles forever. Face to face with Jesus, they had admitted openly what each of them had held in his heart secretly for weeks. "Jesus is the Messiah."

There, they had said it out loud. They knew it; now it was out in the open. He was the Redeemer sent from God. He was the promised Savior of the world. He was God Himself, sent to them in the form of a man. What would have been unthinkable statements only a short time ago were now proclaimed directly to their Redeemer. They had said it out loud and now they wanted to proclaim it to the world. The Messiah had come and they were the first to realize it.

Can you imagine their joy? Every expression, every body movement told Jesus they were going to herald the wonderful news to the whole world. Their Lord had come to them. Their minds raced to think who they would tell first. Every thought centered on how they could spread the news of this wonderful event as quickly as possible. They knew at that moment that it was their privilege to proclaim to everyone that they knew what their forefathers had only dreamed about. What an exciting opportunity! What an astounding privilege! Each one knew he had found his life's purpose.

Jesus, however, could see what was on their minds. He knew what they were about to do. He also knew that if He let them do what they intended to do, they would hinder Father God's plan. If they had their way, factions of both believers and non-believers would arise. They would become formidable opposing forces as the believers attempted to raise Him to the kingly status He so deserved as the Savior. However, it would confuse the issue and possibly halt the crucifixion because they were attempting to crown a spiritual King in the physical realm. He had to stop them. They were trying to mix oil and water; and more important, it was detrimental to the Father's plan.

"Don't tell anyone who I am," He said to their astonishment. In essence, He was saying that no one should know His identity before the appointed time. Some of those who would eventually repent and come to believe in His Lordship would be needed to comprise part of the mob that would demand He be crucified. He had to stand alone, despised and scorned. He went on to show them He had to die. When what had to happen was completed, they would be able to understand why Jesus wanted them to keep quiet during this time.

After all of the prophecies were fulfilled, after all of the enemies of the gospel were defeated, they could and would tell everyone. In that timeframe, Jesus would ask each of His disciples to spend their lives telling people Who He was. In fact, all of His teachings required that if they were to follow Him, they would have to live their lives before people as He did, so that it would be unmistakable Who their Lord was. People who knew them would also know Jesus because of the lives they lived. People "saw" Jesus when they were with His followers. Jesus told them: "If you abide in My word [hold fast to My teachings and live in accordance with them], you are truly My disciples." (John 8:31 AMP)

After the cross, His followers could "say" He was the Messiah not just with their mouths, but by their every action because He lived in them. As part of the heritage that was won for them at the cross, they experienced the same kind of miracles that He did. They imparted His provision to others, filling their needs. Some were imprisoned, slain by the sword, beheaded, or went to the arena, losing their lives for His sake. They loved as their Master loved, lived sacrificially, and laid their lives down without question, following His example. Many in their community saw that Jesus was the risen Christ, the Messiah of the world, because of the lives His disciples lived.

For centuries now, people have said that Jesus Christ is the only Lord. Some say He is Lord because of what they have been told, or what they've read, or what they feel by way of their own interpretations and personal wisdom. Some have proclaimed Jesus and have added their own ideas to His Word, leading others astray through that deception. Many true believers have for centuries, however, proclaimed the fact that He is all that He said He was by living crucified, fruitful, significant lives before others. They have proclaimed loud and clear the finality of the work of the cross and the empty grave by living as He would before those around them. They have not only said that Jesus is Lord of all with their mouths, but they have confirmed all of the power of Calvary's cross by their changed lives.

Now It's Our Turn to be Men of Significance to God and to Others

So now it all comes down to each of us who is living in these appointed times and given the command to proclaim what we know in our hearts to be true from the Word of God. We are commissioned to tell those who have not heard clearly that Jesus is Lord. With that commission in mind, this question must arise: Who are you "saying" that Jesus is? Does your unsaved neighbor have an opportunity to know Him because of the way you conduct your life? How about your boss or your work associates? Better still, who is the Jesus that is proclaimed to your family and, subsequently, by your family?

Jesus lived and died for each of us out of a love that is beyond our wildest imaginations. His mercy allowed us to come to Him when we deserved only condemnation for our actions. He now asks you and me to tell others of that love. You can tell them loudly and clearly by demonstrating that kind of love in your prayer closet, your communication of the good news of the Gospel; and most importantly, through your example. Live His life before them and they will see Jesus.

Become Trustworthy Men of God

Acts 15:36-40 AMP   And after some time Paul said to Barnabas, Come, let us go back and again visit and help and minister to the brethren in every town where we made known the message of the Lord, and see how they are getting along.

37) Now Barnabas wanted to take with them John called Mark [his near relative].

38) But Paul did not think it best to have along with them the one who had quit and deserted them in Pamphylia and had not gone on with them to the work.

39) And there followed a sharp disagreement between them, so that they separated from each other, and Barnabas took Mark with him and sailed away to Cyprus.

40) But Paul selected Silas and set out, being commended by the brethren to the grace (the favor and mercy) of the Lord.

Paul couldn't trust Mark at this time in his spiritual walk. Mark had deserted them when the going got rough in another city, so Paul knew it wasn't wise to have someone who had previously not covered his back on this next journey. He could love him; but he was going into places where it would be dangerous and Satan would be setting traps, so he couldn't afford to risk his God-given mission because of the weakness of someone else. His discernment of the character of Mark and his subsequent action of taking someone else with him had little to do with fear; it had a lot to do with wisdom.

This brings up a highly underrated element in the body of Christ - associations. The flagrant disobedience and heartbreak of being unequally yoked with those who are not in Christ needs no discussion. The warning against covenanting with unbelievers is quite clear throughout the Word. (Still, many believers choose to ignore this warning, usually for their own gain, and suffer the consequences.) Something else that is rarely considered, however, is the astounding folly of joining with someone who claims to know and follow Christ, yet has proven himself to be untrustworthy in the past.

Violations of a trust are a very big deal to God. How can He use those He can't trust? How can anyone see Jesus in those who have selfish, carnal attitudes? How can those who call themselves followers of Jesus consistently violate every principle established at the cross as they continue to hurt their brothers and sisters in Christ and those in the world? God considers it a violation because it misrepresents the character of Jesus!

There are such people in the body of Christ. They have proven themselves unworthy of our trust. They have hidden agendas and ulterior motives for joining with us and with others. They will violate any trust for their own good, sometimes causing great harm. They will use people and ministries for their own gain or to enhance their reputations or their spiritual standing with others.

If you have been harmed by such wounded people, you must forgive them; but be wise in your associations with them. If they have seen their error, you need to make every attempt to restore your relationship and love them as you would love any brother or sister in Christ who has repented of their mistakes; and at the same time, walk cautiously as you observe their changes.

However, until they prove themselves trustworthy again over time, it would be foolish to make associations with them at any level where there is the potential to cause problems for the reputation of Christ, your family, or your ministry. Paul would have placed his life and his mission in jeopardy if he had taken Mark with him on a potentially dangerous journey. Mark needed to grow past his spiritual immaturity.

[Remember, others are functioning as best they can. You are to exhibit the character of Jesus to them. It is His job to change them.]

The idea of joining only with those who are proven trustworthy - those who only desire the heart of Jesus in their lives- is becoming more and more important as God's timetable plays out. We must always nurture those who are young in the faith, but allow ourselves to become vulnerable only to those who have a Christ-like maturity. The character traits of Jesus will be the litmus test in choosing friends and making associations as the world becomes darker and the body of Christ is the light that the darkness must put out.

Time to Move in the Love of Jesus

With that in mind, it becomes necessary to consider minimizing any vulnerability you now have with people not worthy of trust, so that God can bless you with His presence in what you do, just as Paul did. It's time for you to allow God to connect you with those who understand what it is to live in covenant with God and with others. On the flip side, if you have violated any trust in the past, it would be wise to do whatever it takes to make things right with whomever you have offended before you meet God face to face. Enough said!

<u>Examining the Early Church Blueprint</u>

The Life of Jesus

Jesus loved deeper than any person ever born of woman and yet those who were spiritually impotent in the world saw Him as a threat to the way they wanted to live. His single direction for right living boiled the potatoes of those who had other ideas of what was right and wrong. His immovable commitment to the way His Father in heaven chose to express His love for all of mankind demanded that either a person conform to the provision of the cross or walk away from it. He walked with those who

261

chose to walk as He did. In fact, His establishment of an immovable benchmark for God's right kind of life was so disagreeable to the spiritually impotent, they had to eliminate its Proponent, hoping that it would go away. Jesus was in the way of those who chose to follow their own version of right and wrong. He still is!

The Cross of Christ

In the same way that the life of Jesus was a stumbling block to the way the world wanted to live when He walked this earth, the unyielding cross of Christ is detestable to the way the world desires to function wherever the cross is firmly planted. It is an undeniable threat to those who are opposed to God's right way of living and the pattern He set for eternal association with Him. It is the burr under the saddle that will never go away and the light that can never be extinguished. It is the center point of all eternity. All those who lived before it was planted on an obscure hill called Calvary looked forward to it, whether they knew it or not. All those who were born after it hosted the mangled body of Jesus will look back on it, either with immense gratitude or overwhelming remorse.

From Our Father's Heart

You need to begin the quest for those whom you can trust.
The time is coming when it will be very important
to understand who your friends and holy alliances are.
Spiritual discernment will be the key to your safety.
Be especially aware of those who seem to be with you,
but have a hidden agenda
and are out to destroy the work that I have given you.
Watch for jealousies.
Cherish your anointing.
Beware of those who only want to distract you
and consume your time in endless controversies.
In the times ahead, I will send many alliances your way.
Mark them by their integrity regarding My Word.
Watch their lifestyles.
Judge their priorities according to My Word.
Allow Me to show you truth
concerning their positions in your life.

Holy Alliances

As a remedy to the weakness and immaturity within the body of Christ and in preparation for the coming perilous times, God Himself is reestablishing the life and character of Jesus in His church through holy

262

alliances, kinsman friendships, and covenant relationships. He is taking charge of the relationships He plans to join together to accomplish His work in the near future. Becoming trustworthy and joining with those who are trustworthy is the pattern of the first century church. You will want to make yourself ready for this time by becoming a trustworthy follower of Jesus, if you desire to find favor within groups of significant people who are also trustworthy.

In the coming, more-than-likely very challenging days - if you are trustworthy yourself - watch for specific people the Lord will place in your midst as a holy alliance. If you are fickle, foolish, immature, and self-consumed in your relationships, don't expect the Lord to bring holy alliances your way, because He will not allow you to harm His children and distract them from fulfilling His purpose for their lives. Until you repent of your ways and have a heart to live your life for the benefit of others and for the benefit of God's plan, you will basically find yourself on your own or in league with others just like you. I would call these people the spiritually insignificant, cowering masses. It's your choice.

If however, you desire to live the way Jesus lived, God will place you with others of the same heart and mindset, Holy Spirit-inspired obedience, and like-minded direction. You will be given the opportunity to enter into an unbreakable alliance with them, sealed, protected, and enforced by God Himself for the purpose of accomplishing specific tasks and Holy Spirit-led projects to further the kingdom of God in these last days. It will be the most wonderfully fulfilling, remarkable time since the cross and the covenant heart of Jesus spilled out spiritual integrity over those who could receive it. Husbands and wives who understand that they have been joined together for far more than living in moderate harmony and success, business associates who have only the goals and desires of God as the basis for their association, friends who establish a covenant relationship in order to accomplish God's plan for their lives will soon be the norm or survival will be non-existent for believers in need.

God Loves Honorable Covenants

God has established the most powerful, unbreakable, eternal covenant with us through Jesus! Before that was accomplished, Father God established many other covenants with trustworthy Old Testament figures to propel mankind closer to the cross of Christ. He established covenant in long ago generations for their protection and safety, as they would covenant one with another. He is doing the same today.

God Himself will anoint and reinforce your relationship with Him in very visible ways. He will anoint your marriage so that it is a brilliant representation of the relationship between Jesus and the church. He will anoint your children and your children's children to follow in the footsteps of Jesus. He will bring forth holy business alliances for the purpose of fulfilling His will and flowing resources to accomplish His plans through trustworthy stewards. He will create kinsman friendships for the protection of you and your family during perilous times. He will do all of this so His plan on earth can go forth and because you have submitted to Him to make you trustworthy with the stewardships He has given you.

God is in the business of doing these things not only so that none should perish, but also that they will be brought to maturity in Him. It is part of His plan that spiritually potent men properly oversee the offices He has given them so that others can see Jesus. This kind of life has never been expected on our part, because He hasn't had enough trustworthy men to make it clearly visible. That is not the way it will be for the coming church, as they wait for the return of Jesus and live His kind of life while they wait. His real church, those who allow His life to flow through them, will be engulfed with powerful holy alliances, unbreakable covenant relationships among valiant men, women, and children, and family-like kinsmen friendships that overcome anything the enemy has in store for them.

Someone Who Knew the Power of Covenant Relationships

A while ago, I had the privilege of leading a motorcycle gang member to the Lord. The biggest obstacle that had to be overcome in showing him that he needed Jesus was his observation of those who said they followed Him. He spent several weeks observing the church and after talking, listening, and questioning their hearts, he wanted nothing to do with them. He saw them perform as back-stabbing, untrustworthy hypocrites, very much different from the One they said they followed.

You see, he was in covenant with his fellow bikers, who abided by a code of honor. Granted, it was their own code and form of honor, but it was followed to the letter and rigidly enforced. They had committed to always cover their brother's back. Because of this, he knew and understood covenant associations the same as Paul did in his generation. He saw that the church had no grasp of how to stand for one another against all opposition. As he observed the church, his comment to me was, "I have hundreds of people who have promised to give their lives for me if necessary. I have stood back to back with people I could trust with my life when it was on the line. There isn't one person here in this building that would do that for me or for anyone else."

He was right! The body of Christ is not in covenant with one another, even though we say we are. We violate friendships and shoot our wounded, all in the name of Jesus. Worse than that, we violate our promises to God even though we are in covenant with Him. We have told Him that He owns our lives and then we function daily as if we care very little about the example for living that He set for us. It's time we started to act as He did or stop saying that we follow Him, because we don't live it.

Holy alliances and covenant relationships among valiant men and women of God, who are joined in fellowship, are the actual church of Jesus Christ and the exhibition of His character. If you examine the blueprint God established for the early church, you will discover that it's a group of men and women who established covenant relationship for the purpose of proclaiming and living the life, death, and resurrection of Jesus Christ before one another and the world.

(Note: Our novel, <u>A White Stone,</u> is an inspiring testimony of covenant relationships and holy alliances lived out to the glory of God during very perilous times, similar to those that are on the horizon. You will find this book and other tools for growth on our website, www.the101group.com.)

Chapter 21
MASH icu Study Questions

1) Are you a trustworthy friend to others, as trustworthy as Jesus is with your life?   Y/N

Why or why not? Journal or discuss.

Father,

I really don't understand the concept of laying my life down for another and yet I say that I'm a follower of Jesus' ways. I have violated the commands You have given me regarding my relationships with others. I have lied to You about caring for even those close to me, when I said that I loved them. I am a threat to them by my selfishness. Forgive me, Lord. Make my heart the same as the heart of Jesus toward others. Thank You, Lord!

Chapter 22

A Significant Fellowship

You are to be the church.

Acts 4:29-35 NIV *"Now, Lord, consider their threats and enable your servants to speak your word with great boldness.*

30) Stretch out your hand to heal and perform miraculous signs and wonders through the name of your holy servant Jesus."

31) After they prayed, the place where they were meeting was shaken. And they were all filled with the Holy Spirit and spoke the word of God boldly.

32) All the believers were one in heart and mind. No one claimed that any of his possessions was his own, but they shared everything they had.

33) With great power the apostles continued to testify to the resurrection of the Lord Jesus, and much grace was upon them all.

34) There were no needy persons among them. For from time to time those who owned lands or houses sold them, brought the money from the sales

35) and put it at the apostles' feet, and it was distributed to anyone as he had need.

Far from being huddling, fearful masses who prayed for protection from all the bad guys, the church of Jesus Christ flowed in the brilliant light of the life of Jesus. Prayers for boldness replaced prayers for protection. Petitions of love for the best interest of others replaced self-serving prayers for personal safety or gain. The church of Jesus Christ, as individuals, looked like Jesus, acted as Jesus would act; and prayed as Jesus taught them. In its purity, it was the embodiment of the One they said they followed. They were called Christians because they showed others the character of Christ in the way they lived.

Over the years and throughout the centuries since the cross, God has raised up fellowships of people, joined together to proclaim the death and resurrection of Jesus and exhibit the lifestyle He gave them. People, who understood the covenant into which they had entered with God and subsequently with each other, gathered to study the Word God had given them and give praise to Him by caring for His honor and each other's needs. The Word of God called these believers His church.

Fellowships were started by men and their families to encourage one another and to study and exhibit the purity of the life of Jesus. Often an individual man would sense a calling on his life to lead others into a relationship with his Lord and accept the responsibility of seeing that they were discipled, nurtured in their newfound faith, and held close while they grew in Christ. Under his tutelage, responsible men, who exhibited significant lives before God, would be called upon to assist him in his vision and implement the duties of caring for the fellowship with him.

The leader and these men were stellar examples, chosen by God to represent Jesus to the world through the lives they lived and the way their families honored God. It started with a man who, along with his family, lived a significant life before God. He gathered men around him who had the same understanding and ability to live a significant life before God, who then taught other men and their families to do the same.

Titus 1:6-9 AMP [These elders should be] men who are of unquestionable integrity and are irreproachable, the husband of [but] one wife, whose children are [well trained and are] believers, not open to the accusation of being loose in morals and conduct or unruly and disorderly.

7) For the bishop (an overseer) as God's steward must be blameless, not self-willed or arrogant or presumptuous; he must not be quick-tempered or given to drink or pugnacious (brawling, violent); he must not be grasping and greedy for filthy lucre (financial gain);

8) But he must be hospitable (loving and a friend to believers, especially to strangers and foreigners); [he must be] a lover of goodness [of good people and good things], sober-minded (sensible, discreet), upright and fair-minded, a devout man and religiously correct, temperate and keeping himself in hand.

9) He must hold fast to the sure and trustworthy Word of God as he was taught it, so that he may be able both to give stimulating instruction and encouragement in sound (wholesome) doctrine and to refute and convict those who contradict and oppose it [showing the wayward their error].

270

If That Pattern Thrived Today

If the pattern on the previous page thrived today, the church would take on a Christ-like persona. It would consist of men who are living out their offices of husband and father in covenant with one another, joined together to live rightly before God and teaching all who choose to listen to do the same. It would exhibit families who are committed to honoring God with their lives and personal wholeness, prospering in the life of Jesus and focused on joining together for the good of others and each other. The members would seek the best interests of those around them before their own while boldly proclaiming and defending the honor of Jesus. It would be a fabulous, dynamic portrayal of the character of Christ.

The church would be a place of safety and healing for anyone who sought it and a place of conviction to those who wanted their own way. It would be the expression of the life of Jesus Christ, lived out within its fellowship and in the midst of those around it. It would be a place where you would make the choice to either follow the life pattern that Jesus established or find another place that didn't expect you to be an imitator of Christ. Full of the compassions of Jesus and endued with the power of the Holy Spirit, this body of believers would be a shining representation of the incredibly misunderstood love of God to a lost and dying world which would either embrace the life of Christ they saw in it or be repelled by its brilliance. *[For further study, read the entire book of Titus.]*

What Has Happened

I believe the heart of God has been broken over and over as on-fire young men enter pastoral school with a calling on their lives to lead others to a deep relationship with Jesus and graduate with much knowledge on how to build a church, but little zeal left for Jesus and His first century ways. Somehow, the purity of His heart was converted into a mechanical formula for building a church in the ways of the pharisaical experts over the years. Now, I realize this is not always the case, but it seems to happen often enough to warrant addressing it as pertinent to our study.

If recent history repeats itself, this young pastor is now thrown into the mainstream tide. Beginning as a youth pastor because he is young, he is told that numbers are important and that programs and methods will make his numbers respectable. He is sent to many conferences and seminars on church growth and the needs of youth and how to inspire them to follow in his footsteps in regard to what it means to be a Christian.

Over the years, he becomes fully indoctrinated in the ways of his particular denomination or non-denomination and eventually becomes a senior pastor, who leads others in the way he was taught to follow Jesus. As a leader of others, he guides them into what he knows, which is based on what he was taught in a Bible college or seminary. Sincere, dedicated, but trapped in the vice of tradition, he gives what he has been given by those who initially dampened his zeal and taught him how to build a church, rather than a relationship with the Lord. This pattern has been repeated over the years to this present day.

The Church of Christ and the Cross

To the Pastor

Pastor, I'm sure you're well aware of your accountability before God for the spiritual lives of those with whom you've been entrusted. You know that you will stand before Him one day and be judged as a teacher of His Word and want nothing more than to please Him. Because of your integrity, you won't want to be known by God for preaching a watered-down version of the work of the cross and exhibiting a weak Christian lifestyle. If you have read this far, more than likely the Holy Spirit has been calling to you for some time; so your heart is ready for any changes needed, and getting right with God is far more important than offending those who would stop you from doing so.

If you're still not convinced you need to make the changes presented in this book, I pray you'll spend some time with the Lord to hear His heart. Having a reputation with God as someone who focused on building a large but lukewarm congregation will not bode well for any pastor. If you are not willing to provide an atmosphere for those who come to you so they can become all they can be in Christ Jesus, please examine your heart. It will benefit those in your care to be led by someone who will give them an opportunity to live wholeheartedly for Christ, especially by his example.

If you do not want to live up to your potential in Christ, you are a stumbling block to those who follow your example and your teaching. If you are a blind guide leading others to destruction, you will be held accountable for your life and the lives of those you say you serve. I'm sure you're well aware that this is no game as far as Father God is concerned.

Hosea 4:6a AMP My people are destroyed for lack of knowledge; because you [the priestly nation] have rejected knowledge...

2 Peter 2:3 NIV In their greed these teachers will exploit you with stories they have made up. Their condemnation has long been hanging over them, and their destruction has not been sleeping.

272

Let's for a moment consider the welfare of the pastor and his stewardship before God. If he is spiritually impotent because of fear and his impotence infects his congregation, is he not in grave danger? Aren't his actions in violation of the Word of God? Shouldn't he and everyone else who teaches the Word of God be more concerned about offending God than offending people? If not, could the church itself have succumbed to the lies of the enemy?

James. 3:1 AMP Not many [of you] should become teachers (self-constituted censors and reprovers of others), my brethren, for you know that we [teachers] will be judged by a higher standard and with greater severity [than other people; thus we assume the greater accountability and the more condemnation].

Pastor, isn't it your job to provide a fertile place for those who come to you to learn to love Jesus and represent Him in their circle of influence? Your job is not to be the biggest, the best, the most well-known, or the most popular. You are to guide others to Jesus and equip them for present and future service. You are to be a proponent of reestablishing the offices of husband and father in the men in your charge, a dominant force for revival by living that life yourself and guiding your men to Christ-like living in all they do. Whatever stops you from rebuilding your fellowship according to the first century blueprint of believers must be eliminated from your life, or at least modified so God can accomplish His plan.

A very good pastor friend of mine challenged his leadership to live rightly before the Lord. He said something like this. *"Maybe the skepticism in the church comes from the people in the pew seeing those who are over them in the Lord doing things they should not do. As ministers and leaders in the church, we, more so than others, should seek to 'avoid every kind of evil.' I'm going to ask all of my leaders to come forth, elders, pastoral staff, ministerial staff. I want this church to be able to believe in its leadership. I want to do away with any skepticism, so I am going to give a charge to these standing before you. As leaders, this message should cause us to either rejoice because you are already living this way, or repent of the things in your life that should not be there; or if you cannot do either one of those two things - you cannot either rejoice or repent - then you need to resign."* **Wow!**

Pastor, as you know, you are to be the example to men who are hearing the call of God on their lives and in the process of regaining their spiritual identity. If your marriage is out of order, it must be fixed. If your children are not serving Christ, do whatever you need to do to bring them back to Him. If your board of directors or your elders hinder your ability to guide others to the power of the cross and the absolute wealth found in Jesus, please reevaluate your association with them.

Join with men who have repented of their impotence and are being healed. God is waiting for you with open arms. Allow Him to show you any areas that need to be addressed within your fellowship, and then make whatever changes are necessary in your life that will allow you to follow His criteria for your office of guiding others to Him.

Walk Fearlessly with Your God

Never fear what will happen if you rebuild your church or build another church on the foundation of the crucified life, one whose men are shaking off the impotence in which they've lived for so long. Never fear challenging your congregation to follow hard after God and doing what is necessary in their lives to rescue their marriages or their children. You may lose those members who are playing religious games with God; but, in reality, those members have been a stumbling block to the work of God all along.

There are hungry hearts who really desire to follow Jesus that need your focused effort. You may lose a significant number of warm bodies with cold hearts if you teach, preach, and live the crucified life; but you'll find yourself in fellowship with warm, loving hearts toward God. You'll become an honorable leader and a valiant guide to those walking in covenant with God and with others. Most of all, you'll be pleasing God. You'll be able to present your significant life to Him face to face and many others will do the same because of your integrity.

To the Youth Pastor

It is quite important to say that your accountability to God is great, but it more than likely has become minimized in your eyes if you learned an inaccurate concept of what God desires in a youth group. If that is the case, in all likelihood, you are ineffective in guiding youth to a deep, intimate relationship with Jesus, because you never learned how to go there yourself. If the typical church growth traditions hold true, most demands on you as a youth pastor center around the numbers you can acquire, rather than on the quality of the relationship you are helping the youth to develop with the Lord. If you were to observe your youth group from God's perspective, your work to this point could look to Him as little more than a spiritual baby sitting service and a relatively safe social setting for young people. Unfortunately, they remain far from the intimate walk the Lord desires for them. Are you content with that?

Possibly, you have acquired a belief that a deep, wealthy relationship with Jesus comes only after a person grows past being a teenager and into adulthood. That belief is straight from the pit of hell! It is not true and never will be. If you are not leading the youth with whom God has entrusted you toward a continually deeper relationship with Jesus and equipping them to lead others to Him, your ministry may well be of little effect in advancing His kingdom with power.

God desires to move on the hearts of young people. He desires them to be equipped for the perilous times and seasons that are on the horizon. They are the future. He is calling them to be Christ-like, not like the world while spouting Christian phrases and sporting Christian symbols on their t-shirts. What is so amazing is most young people - without knowing it - desire a deep, meaningful relationship with the Lord. They are looking for the love that can only be found in Jesus. Most of them are rebelling against the kind of world you are asking them to partially embrace. Most of them are craving the understanding of their personal value and want real direction for their lives. Are you helping that desire or hindering it by preaching a mediocre life through your teaching or the example of your life?

Young people are often viewed as having little desire or even as incapable of walking in deep spiritual wealth and Christ-like character. Somehow - but very understandable if you know Satan's plot to hinder the work of God - the idea that God intends our youth to emulate Jesus in all they say and do is not even considered by many youth pastors. More than likely you, their youth pastor, were never guided to seek a deep relationship with Jesus by your mentor or youth pastor. Is it possible that you are teaching others to become impotent adults? Are you in spiritual danger yourself and leading others into spiritually dangerous waters?

If the above scenario describes you, you need to change! It is God's ardent desire because of His great unconditional love for you! Jesus deserves more from you! So do the young people in your group.

It's time to truly learn how to love Jesus. It's time to seek Him until you receive His heart for young people. You need to become like Him, so others can see who He really is and desire Him themselves. After you've been with Him and after He is your only priority, then take an assessment of your ministry. You need to look around and see if you have the freedom to function according to the plan God desires for you and for the sake of those He desires to bring to you.

God Desires to Use You!

If you love Jesus deeply and have a desire to lead others to a steadfast intimacy with Him, God has appointed you for this time. In the coming days, the youth groups in this land will need to be places of safety.

They will be rescue missions from the world, as they should have been all along. As men respond to their office as fathers and begin investing in their sons and daughters, they will need trustworthy youth pastors to reinforce and teach what God is providing to heal their children. Loud music, videos, and spiritual games will not be enough to hold the hearts of these troubled people. Fathers will not allow you to destroy what God desires to do in their sons and daughters through any immaturity or ignorance on your part. You need to have the real Jesus on tap. You must be willing to invest in these young people with the same heart, the same passion, and the same dedication He has.

You have an incredible opportunity to participate with God in turning the heart of your generation toward Him. Cease conforming to the stereotype of who you are to be if you're a youth pastor. Find out what God considers successful and go after it, no matter what the consequences may be. If your pastor doesn't see the need for a vibrant, on fire, praying youth group that's willing to pay the price to hold young people close while they are on their way to spiritual healing, pray for him. If, over time, your fellowship can't provide the support you need to train up young men and women to be all they can be in Christ, you may need to relocate to help fulfill the Lord's desires for His young people.

Chapter 22
MASH icu Study Questions

1) Are you willing to make whatever changes are necessary that will allow you to follow God as a true leader of others?   Y/N

If not, why not? Journal or discuss.

2) What changes do you now know you need to implement?

Father,

Break my heart. Cause me to see my life as You see it. I claim to be a teacher who represents You and presents the life of Jesus so that others can become like Him. I need to make changes. Give me the power to do so. Thank You, Lord!

Phil. 1:11 AMP May you abound in and be filled with the fruits of righteousness (of right standing with God and right doing) which come through Jesus Christ (the Anointed One), to the honor and praise of God [that His glory may be both manifested and recognized].

Chapter 23

Valiant Men of God

There is never a time to be angry, condescending, or combative when you are moving in Christ.

"The price may be everything," Barry said to Nick and Judy, as he held Connie's hand under the restaurant table. Connie silently prayed as she and Barry had done so often for the harried couple, ever since Barry had told her about the conversation he had with Nick in the gym. Together they had covenanted to hold Nick, Judy, and their son Tony before the Lord until somehow the family would find answers for their lives.

The phone call from Nick on Wednesday to set up this meeting thrilled the thriving couple. Knowing that reaching out for help was the beginning step to healing, they enthusiastically responded to Nick's desire to meet and prayed they would have unlimited love toward the couple and their son, vowing to do whatever it took to help them through this time.

Nick and Judy reassured Barry that they had counted the cost. They knew that healing for Tony would begin with them and they were willing to do whatever it took to rescue him from his life, just as Barry and Connie had done with their daughter Sarah. Judy gave Connie a determined glance. Connie smiled at her, which reassured Judy they were no longer alone.

"OK," Barry began. "Let's get on with this." Nick and Judy looked intently at Barry, anticipating their game plan. "Our pastor, Pastor Gary, has been told by the Lord to make his fellowship one of significance to the Lord. He has restructured everything to address the impotence of men and the restoration of families. Part of that plan is the rescue operations for the children of those men and women who hear the call of God and choose to do something about it. Before we came here tonight, he offered whatever resources he and those who are with him have to help you. There are about twenty of us so far, who have covenanted everything we have to get right before God ourselves and help anyone else who chooses to do the same. Some of them are part of our youth pastor's adult advisory team. They have already started praying and some of the guys who are heading for significant lives in the youth group are ready to invest in Tony. They are on their way to overcoming the ways of the world, and want to help him. We are at your disposal and we're all going to walk through this with you."

Throughout the eventful evening, a blueprint of hope was laid out before Nick and Judy, one that would put one more family back on the path to significance as God intended. Who would have thought that in a corner table of a small restaurant in an obscure town, the eternal work of the cross of Christ and the humble people who submitted themselves to that work would once more thwart the enemy's plans against a family of God by the power of the Holy Spirit? One more family now had the opportunity to journey the path toward a significant life in Christ, which would more than likely impact many in generations to come.

You Need to Support Your Fellowship and Your Pastor

Men, it's time to please God and lead others to do the same! The marriage covenant and the family unit that is guided by a Christ-like husband and father is God's foundational unit for a strong fellowship. Living in concert with the Word of God, Christ-centered families clearly demonstrate the relationship Christ has with His church to the unbelieving world. It is the tangible presentation of the life of Christ in action.

If you belong to a body of believers who understand the demonstration and the accountability of their lives before God and you are led by a pastor who is focusing on addressing the impotence of men and the restoration of families in his congregation, you need to get behind that work with every fiber of your being and all of the resources you have. Now is not the time to play the typical church game. Father God is waiting for you to respond to His heart and His plans for the coming times. It is vital that you invest yourself and your family's resources to further the vision of your pastor and his calling to make the family unit the backbone of your fellowship. Join with him and other men to set up a game plan for a strong fellowship that is capable of receiving men and families who need to turn their lives around and are willing to surrender to the Holy Spirit to do so.

You may possibly decide to implement our MASH icu program to help facilitate a strong men's support group. The world needs to see godly families in action under the leadership of a godly pastor, working with God-focused men who have responded to the present call to build significant lives to present to their Lord. God wants to use your church to reach those who need to see Jesus in action.

280

The world has no answers. The cold, dead church has only a form of godliness yet denies His power. God, however, is re-establishing fellowships of covenanted believers, led by men who desire to leave a significant heritage and exhibit a pattern of right living before God. He is assembling bodies of men and their loved ones who have made the commitment to be restored as fertile representatives of Jesus Christ in fellowships that have fully submitted to God, so the life of Jesus can flow unhindered in each and every member. Today's world needs to see that kind of fellowship. Because there is such a desperate need, God will bring His presence to His kind of fellowship in order to restore His people and honor the work of the cross. It is the spiritual antidote for the rapidly developing apostate church, which was foretold as part of the closing hours of God's timetable.

Church can no longer be just a Sunday thing for you if you name yourself as a follower of the ways of Jesus. You can no longer demand that the pastor spoon feed you what the Holy Spirit is saying to everyone who will listen. You have an obligation to hear from God for yourself and your personal circle of influence. Your spiritual maturity will allow your pastor to devote his time to prayer in seeking direction for his flock and its impact on your community rather than babysitting its members.

Full of the Holy Spirit and in an advocate alliance with other men who understand their spiritual responsibility, your commitment to walk in a significant life in Christ in concert with your commitment to your pastor, your family, and the other families in your fellowship will allow that fellowship to become a place of safety and growth for others who need to see Jesus in action. It's time to take responsibility for who you are in Christ, devote yourself to the tasks He gives you; and help others with their lives. You need to do whatever it takes and give whatever is needed to help your fellowship become significant to those who need to see a living example of the power of the cross of Jesus Christ, if you desire to present a significant life to God yourself. You need to become an integral part of making your fellowship effective so the work of God can go forth under the full and complete Lordship of Jesus Christ and in His kind of service to others.

Time to Move Very, Very Carefully and Only in the Love of Jesus

However, if your pastor is not heading deep into the heart of God and conducts church in a business-as-usual fashion, initiating programs (the outward appearance) to get the job done without focusing on the development of Christ-like character and commitment in his men (the inner arena where God assesses things,) you may need to find one who is. You need to find other men who are seeking hard after God and join with them in fellowship. As I said before, you may possibly be led to set up your own MASH icu group. Your spiritual life and the lives of your family depend on it. To remain in a weak, worldly fellowship that is led by a pastor who cannot help you get to where God is calling you is deadly to whatever God is doing in you. You have two choices: One, if God tells you to stay where you are, then you need to pray so that your pastor will truly submit himself to God and then trust the Lord to supply other avenues for you to grow in Christ. Two, if He tells you to go, then find a church that's functioning the way the church of Jesus Christ should function, which includes a positive support, sold-out men's group, a vibrant women's ministry, and for the sake of your children, a dynamic youth group that understands the need for each participant to commit to the complete Lordship of Jesus.

Traditions serve no purpose if they minimize the power of God and His desire for those who are in Jesus. Denominations that once may have been vibrant and alive in Christ, but have since become not much more than Sunday morning time fillers, are harmful to you if you really desire to move on with God. They will eventually rob you of what the Lord desires to do in you. Shake yourself and your family loose from their stranglehold on your spiritual life.

When you stand before God, He will care little about what church you attended. He will, however, care very much about how you represented Jesus to your world and how you directed your family and those around you to do the same. He will determine the importance of your legacy based on how closely you followed the life of Jesus and how well you taught others to do the same through your actions as well as your words.

Find a vibrant fellowship home where you and your family are encouraged to go deep with God, one that has removed the carnal limits that hinder the marvelous relationship you can have in Jesus since you have repented. If you can't find one that suits your needs and is spiritually safe for your family, take the responsibility to start one in your home. The Bible never demands that you go to an established church. It only states that you do not forsake the fellowshipping of believers.

Hebrews 10:24-25 NIV And let us consider how we may spur one another on toward love and good deeds.

25) Let us not give up meeting together, as some are in the habit of doing, but let us encourage one another- and all the more as you see the Day approaching.

Find other men and their families who are really seeking Jesus to join you in covenant. That's the way the first century church got started and prospered, until it deteriorated into a big, immovable institution. That's the way the persecuted church remains alive in Christ all over the world. Many established churches of today began in a vacant building, a living room, or a store front, led by a sincere, sold-out man on fire for God and for the purity of the Word to go forth to those who believed the same as he did. Pray! Pray! Then pray some more!

Although your credentials are given to you by the Holy Spirit as a sold-out believer, get your certification from a reliable source if you believe you should. Trust the Lord to show you how to accomplish that. In addition to church programs and Bible colleges, there are some legitimate parachurch ministries and correspondence courses that may suit your situation. Consider finding some godly men to mentor you as you press on. Take night courses if necessary. You may desire to sign up for some kind of leadership courses for men. (We provide many materials on our web site, www.the101group.com. See if these in-depth studies on living a significant, overcoming life are for you. If they're not for you, then find what you need and commit to it.)

Where people honestly gather in the Name of Jesus, He is in their midst. Where He is present, where He is welcome, honored and lifted high, where He is glorified, that is the church. That is the only true church! You must join that church somewhere or begin that church yourself. If you don't, you will become a casualty among the cold and spiritually dead. You need to become an advocate leader who fears God, but like Teflon in regard to the fears of the world and dead, apostate religion.

1) Are you willing to do whatever it takes to help bring those around you closer to Jesus?   Y /N

2) Are you willing to do whatever it takes to take on the character of Jesus to accomplish it?   Y/N

3) Have you ever seen your life as a tool to be used by the Lord to prepare future generations to exhibit the character of Jesus to those who might hate them?   Y/N

Father,

I now know that I am directly and indirectly accountable so that future generations within my sphere of influence will be able to show others Jesus. I'm responsible to live as Jesus lived so that those who see me see Him. Give me what is needed to live as He lived. I need You! Thank You, Lord!

Until we, as men, approach our relationship with God from an eternal perspective - sensitive to His reasons for creating us and realistically facing our spiritual impotence - we will remain weak, atrophied representatives of Jesus, who are unable to even desire to live as He did in front of those who need Him.

Chapter 24

Maybe Today!

The joy of presenting a significant life to Father God

Time to Prepare Others for Tomorrow

Gentlemen, as men of God, we are long overdue in investing in those who will invest in others. Merry and I believe that everything mentioned in this book is simply Christianity 101. All of the statements and the heart positions of repentance and love are basic Christianity for those who say they follow Jesus. Although some of the statements may seem radical or very direct, they appear that way only because we have migrated far away from the life God planned for us, which was lived out by the first century followers of Christ. Our lives so little resemble the significant lives of those saints, that getting back to the standards by which they lived seems like a radical change in our comfortable, selfish world.

Everything we have presented in this book can be implemented quite readily in our present-day society, where things are relatively comfortable, employment is possible, carnal dreams can some day be fulfilled, education is available, and the great American dream is still reachable with hard work and diligent effort. But what happens when things change?

Jeremiah 12:5 AMP [But the Lord rebukes Jeremiah's impatience, saying] If you have raced with men on foot and they have tired you out, then how can you compete with horses? And if [you take to flight] in a land of peace where you feel secure, then what will you do [when you tread the tangled maze of jungle haunted by lions] in the swelling and flooding of the Jordan?

I am convinced there is a season of great peril coming very soon upon this land. (It may already be here, depending on when you read this.)

287

Over the centuries, the enemies of God have continually attempted to minimize the work of the Lord and destroy the work of the cross. The coming peril will be as nothing you and I have seen before. It could very well be the time when unparalleled change will encompass the whole world, eventually allowing the antichrist to emerge and set himself up as God in the temple in Jerusalem. However, God will not be mocked. God will, in His perfect timing, defend His Word and those who defend it with Him. His Word will prevail.

For too long, however, most of the church of Jesus Christ has been rendered powerless to exhibit Him to a lost and dying world because they have not overcome the world and its ways themselves. I believe the present call to the men of God is part of the Holy Spirit's end-time revival call and a preparation call for future generations. When the enemy comes in like a flood, the Spirit of the Lord will raise up a standard against him (See Isaiah 59:19). The standard will always be the powerful character of Christ exhibited in those who are His. If you are reading this, more than likely you are being called to be part of that standard.

With a calling comes a responsibility. The knowledge of that responsibility is often used by God to weed out those who would like to be part of what He is doing, but are unwilling to pay the price. This book is part of the weeding out process. Those who see the responsibility and the refinement it will cost them delight in the fact that their submission is a privilege and their commitment is an opportunity to please and honor God. Those who don't, set the calling of the Holy Spirit aside and go about their business-as-usual lives, lives that are insignificant in God's economy.

If you are part of the impotent crowd, you will not be able to see the need to even enlist as one of those who will be part of the standard that God is raising up. The cost will simply be too high. You have been spiritually made impotent and have no desire to fulfill the spiritual call presented to you. You may go through your entire life blissfully unaware of how far you are from who the Lord really wants you to be. Your spiritual life has been sidelined and a nice, warm place on the bench is eternally reserved for you. In times of great distress, you will more than likely even come against the anointed of God, those who are walking daily in the character of Christ. Unless you surrender fully to the heralding of the Holy Spirit to become who you are called to be in Jesus, you will remain impotent and unable to discern what the Lord is doing, blindly following those who are not part of His end-time generation disciples.

But take hope! Your name is not carved solidly into that bench on the sidelines in the heart of God. It can be removed at some future date, if you come to the realization that your actions in this life have been insignificant in God's eyes and choose to do something about it. If you are being called this very moment and feel a new desire stirring in your spirit to be part of God's anointed, vibrant representatives of Jesus to this endtime generation, you need to act now, while He still can be found. Shaking loose from spiritual impotence is hard work. The price is high; it will cost you everything you hold dear that is outside of the plan of God for your life. So what; it will be worth it! Most of all, it will honor Jesus and His work of the cross.

From Our Father's Heart

I have told you that I will be putting holy alliances together.
These are relationships that you will be able to trust completely.
They are designed to accomplish My will in the times ahead.
They will be My kind of alliances, held together by My power,
not the power of the flesh.
These "covenant relationships" will be the example
of what My church should be.
They will not fall apart because of the intrusions
that the world and the church place on them.
Tried in the fire of affliction
and having stood the test of the enemy's onslaught,
I will be able to use the gifts and talents of one party
to complement the other and fulfill any task
that is ordained for their particular association.
What a joy it will be to see trustworthy friends
who work together to accomplish My will
and represent My church
as I want My church to function one with another.
Soon, I will also establish safe harbors throughout the land,
similar to My "cities of refuge."
They will be places where My presence dwells
to protect those who are implementing My plans.
These will not necessarily be communities or large areas.
They might be a single home, building, or piece of land.
People that I trust will be able to function there
when there is little else being accomplished in the land.
Supernatural forces will oversee these places
to keep out intruders as long as I desire.
They will not be for the faint of heart
who desire to save themselves.
Those who dwell in these havens
will have given away their lives long ago,
hold on to nothing but My Word, and desire to do only My will.
When the land burns,
these places will bring forth the refreshing water of My Word
and the life of My Son to a parched land.

What if Our Relatively Comfortable World Changes Radically?

Because history bears out the accuracy of the prophecies in the Word of God, we know there will come a time in the future that ushers in the coming of the Lord. Incredible things will happen prior to the event itself and it will be very difficult for followers of Jesus Christ. The freedom to worship Jesus and express His love to others, which we enjoy at this writing, will be greatly hindered or non-existent.

All but the most naive need only look around and see that, whether or not these are the closing days of history or just another time when the forces of evil are attempting to extinguish the light of Christ, something about our world is changing drastically. Evil men with evil hearts are exhibiting their agenda and forcefully attempting to demand that it be embraced by everyone else.

Persecution is really nothing new, for it has taken place in many past generations. If this exhibition plays out as it has in the past, the Christian principles and the freedoms that we have relied upon in the United States will soon be hindered wherever possible and more than likely eliminated at some time in the future. This may happen in our generation, our children's generation, or our grandchildren's generation; but it will happen one day.

As men who will be held accountable for the direction we have given those in our generation and for how we have trained future generations to follow Jesus, what kind of presentation of His life should we be exhibiting so that those who see us will be able to survive and even prosper in difficult times – no matter what timeframe, end-time or otherwise? How do we prepare our wives and our families for a possible time when there is no one but Jesus they can rely on? How will we train them to seek the Lord so they don't curse God and die when the pressures of life are so overpowering that the handles of safety they have found to be a refuge are removed and He is the only hope they have left? How will we teach them to teach and reach others?

In my study of the persecuted church, I have found a golden thread of wisdom that is expressed one way or another by anyone who prospered during their ordeal, even the heaviest persecution, the most severe torture, or the longest imprisonment. It is the spiritual guideline that allowed those who followed it to stand as overcomers before the Lord, having neither cursed those who harmed them nor denied Who He is even under the direst of circumstances.

In each instance, the two principles of <u>prayer and living right before God</u> saw them through the hardest of times and allowed the persecuted to prosper, even pass on the completed work of the cross in them to others. Because it is the heart of Jesus from the cross as He forgave those who crucified Him, it is the power of the cross demonstrated in every generation that needs it. Although you can rely on God to meet you with His power supernaturally whenever it is needed, that forgiving heart, that powerful life, that significant way of living, however, will normally not be attainable at the point where times get really tough. It must be sought after, developed, and nurtured long before any difficulties arise.

[If you say you are a follower of Jesus, your primary goal in life should be to become an accurate representative of Him. Anything short of that is really hypocritical.]

Ask God to develop the heart of Jesus in you while things are still relatively calm, so you will not fall apart under pressure and exhibit carnal, fleshly behavior. If you are incapable of exhibiting the character of Christ to your family and directing them to do the same when your life is relatively easy, how can you possibly believe you could do it when things are rough? If you are focused foolishly and determined to remain impotent in a time of relative safety, how will you pass on to future generations the strong guidance and solid basis they will need to follow Christ? Your selfishness will produce future generations of ill-equipped, sickly members of the body of Christ and you will be held accountable.

Prayer and Living Right Before God

No matter how society turns, no matter what your circumstances might be, you can always pray and you can always personally live right before God. In prosperous times, living right before God has a very different application than it does when you are in peril or have come to the end of normal resources for living. Either way, the Holy Spirit is willing and able to show you how that kind of living plays out. No matter what the circumstance, no one can stop you from praying and seeking the Lord for His wisdom to meet whatever challenges come your way.

From the cross, Jesus could have vaporized those who drove the nails in His hands and made His flesh like hamburger. He could have called upon legions of angels to come to His rescue even though one of them would have been enough to destroy those in His immediate world. Instead, He turned to His Father and petitioned on their behalf for their good. Even on the cross, with His very last breath, He lived the kind of life that pleased His Father.

Matthew 26:53-54 NIV "Do you think I cannot call on my Father, and he will at once put at my disposal more than twelve legions of angels?
54) But how then would the Scriptures be fulfilled that say it must happen in this way?"

291

Luke 23:34a NIV Jesus said, "Father, forgive them, for they do not know what they are doing."

Before the cross, when He was standing before Pilate, Jesus could have used His stature as the Lord of All - One much higher than a lowly public official - to bargain for His life or defend His rights. Instead, He submitted to His Father's will, knowing the consequences that were at hand.

John 19:11a NIV Jesus answered, "You would have no power over me if it were not given to you from above..."

When all that needed to be done was accomplished, when the circumstances of His life had been played out to the conclusion His Father intended, Jesus still continued to do what He had done all of His life - He prayed. While He endured the concluding moments of His life, moments that were far from comfortable, He lived them in a way that was honorable and right before God, the same way He had lived throughout His life. Many people in the ensuing generations fulfilled the calling the Lord had for them by applying these same principles.

As in many previous generations, some generation - possibly this one - will have everything taken away that can be taken. Nobody, however, can take away your ability to pray to your heavenly Father if you make it your priority before that time comes. It is your God-given, God-empowered right. Likewise, nobody can take away your privilege of living in a right and honorable way before God, if you learn to live that way long before difficult times become the norm.

Your possessions, your freedoms, your carnal rights, your reputation, and even your very life can all be taken; but no one can force you to deny God or discontinue your communication with Him for direction and strength. If you are sold out to Jesus, no one can stop you from loving even those who want to kill your flesh the way He loves them. They certainly may try, but if you have submitted yourself fully to the Lordship of Jesus Christ in a time of relative safety and freedom, you will be able to live right before Him in difficult times by not denying Him and not hating those who hate you.

Choose to Live Right before God Now

It can't be stated often enough. These character strengths cannot be developed with the snap of a finger, but must be cultivated long before they are needed. Without them, those going through the desperate trials foretold in the Bible for the body of Christ will not be able to function in the character of Christ and will most likely hate their accusers and deny God. If one denies God, hates others, and cannot function in the character of Jesus

292

Christ, what hope does that person have of presenting God with a significant life? That person will live an impotent life to the very end and have nothing to show for it before God.

Even if this present generation is not given the challenges stated above, it will befall some future generation. That means your children or their children or their children will need to have those strengths on tap to be able to overcome. If you love them, you need to pass on what will allow them to stay the course. That goes far beyond having them go to church, make money, or produce a family of spiritually impotent offspring. You need to prepare them in the only way that will give them the opportunity to live a significant life and please God. You need to get right with God yourself and let them see the character of Christ in you. You need to do it now! Everything starts with the decisions you make at this very moment. As a husband and father, it's in your court to live the Christ-like character that's vital for this generation and for generations to come.

There is a wonderfully peaceful and spiritually powerful rhythm and pace for life that's only found by someone who has purposefully immersed himself completely in the ways of God through Jesus Christ. As the world scurries blindly to fulfill an unquenchable emptiness, this joyous spiritual environment in Christ cannot be touched by anything other than God Himself. It cannot be intruded upon by anything the world may have to offer. It cannot be violated by anything the world may attempt to bring its way.

One Final Assessment

If you truly desire to present a significant life to the Lord, it's time to make one final assessment of your life and your relationship with God. How much time do you have presently to really seek the deep things of God that we've talked about throughout these pages? What is filling the needs in your life? What is replacing the quiet place where you will find rest for your soul?

It is important to remember that intimacy with God is never found in places that are busy with life's activities and distractions. He is always found in the quiet places. Remember throughout the Word, that when Jesus sought His Father or wanted others to seek Him, He would find a quiet place away from the din of the activity of life. Overactive environments are Satan's territory. He loves to keep life so "in your face" that you have no time to seek God.

The paces and rhythms to which the world dances are diametrically opposed to the paces and rhythms in which the Lord flows. The world will keep you so busy, so consumed with your "stuff," that you have no time to

293

draw near to God to reverse your impotence. You will need to shake yourself loose from all of it.

To be in harmony with the loving Father Who created you is God's ultimate plan for you. His desire is that you take on the desires of His heart and walk in the ways of Jesus. It is the epitome of success. It is the significant, world overcoming life for which your Father in heaven created you and the life He will fully accept when you hand it back to Him. It is the ultimate fulfillment of everything you have ever desired and will only come about when you rely solely on His strength and not at all on your own.

From Our Father's Heart

I have given you a specific life to live.
It is important to Me that you live it to the fullest.
There are certain people who only you will be able to touch.
There are specific instances
when you are to be a testimony to others.
Every detail of your life is important to Me.
Every instance that you encounter
is part of who you are becoming.
They all add up to who you really are in Me.
At each point in your growth, I move people to you
so that they can observe more of Jesus.
Your experiences and growth help them to become
who I want them to be.
Consider every instance, every encounter,
and every circumstance you face to be worthwhile.
They are building blocks to your completion.
Your life is for you to live as you choose.
I choose for it to be developed into the character of Jesus.
I ask you to do the same.

Your spiritually potent life in Christ verifies the power of the cross and the life Jesus lived to a world that's looking for answers to its emptiness. It solidifies the truth of the Bible. It confirms to others that there really is a God Who loves them and cares about their existence. It is the spiritual magnet that draws everyone to Jesus, the Author and Finisher of their faith. It gives them reason to take their next breath.

Joy in the Journey

The most abundant, significant life anyone could ever live would consist of the following: a certainty that you are greatly loved by God,

294

intimate communion with Him, a daily walk directly in the center of His will; and the ability to flow in His presence in all that you do as His ambassador, commissioned and equipped by the Lord Himself to fulfill His purpose for your life. There should be no other purpose for breathing. What is so remarkable is that when you spend time in His presence, fulfilling His perfect will, you will experience incredible moments, no matter what challenges life throws your way.

My family and I have taken on the phrase "Maybe Today" as an expression of anticipation. To us, it means that maybe today the power of God will so encapsulate us that we will serve Him with all of our hearts. Maybe today He will reveal something more of Himself to us. Maybe today He will provide the heart motive that is needed to serve Him full sway and walk properly in His kingdom while here on this earth. Maybe today He will answer a specific prayer. You get the idea.

The concept of "Maybe Today" has given us a new hope in the wonder of God and the promise of His eventual presence in all we do. In addition to giving us joy in our personal journey, it continually reassures us that all of His promises and power are for us, not just for others. It places a newfound confidence in His continual companionship as we walk together toward Father God. It's time that you fully understand that if you surrender completely to the Lord, "Maybe Today" He will make you a valiant man after His own heart, doing the things you do only because of the presence of Jesus in you.

Choose How to Live Now

So, the choice is really yours. Jesus is presently at your door step. He is asking you through the Holy Spirit to shake yourself loose from the impotence to which most of the men in the modern day, complacently deceived church have succumbed. He is heralding honorable men who call themselves followers of Jesus and choose to devote themselves to the honest heart of God. He is calling men who are determined to exhibit the life and character of Jesus and do whatever is necessary to build a significant legacy and teach others to do the same. You can, this very moment, respond to His call or you can shake it off to remain blissfully unaware of your spiritual impotence until you meet Him face to face and hold little in your hands to offer the Lord.

God is With You!

Finally, remember to prepare your heart to be overwhelmed by the goodness of God, if you choose to walk toward Him for His honor and glory. Even though they may be the hardest steps you have ever taken, your wife, your children, your circle of influence, and future generations need you to take them. God has given you all you need to overcome the world if you will only tap into it through the power of the Holy Spirit. If you do, prepare to live a life that honors Jesus as the Holy Spirit changes you. Just know that the Lord rewards those who diligently seek Him and desires to show Himself strong on your behalf as you walk in a life of significance before Him.

Hebrews 11:6 NIV   And without faith it is impossible to please God, because anyone who comes to him must believe that he exists and that he rewards those who earnestly seek him.

2 Chronicles 16:9a NIV   For the eyes of the Lord range throughout the earth to strengthen those whose hearts are fully committed to him.

Prepare your heart to be overwhelmed when you find joy in the fact that your life pleases God, not for the reward it brings to you, but because it honors Him and the work of the cross. Prepare to be overwhelmed by the goodness of your Abba Father as you turn completely to Him!

1 Peter 2:9 NIV   But you are a chosen people, a royal priesthood, a holy nation, a people belonging to God, that you may declare the praises of him who has called you out of darkness into his wonderful light.

Maybe Today!

Father,

I choose to live only for You. I dedicate my life, my marriage, my family, and all of my associations to You. Please take the little I am able to offer and use it for Your glory. I choose to serve You with all my heart. Thank You for Your patience with me. Thank You for Your power that dwells in me through Jesus so I can truly live a significant, world overcoming life for Your glory and delight.

Signed _____

The MASH icu Support System Materials

This book, **The Father Factor**, is an intensive study designed to help individuals or groups to initiate the Men After the Savior's Heart intensive care unit (MASH icu) support system. Its content and study questions at the end of each chapter are a springboard for the heart revival necessary to overcome the world as Jesus did. Our other books and resources are also available for further personal support and assistance to you as you pursue God.

A White Stone is an engrossing novel that clearly demonstrates how one life changed and empowered by the Holy Spirit can significantly affect the circle of influence given to the man or woman who follows after the Lord. Join a diverse group of individuals from all walks of life who are challenged to depend solely on God; and watch as those who say "Yes" meet their loving heavenly Father at every turn, while those who rely on their own plans reel from the chaos of a world that no longer holds any answers.

In its sequel, **The Elect**, follow Ben Fairchild, Reefer McGee, Gloria Manly, and Tim Hanek as they navigate life on this earth when God's invisible spiritual order is allowed to function differently. Discover what it truly means to know God - to really live for Him, even in the most challenging times. The Elect will take you to places that require answers and answer questions that may dwell in the quiet places of your heart.

The Overcoming Life guidebook is meant to be a lifetime "operations manual" for navigating your journey with the Lord. Far more than a workbook, it is a journaling resource to have on hand as the Lord imparts His wealth to you. Whether you choose to experience this resource from cover to cover, or work with particular sections as the Lord leads, it's a valuable asset to your spiritual growth arsenal.

All seven of our **From Our Father's Heart** books are an oasis of encouraging words from the Lord to help move you along the straight path to healing and wholeness.

Manna Moments is the perfect night stand companion. Full of encouragement, exhortation, Bible verses, heartwarming stories, and just plain devotion to Jesus, this series of messages will bring a wonderful assurance of the love of Father God your way and help direct you to a secure place as a child on His lap as you read and hide under the shadow of His wings.

Check out our blogs!

Our "From Our Father's Heart" messages and "Mash icu" blogs are daily opportunities for the Lord to touch, exhort, and encourage you on your journey with Him. If you teach others or need a catalyst for each day's devotions, they are resource libraries available to you whenever you need them. To sign up for these daily messages, visit our website: www.the101group.com.

For more information about using the **MASH icu support system** in an already established men's group or starting your own group, visit our website: www.the101group.com, or contact us at jim@awhitestone.com.

Books in progress:

God's Final Frontier is a flat-out down-to-earth description of who we are in Christ, and what our amazing Father has provided for us even through the darkest of times.

Hidden Manna is a comprehensive one-year daily devotional that will hold you close year round. It's a collection of words from the Lord that will remind you Who God really is and how much He desires to be involved in your life at every turn.

Resting in God is a series of short sessions that can help bring you to a place of total surrender to the Lord. It's designed to be a personal or group study for those who desire to find the depth of God's covenant through Jesus and walk in it.

[Everything begins with prayer. Everything ends with prayer.
Everything is accomplished through prayer and submission.]

66912227R00181

Made in the USA
Lexington, KY
27 August 2017